Beyond Tolerance

Philip Jenkins

BEYOND
TOLERANCE

CHILD PORNOGRAPHY

ON THE INTERNET

New York University Press

New York and London

NEW YORK UNIVERSITY PRESS
New York and London
www.nyupress.org

First published in paperback in 2003

Library of Congress Cataloging-in-Publication Data
Jenkins, Philip, 1952–
Beyond tolerance : child pornography on the Internet /
Philip Jenkins.
p.   cm.
Includes bibliographical references and index.
ISBN 0-8147-4262-9 (cloth : alk. paper)
ISBN 0-8147-4263-7 (paper : alk. paper)
1. Children in pornography. 2. Internet pornography.   I. Title.
HQ471 .J45 2001
363.4'7—dc21   2001001250

New York University Press books are printed on acid-free paper,
and their binding materials are chosen for strength and durability.

Manufactured in the United States of America
10 9 8 7 6 5 4 3 2 1

CONTENTS

Contents

ACKNOWLEDGMENTS

I am very grateful to Kathryn Hume and Joel Best for advice and comments concerning this project, and particularly for having read the manuscript.

NOTE ON USAGE

Throughout the book, I quote extensively from Internet newsgroups and bulletin boards, where the level of writing, grammar, and spelling is often abysmal. To reflect the tone of these groups accurately, I have left the original text unchanged without the very frequent use of "*sic*," which would normally be appropriate. On another point, it is customary today to strive for gender-neutral writing, eliminating the use of male-specific pronouns to cover the whole of humanity. In this book, however, I generally speak of the average patron of child pornography as "he" and "him," based on the well-substantiated observation that males constitute the overwhelming (but not exclusive) majority of individuals ever identified as makers or users of this type of material. In the context of the bulletin boards studied, the use of pseudonyms makes it impossible to tell the real identity or gender of the participants with complete assurance, but I have little doubt that virtually all are male.

GLOSSARY

abpep-t	*alt.binaries.pictures.erotica.pre-teen*
abpee-t	*alt.binaries.pictures.erotica.early-teen*
abpell	*alt.binaries.pictures.erotica.ll-series*
AOL	America Online
BBS OR bbs	bulletin board system
bubba	prison, or the criminal justice system
b/w	black and white
CDA	Communications Decency Act
CP	child pornography
d/l	download
FAQ	frequently asked questions
flame	an abusive, excessive, or "overkill" response to news-group postings
gif	graphics interchange format (an image format)
hc OR h/c	hard-core
hd	hard drive
html	hypertext markup language, the language in which Web pages are written
http	hypertext transfer protocol, which permits Web browsers to communicate with servers
icq	"I Seek You," program permitting real-time online conversation
IP	Internet protocol
IRC	Internet relay chat
ISP	Internet service provider
jpg	joint photographic experts group (image format)
kp	kiddie porn OR Kinder Porno (German)

LEA	law enforcement agency/agencies
loli/lolita	underage girl, generally at or below the age of puberty
lurker	one who observes the proceedings in a chat room or bulletin board without contributing
MCLT	"my collection of lolitas and teens"
mpg	moving pictures experts group (format for movies)
newbie	novice
ng	newsgroup
on-topic	common euphemism for "child pornography" in the subculture
pedo	pedophile
peeps	"peepers," individuals who view child pornography online
pt	pre-teen
PW	password
reg	regular
SC OR S/C	soft-core
sysop	system operator
troll	a disruptive or malicious participant in a chat room or bulletin board
u/l	upload
URL	uniform resource locator, the addressing information that a browser client needs to connect to a particular page
Y/N	yes-or-no

ONE

Out of Control?

In fact, extremely few persons actually get arrested and
sent to jail, that is a myth really. There are thousands of
vhs's out there, many from 1999, thousands of people present at this bbs [bulletin board] and millions of loli-lovers
in various countries, yet you only see a couple of persons
getting arrested, and the media writes about it like they
have been busting Al Capone.

—Godfather Corleone, Maestro board,
January 24, 2000

Over the last decade, politicians have often been agitated by the issue of
Internet regulation, and they have usually couched their concerns in
terms of protecting children. How can the young be kept clear of the
"back alleys of the Internet," where they might encounter disturbing
adult imagery? Might children be lured online by cults or hate groups?
On the other side of the debate, opponents of regulation counter that re-
pressing overt sexual or extremist material threatens to damage access to
genuinely important information or literary work. Yet throughout these
charged discussions runs a consensus that regulation *could* work in practice; that a law passed against, say, pornography or hate propaganda
might actually sweep those materials from the World Wide Web or at
least keep people away from them; that, given the chance, censorship
might work. But is this idea plausible? That it is not—that regulation
can, in fact, achieve remarkably little—may be suggested by the easy
availability on the Internet of what is probably the most reprehensible

material of all, the most stigmatized, and the most rigidly prohibited: namely, child pornography.

When hearing debates about Net regulation, we might usefully remember the case of "Helena," probably a British girl, who, tragically, may be one of the best-known sex stars on the Web. In the late 1980s, as a little girl of seven or eight, Helena became the subject of a photo series that depicted her not only in all the familiar nude poses of hardcore pornography but also showed her in numerous sex acts with Gavin, a boy of about the same age. Both are shown having sex with an adult man, presumably Helena's father. The images are collectively known by various names but the commonest is "hel-lo," that is, "Helena/lolita." Since their first appearance they have had an astonishing afterlife; probably not a day has passed without the hel-lo images appearing anew on some electronic server somewhere in the world, and they are cherished by thousands of collectors worldwide. They seem to be the standard starter kit for child porn novices. In addition, Helena's pictures form part of a much larger series, known under titles such as hel-anal, hel-cum, and hel-louise. Hel-lo itself was recently described by a child porn enthusiast as "the greatest HC [hard-core] series ever made! She was 'acting' since she was a toddler until she was twelve years old, which means there are thousands of pics of her in action out there somewhere! No other series compares!!!"[1]

Or we might consider the more recent KG and KX series, the "kindergarten" photos, which together represent perhaps the most prized collections currently available on the Net. KG is a series of hundreds (maybe thousands) of nude images of several very young girls, mainly between the ages of three and six years old, with each item including the girl's name—Helga, Inga, and so on. The photographs date from the mid-1990s, and they likely derive from either Germany or Scandinavia. In the words of one fan of the series, "Once upon a time. There was a chemist that had earned his Ph.D. Well, he got married and along with his wife opened up a day care center. Well, as the story goes, he managed to take pictures of lots and lots of things. Eventually he got busted."[2] The KG collection exists alongside a still more sought-after version, KX, which depicts the same children in hard-core sexual situations with one or more men. Put simply, most are pictures of four- and five-year-old girls performing oral sex and masturbation on adult men. The immense popularity of the KG images ensured an enthusiastic market for KX, which entered general circulation in early 2000.

The popularity of hel-lo and KX has been achieved despite the utterly illegal nature of such collections. Surely there is not a country in the world where it is legal to carry out the acts portrayed, to record them on film, to post the images on a server, or to possess them in any form whatever, hard copy or electronic. In most countries, the penalties for any of these behaviors are extremely severe: governments in most advanced countries have passed draconian prohibitory laws that often provide harsh prison terms for mere possession of child porn, let alone its distribution or manufacture. Sanctions against such hard-core pictures are especially tough in Japan and the Scandinavian nations, which have traditionally been quite easygoing about softer materials. And yet, not all the world's censorship laws, backed by the direst threats of prison and social ruin, have prevented these series from being readily available for anyone who wants them.

Just how easy it is to find these materials needs to be emphasized. Both the price and the quality of illegal commodities are greatly affected by the relative success of law enforcement intervention. When, for instance, police and customs are waging a particularly successful war against the cocaine trade, making major seizures, the price of cocaine on American streets rises steeply, while the quality of the substance being retailed falls dramatically. Conversely, weaker police responses are reflected in bargain-basement prices and higher purity at street level. Applying this analogy to child pornography produces disturbing results. In the mid-1970s, a child porn magazine containing thirty or so pictures might cost ten dollars in an American city. Today, the entire contents of that same magazine are available through the Internet for free, as are tens of thousands of other, more recent counterparts. A month or so of free Web surfing could easily accumulate a child porn library of several thousand images. The only payments or charges involved would be the standard fees for computer connect time and the cost of materials, such as Zip disks. Prices in the child porn world have not just fallen, they have all but been eliminated. "Quality" has also improved immeasurably, in terms of the range of materials on offer. Arguably, the images now coming online are ever more explicit and hard core. Applying the drug analogy suggests that the role of law enforcement in regulating supply is approximately zero. I want to keep this problem in perspective, since the actual numbers of traffickers are not vast—we are probably talking about a subculture numbering in the tens of thousands worldwide, together with a significant number of casual browsers—but even so, the scale of the enterprise they support is depressing, as is the constant infusion of new materials.

For many reasons, this is one area where enforcement should, in theory, have been quite successful. Since child pornography first entered the public consciousness in the mid-1970s, any involvement with such materials has commonly been regarded as an extreme and unforgivable form of deviance. Many other forms of deviant behavior have their reputable defenders or at least libertarians who assert that these activities should not be severely penalized: drug use has its defenders, as do exhibitionism, public sex, and even bestiality. For child pornography, however, there is no such tolerance, no minoritarian school that upholds the rights of individuals to pursue their private pleasures.

The reasons for this stigmatization are not hard to understand. By definition, the subjects of child pornography cannot give any form of informed or legal consent to their involvement in this trade, and it is a reasonable suspicion that, even when children are just depicted nude, they are subject to actual molestation. A broad public consensus accepts the assertion that possession or use of this kind of material is the direct cause of actual criminal behavior, a contention that commands nothing like the same respect when purely adult material is under debate. Feminist activists have long argued, "Pornography is the theory; rape is the practice"; a corollary declares that "child pornography is the theory, molestation is the practice." Helena and Gavin were certainly molested, as were the KX kindergartners: we have the pictures to prove it. Conceivably, too, some viewers of these images might be induced to carry their own fantasies into reality. In the 1982 case of *New York v. Ferber*, the U.S. Supreme Court stated, "The distribution of photographs and films depicting sexual activity by juveniles is intrinsically related to the sexual abuse of children . . . the materials produced are a permanent record of the children's participation and the harm to the child is exacerbated by their circulation."[3] Some critics go further and see a direct stimulus to child abduction or murder. Yet even the hardest child pornography materials continue to be easily accessible for anyone with appropriate technical expertise.

For debates over Internet regulation, the implications are alarming. If we cannot suppress items such as hel-lo and KX, what can we hope to achieve by regulating any lesser atrocities on the Net? The case of child pornography also throws into relief the other concerns that are so often expressed about the Internet. Why is so much attention focused on quite innocuous forms of adult material, while something as pernicious as child pornography circulates with such relative ease? Consistently, politicians, media, and law enforcement agencies have massively over-responded to relatively mild forms of online obscenity while failing to grasp the realities or scale of the more serious electronic market. Their only excuse is that the electronic child porn world remains so very poorly known, so obscure even to law enforcement professionals.

Goals

I have three goals in writing this book.

First, I suggest that child pornography offers a critical case study for efforts to regulate the Internet, to enforce the law in cyberspace. The paramount question is, what law? The subculture operates beyond the boundaries of any particular state or legal jurisdiction and represents a new pattern of globalized crime and deviance. Just *where* is the Internet? The foolishness of the question is self-evident: the Net is neither a place nor a thing but a construct of millions of individual servers, which we happen to describe through the visual metaphor of a net or a web. If our cultural traditions were different, we might equally well imagine it as a symphony or a concatenation of smells or tastes. It is an assemblage, a congeries, and it has no tangible reality located in any single nation-state. When you get there, there is no *there* there. So how can a state regulate it? Child pornography raises to an acute degree the fundamental issues about international law and jurisdiction posed by the Internet and electronic commerce. This emerging global market in illicit commodities poses challenges that law enforcement agencies worldwide have only begun to contemplate. Based on this example, we can see that enforcement clearly is not working at present; but might any future policies might be more successful? Is the Net truly beyond control? I argue that while the total elimination of electronic child porn is impossible, nevertheless a massive reduction could be achieved, but it would require a transformation of present law enforcement tactics and priorities.[4]

Everything depends on the way in which we conceive of the child porn problem, which presently is scarcely even recognized as a distinct problem. This brings me to my second goal, understanding why society in general has such a distorted view of the child porn issue. Many scholars work on how social problems are constructed, why we see issues as gravely threatening at one time rather than another, but it is rarer to pay attention to what might be called unconstructed problems. Some phenomena that prima facie seem harmful or destructive can continue for years without people paying much attention to them or without them entering public discourse. Through the 1980s, for instance, there were several hundred violent attacks on abortion-related facilities in the United States, in what some observers viewed as an extremely serious wave of terrorism. In the media and in political discourse, however, the word *terrorism* was virtually never used in this context until a change of national administration in 1993. Hitherto, the incidents were generally viewed as discrete events, not part of a single problem or crisis, so that they lacked a label such as "abortion-related terrorism."

The fact that this problem remained unconstructed says much about how the mass media report social issues. All too often, news seems to be defined as reporting what bureaucracies say and do, and in matters of crime and justice, the media at their worst define issues in terms of the latest press releases from federal agencies. If the Drug Enforcement Agency declares that drug X is about to become an epidemic, this fact is duly reported with minimal comment or criticism. If, by contrast, agencies refuse to define an issue as grave or threatening, then the media follow suit. The FBI denied for years that abortion-related violence was terrorism, and so it was not classified thus, whether in newspapers, television reports, or the works of academic experts.[5] In the case of sexual threats to children on the Internet, federal agencies speak mainly in terms of online seduction, or pedophiles stalking victims via computers, an area in which police can hope to achieve results. In consequence, the larger problem is popularly defined in terms of cyberstalking. Serious child pornography trafficking is thus ignored, or at least left unconstructed. What is not recognized as a problem is not studied, and the less we know about the phenomenon, the less incentive there is for research or intervention. If we don't see a menace, we are not even trying to fight it.

Third, I believe that the child porn phenomenon raises doubts about most present theories of deviant organization. There exists a remarkably cosmopolitan "bandit culture" of suppliers and consumers of child pornography, which sustains a worldwide criminal market of unprecedented geographical scope. This underworld represents a new type of social organization, made possible by novel forms of technology and characterized by types of interaction that would have been inconceivable only a few years ago; the attendant subculture cries out to be explored.

Discovering Child Pornography

To explain this study, I have to devote some time to describing my methodology and the still more basic question of how I became involved with this research.

My scholarly work over the last few years has involved deconstructing public perceptions of social problems. I have tried to debunk myths surrounding such issues as serial murder, clergy child abuse, and synthetic drugs. In 1998, I published the book *Moral Panic,* which was a history of ideas of child abuse and molestation over the past century or so, and as part of this, I described the then-recent controversy over the various dangers that children encountered on the Internet. Calls for government action against online obscenity and "cyberporn" resulted in the controversial Communications Decency Act (CDA) of 1995, a sweeping censorship measure that was eventually struck down by the U.S. Supreme Court.[6] As a follow-up to my study, I became interested in the whole area of Internet pornography, which was surrounded by so many myths and misstatements, and this led me to imagine a book on Internet-related moral panics. Initially, I had no intention of dealing with the child pornography issue, but quite early on I was startled to find materials of this sort, as well as indications that a substantial traffic existed.

The reason I was so surprised is that hitherto I had thought that allegations concerning child pornography on the Web were largely bogus. My attitude was conditioned by my knowledge of general anti-porn rhetoric, which tries to stigmatize "normal" consensual adult materials by contextualizing them together with the most unacceptable content—namely, child pornography, extreme sadomasochistic portrayals, and even so-called snuff films.[7] To win the widest possible support for repressive measures, activists assert that obscenity is not merely a consensual crime but involves harm to those unable to give consent; any suggestion that this is "victimless" activity must be countered by examples of actual and severe harm. On both counts, child pornography is an excellent rhetorical weapon; hence the far-reaching claims since the 1970s about the supposed scale of this activity.

It is useful to define terms here, to achieve a precision that was so conspicuously lacking in the CDA debate. Since so much has been written about the dangers that electronic technologies pose to children, it is helpful to differentiate between three related but separate areas. These areas involve *cyberstalkers,* or predatory individuals who seek to contact and seduce children online; *cyberporn,* or children gaining electronic access to adult pornographic materials; and *child pornography,* the distribution of obscene or indecent images of underaged subjects.[8] Although

the three are radically different in their nature and in the response demanded, they are confounded partly through a genuine failure to understand the Internet and partly as a deliberate tactic by politicians seeking to expand censorship of adult materials. In the CDA campaign,
politicians capitalized on public outrage against cyberstalkers and child
pornography to stir anger at the circulation of any sexually oriented material on the Net, and thus to support legislation against cyberporn,
which was the movement's real target.

Despite activists' claims to the contrary, child porn is extremely difficult to obtain through non-electronic means and has been so for twenty
years, so I initially believed it was equally rare on the Web. I was wrong.
It is a substantial presence, and much of the material out there is worse
than most of us can imagine, in terms of the types of activity depicted and
the ages of the children portrayed. This is not just a case of soft-core pictures of precociously seductive fifteen-year-olds. Having spent a decade
arguing that various social menaces were vastly overblown—that serial
killers and molesters did not lurk behind every tree, nor pedophile priests
in every rectory—I now found myself in the disconcerting position of
seeking to *raise* public concern about a quite authentic problem that has
been neglected.

This is a curious position for someone who defines himself as a libertarian, who fits poorly into most existing schemes of political affiliations.
As a general principle, I believe that criminal law should be kept as far removed as possible from issues of personal morality. I am in no sense an
anti-smut activist, and I reject efforts to restrict sexually explicit adult
material, whether these attempts derive from religious or moralistic be-
lievers on the right or from feminists on the left. I know of no convincing evidence that pornography causes harm or incites illegal behavior
where both subjects and consumers are consenting adults, and I believe
there are convincing arguments that adult porn can be actively beneficial
and liberating for both sexes.

Having said this, I now find myself involved in a project that could
well arouse anger about sexual materials online and could conceivably
be used as ammunition in political campaigns to regulate the Internet

and to repress obscenity and/or indecency. The difference, of course, lies in the area of consent, where a clear distinction exists between sexual material depicting adults and that focusing on children. There is no reason to challenge the basic assumption that a child pornography industry does indeed inflict severe harm upon those who cannot give consent, and that is grounds for suppression, if indeed it is possible. I would like to see pictures such as KX suppressed permanently, and if that cannot be achieved, then at a minimum the flow of new images might be contained. At the same time, I want to differentiate sharply between such productions and the world of adult materials, where the issues involved are utterly different.

What We Do Not Know

Having discovered the child porn culture on the Internet, the next question from an academic standpoint was what to do with it, and peculiar problems face any investigator. This is apparent from the stunning lack of available information on the current realities of child porn. Most academic or journalistic American accounts of child pornography were researched and written during the intense panic over this phenomenon in the late 1970s and early 1980s, and the books most cited generally have publication dates in the mid- to late 1980s. Little has appeared since then because, at least in the United States, the ferocious legal prohibitions on viewing child porn images have had the effect of virtually banning research. The existing literature thus describes a world of magazines and videos that has now been obsolete for over a decade and ignores the computer revolution that transformed this particular deviant subculture in the mid-1980s, a decade before the mainstream discovered the Internet. (There are some distinguished European studies, but not all are available in English).[9]

When popular magazines mention computers in the context of child pornography or pedophilia, it is usually in the context of children being seduced or stalked by predatory adults whom they encounter online. We now have a whole genre of stories, all basically drawing on the same repetoire of themes, telling of the pursuit and seduction of a young person by a pedophile and the protective measures deployed by parents. Often, too, we hear how adults take the law into their own hands by venturing forth onto the electronic frontier to entrap predators. Accounts of police actions in this area focus on the same theme, "cybersex cops" pursuing stalkers and seducers. One well-publicized recent book on dangers to children was Katherine Tarbox's *Katie.com*, which tells the story of a thirteen-year-old girl seduced by a middle-aged man whom she met on the Internet. The story received wide play in popular magazines such as *Time* and *People Weekly*.[10] Cyberstalking, "chatting with the enemy," is a sufficiently important danger in its own right, but it has next to nothing to do with the underworld that supplies and consumes KX and hel-lo.

As a result of media neglect, the child porn problem remains largely unconstructed. Even well-informed commentators dismiss the CP subculture as a moralist myth, perhaps a kind of conservative urban legend, like snuff films. In her study of Internet censorship debates, *Net.Wars*, Wendy Grossman occasionally refers to child porn as one of the factors leading people to support restrictions, though in reality (she asserts) only a "small amount of material . . . shows up on the Net." She also writes that "many of the newsgroups with names like *alt.binaries.pictures.erotica.children* were probably started as tasteless jokes, and are largely taken up with messages flaming the groups." This remark is ironic, since *alt.binaries.pictures.erotica.pre-teen* (*abpep-t*) is an all too real phenomenon: by late 2000, *abpep-t* boasted some forty thousand postings, mainly images of young girls ranging from toddlers through young adolescents. As we will see, this newsgroup has for years served as a central institution of the kiddie porn Net culture. In *Erotic Innocence*, his magnificent book on contemporary attitudes to childhood sexuality, James Kincaid writes that in the mid-1990s, "researchers found nothing on the Internet that is not also in adult bookstores," though there might be a marginal trade in child porn, "a cottage industry of sorts, a wary trading of photos and old magazines back and forth among a small number of people." Otherwise, he argues, the only people distributing child porn online are government agencies, seeking to bait traps for pedophiles. In *Obscene*

Profits, the most comprehensive study of Internet pornography to date, Frederick S. Lane mentions child porn only when discussing how purveyors of adult materials face legal difficulties through accidentally including underage images on their sites. The book repeatedly tells us about how entrepreneurs do *not* intentionally distribute child porn but says nothing about those who do.

Another major work on commercialized sex is Laurence O'Toole's *Pornocopia*. After describing a celebrated child porn arrest in Great Britain (the "Operation Starburst" affair), O'Toole argued:

> When . . . the hullabaloo over transnational Internet child porn rings ultimately amounts (in the UK at least) to the possession of three images dating back a quarter of a century, people are bound to wonder about the true nature or extent of the dangers of child porn in cyberspace . . . a lot of the materials described as "child porn" are in fact nude pictures of children taken from art-work, family albums and naturist materials.

Many of the materials indeed fall into these categories, but thousands more images do not; and whereas a large number date back a quarter of a century, many others were made last year. But even if O'Toole were exactly correct in his argument, the basic point remains that all the images he mentions are highly condemned under the codes of all advanced nations; so just how do they circulate with relative impunity?[11]

The lack of interest by media and scholars is not hard to understand. Above all, the condemnation of child pornography seems so universal and explicit that there is hardly any point in undertaking research: what is there to explore? Also, the technical issues involved can initially seem forbidding to a non-specialist. Those active in the subculture must be familiar with a variety of terms and techniques, a world of proxies and firewalls, of Zips and anonymizers. Researchers must be able not only to appreciate these details but also to place the subculture in a global context, to understand the subtle legal and cultural distinctions between, say, Japan and the United States, Sweden and the United Kingdom. Some of the major sites require knowledge of other languages, including German and Japanese. No journalists seem to have had the interest to pursue these issues, or to convince editors that the topic merits the space that would be required to explain them thoroughly. Without the raw materials provided by journalistic writing, academics and professionals are stymied.

Statistics

Official statistics (arrests and prosecutions) are equally problematic, since these never include the vast majority of offenders. Instead, such records tell us about those inept and seemingly atypical offenders who fail to take the obvious precautions and who get caught. If, for instance, we wanted to study the child porn world from media or official sources, we might collect media reports of investigations and arrests, of the sort that appear regularly in most advanced nations. Over the last couple of years, regional newspapers in the United States have reported hundreds of such stories, involving all sorts of individuals, including priests, politicians, police officers, and executives, as well as ordinary citizens. Such stories mainly hit the headlines when they involve teachers or others working with youth, but celebrities are also newsworthy. One high-profile case featured the veteran 1970s rock singer Gary Glitter, who was arrested in 1997 after images of nude children were found on a computer that he took for repair. He was found to possess several thousand such pictures, described in court hearings as "filthy and revolting" and "of the very, very, worst possible type." In 1998, an internationally respected geology professor at Yale University was found to have thousands of child porn pictures on his computer, in addition to owning videos of boys performing sexual acts.[12]

But such instances represent only the tip of an iceberg. To quote one of the gurus of the electronic child porn world, "Godfather Corleone":

> Looking at the enormous amount of lolita-lovers out there, very, very few get arrested, the opposite of what most newbies [novices] seem to believe is the case, those that actually do get arrested, do not get

arrested for downloading or uploading to *abpep-t* or visiting sites. Most people that get arrested do so for the following reasons: 1. they had to repair their PC when those repairing the PC discovered pics on the harddrive. 2. they have been trading thru e-mail. 3. they have been using ICQ / IRC [chat lines] for lolita business.[13]

Both trading and chat lines are deadly because one is dealing with faceless individuals who often turn out to be police officers masquerading either as fellow enthusiasts or as underage girls; avoiding such chat facilities is a primary rule offered to novices in this underworld. Another participant on a child porn bulletin board, "Granpa Bob," claimed that recent arrests in the United States could be categorized as follows: "It was basically 75% caught e-mail trading with an LEA [law enforcement agency], 20% by computer repair shops, and 1% caught by either association with known traders or by do-gooders reporting them."[14] It is very rare for individuals to be arrested for posting child porn and virtually unheard of to be caught "just looking."

In the vast majority of cases that come to court, child pornographers are caught for another, unrelated offense such as molestation, which leads to the serendipitous discovery of a collection of images. Though no case is wholly typical, a fairly representative example involves the man in Revere, Massachusetts, who was arrested after a young boy complained that he had been videotaped while having sex. When police searched the suspect's premises, they found four thousand computerized images of underage boys, as well as a hundred indecent videotapes. In a well-publicized case in northern California in 2000, child porn charges surfaced as an incidental element in a suspected murder investigation. Even where porn alone is the major issue at stake, offenders have almost gone out of their way to draw attention to themselves, for instance, by viewing illegal materials on computers in public libraries![15] As long as enthusiasts maintain their interests solely within the virtual realm, observing pictures but not seeking to collect or apply the electronic fantasies in the world of lived action, they appear to be safe from detection. The virtual world genuinely is protected territory. To this extent, we can agree with the

seemingly hyperbolic claim made by child protection activist Barry Crimmins in 1995 that the Internet had permitted "the *de facto* decriminal-
ization of child pornography."[16]

Since it is chiefly novices who get caught, experienced members of
the subculture have little but contempt for the capacities of "LEA." In
a recent exchange on the boards, one poster suggested an ingenious
tactic that might, in theory, serve to entrap many child porn fans and
asked whether police were likely to deploy it.[17] Responses were sarcas-
tically dismissive:

> * **Godfather Corleone** > I don't really think the LEA work that way as
> I'm sure they have better things to do which they know are more effi-
> cient. For instance, trying to catch newbies trading per e-mail or new-
> bies visiting IRC etc.
> * **Kidflash** > LEA is not smart enough or have time to do such things.

By definition, studies of arrests or convictions reveal only the failures in
the electronic child porn world. The cases that come to light fulfill a kind
of Darwinian function, since they remove from the subculture those least
fit to adapt and survive and thus ensure the efficiency of those who remain. Nor can figures for arrests tell us much about the scale or the ge-
ography of electronic trafficking. If a hundred men were suddenly arrested for computer child porn offenses in Los Angeles, this would not
necessarily show that Los Angeles is a particular center for this activity
but would rather indicate the interests and technical abilities of law enforcement agencies in that area. Perhaps such a campaign would further
reveal that child pornographers in this region are singularly neglectful of
security precautions. It is a truism, but criminal statistics measure official
behavior and nothing more.

Media neglect of the child porn world is paralleled at the highest levels of law enforcement and among political leaders. To illustrate this, we
can read the record of a Senate hearing in 1997 on the issue of the *Proliferation of Child Pornography on the Internet*, the witnesses before
which included the head of the federal National Center on Missing
and Exploited Children (NCMEC), as well as FBI director Louis Freeh.

Despite this prestigious lineup, the account offered of child porn was at best rudimentary, at worst simply inaccurate. In his opening address, Senator Judd Gregg noted, "Currently the avenue for distribution of sexually exploitative material is through chat rooms visited primarily by pedophiles and child pornographers. In these chat rooms, the offenders speak freely about their desire to trade pictures."[18] As noted above, none of the many thousands active in the hard-core subculture would dream of participating in such a practice. Very few would be foolish enough to become involved with the online seductions that formed the subject of 80 percent of the evidence before the hearing in question. No witness so much as mentioned any of the key institutions or practices of the subculture, the tricks of the trade, or seemed aware of groups like *abpep-t* (or, indeed, of the newsgroups as such). Much of the discussion thus focused on cyberstalking and cyberporn but very little on child pornography, which was the ostensible justification for the event. Admittedly, this hearing is now several years old, but no recent inquiry or public statement suggests any significant advance in police practice since then. Federal enforcement of child pornography laws in the United States seems entirely geared toward catching the lowest level of offender, and if a bigger fish is ever apprehended, it is by accident.

Just why policing has hitherto been so unsuccessful requires explanation. As we will see, a sizable technological gap exists between criminals and law enforcement, to the advantage of the lawbreakers. Equally critical is the traditional law enforcement approach to major crimes, which are generally assumed to be highly organized by some kind of hierarchical syndicate, such as an organized crime family, a drug gang, or a terrorist movement. In these circumstances, police and prosecutors can wage a fairly literal "war on crime," arresting leaders and their henchmen while disrupting lines of command, control and communication. But such convenient structures are simply lacking in the child porn world. To extend the war analogy, child porn and other computer crimes should rather be seen in terms of a war of the flea, a guerrilla war undertaken by a vast and decentralized phantom enemy totally lacking a command structure. To take one illustration, terrorists dream of creating perfect cell systems, in which no activist knows the identity of more than a handful of comrades. In practice, though, terrorists very rarely succeed in achieving such a degree of insulation, and this failure permits police moles and infiltrators to unravel whole networks. In contrast, the overwhelming majority of child porn enthusiasts have the means of identifying literally none of their co-users, even individuals with whom they have been in electronic contact for a decade. The exceptions to this rule account for the major law enforcement successes, such as the destruction of the so-called Wonderland child porn ring in 1998. But the difficulties facing police are evident. When we factor in the jurisdictional conflicts (organizers in Germany, say, servers in Japan, and users in the United States), we can understand why child porn flourishes, all but unchecked. We can also see from this account that child porn raises to the highest degree issues of control and regulation that surface in almost any area of deviance or dissidence on the Internet, so that any successful measures that evolve in this instance might have much wider application.

Seeing for Ourselves?

If we wish to go beyond merely collecting media accounts or records of prosecutions, with all their limitations and biases, the only alternative is to "go see for yourself"; yet massive problems stand in the way of any such attempt, above all in the shape of legal difficulties.[19] Can anyone other than a police officer study this material without inviting criminal charges?

There is an old tradition of research on deviant cultures, which often, but not necessarily, involves some kind of participant observation. This strategy is felt to be so valuable because subjects in their free state often share their honestly held views and attitudes, while arrested or convicted deviants are all too likely to mold their statements in a way that will best appeal to courts, psychologists, and parole boards. Scholars have used this kind of participant method to study youth gangs, motorcycle gangs, taggers and graffiti artists, extremists of left or right, and participants in sexual subcultures, and in each case there is some threat of legal consequences, criminal prosecution, or personal danger. I quote from the description of a recent collection of essays on *Ethnography at the Edge*:

> Describing their deep involvement with such diverse groups as skinheads, phone sex workers, drug dealers, graffiti artists, and the homeless, many of the authors confess to their own episodes of illegal drug use, drunk driving, weapons violations, assault at gunpoint, obstruction of justice, and arrest while engaged in ethnographic studies.

In one controversial work, Laud Humphreys reported the activities of the *Tea Room Trade*, namely, casual homosexual contacts in public restrooms.[20] But none of these studies involves risks as severe as those found in the child pornography area, and it might be argued that this particular legal environment so constrains the researcher as to make serious research all but impossible. I hope to show that this is not entirely true.

The problem can be simply stated: child pornography is so stigmatized under American law that virtually any contact with the material can lead to a prison sentence. Moreover, the courts have stated that every term in this equation can be interpreted extraordinarily broadly. *Child pornography* involves individuals below the age of eighteen, and *pornography* includes depictions that would be only mildly indecent if adult subjects were involved. Finally, *possession* has acquired an expansive meaning. In the context of computers, one violates the law not only by storing such an image on a hard disk but merely by downloading it. Contrary to popular impression, "downloading" does not refer to the act of deliberately saving an image but merely to pressing on a link that causes an image to appear on the screen. The offense is in the accessing, not the saving. Almost certainly, too, it is not necessary for a prosecutor to show that an accused individual knew that pressing that link would produce a suspect image.

Possession of this kind of material is a strict liability offense. One either does or does not possess it, and none of the conventional let-outs or excuses apply, any more than they would in cases involving, say, heroin.

It is no excuse to say that one was consulting the images for purposes of academic research or journalistic investigation, nor can one claim to be collecting materials to expose and combat the evils of child pornography. In a recent criminal case, journalist Larry Matthews found that it was no defense to claim he was trading obscene images as part of a major investigation into the child porn world, and he was convicted of a serious criminal offense. The trial judge remarked that journalists seeking information about child porn could adequately fulfill their function by attending the trials of perpetrators or by interviewing the victims of the trade. All in all, this would be an excellent way of ensuring that public knowledge of this world is confined to whatever information law enforcement agencies deign to release in their public relations statements.[21]

Viewing child porn material is a criminal offense, in a legal environment in which it is all but impossible for even the most inept of prosecutors to lose a case. Nor, given the horror attached to the offense, is there likely to be much public outcry about judicial railroading: in this area of law, only the most egregious cases of police entrapment have inspired any media complaints whatever. Other avenues are also closed to researchers, since it is inconceivable that an active child pornographer will allow himself to be interviewed or to permit an academic any kind of access to his traffic. These facts explain why, to date, no researcher has attempted to study this market. James Kincaid writes, "If we look for studies of the actual material, the kiddie porn itself, we find nothing, since it is against the law to look at what may exist, much less own it."[22]

For obvious reasons, I share the general reluctance to risk legal consequences, yet there is a solution to the problem of studying this material, one that is far from perfect but at least offers some way of approaching the subculture. Briefly, though virtually any visual images involved in this trade are prohibited, words are subject to constitutional protections. This exception allows the researcher to access freely what we might call the collateral manifestations of the child pornography world, namely, newsgroups, bulletin boards, and message boards. And it is precisely the newsgroups and "pedo boards" that provide the organizing framework for the whole subculture, underworld, community, or industry—the exact term is a matter of debate.

This book is therefore based on verbal, textual material collected from newsgroups and message boards over the last two years. Often these sources are accompanied by pictures that it would be criminal to possess or even to view briefly, but I have circumvented this problem by using a feature available on any computer that prevents images being loaded without my explicit decision. This is achieved simply by deactivating the "autoload images" feature of my Netscape software. It then becomes possible to access a page that may contain child pornography of the most harrowing hard-core variety, but all I will see on my screen are generic icons indicating that photographic material is available or a note that the picture would be (say) 300 x 400 pixels in size, were I to decide to download it—which I do not. I still face potential legal difficulties in that I am leaving a record of the sites I visit, and it is conceivable that some agency observing the traffic would conclude that I was accessing illicit materials and obtain a search warrant for my computer. Although I do not possess a single suspicious image, nor have I downloaded one, the equipment would still be removed until it could be examined, and recent instances suggest that police agencies have a backlog of several years in undertaking such detailed investigations. Since a five-year-old computer is of next to no value, such a seizure would be a de facto confiscation without compensation. This has not happened yet, but I suppose it could.

The other difficulty with this text-only approach is that I do not know from firsthand observation exactly what the material is that I am supposed to be handling, whether what is advertised as child pornography in fact features subjects aged five or thirty-five. Virtually all the so-called lolita sites that are easily discovered on the Internet do, in fact, involve much older women. Still, the nature of the message boards allows me to avoid this problem because the content of so many of the sites is described, analyzed, and criticized in considerable detail and by multiple independent observers. Typically, a person will post a series of images that can be downloaded only in coded Zip format, which is useless without a password that will be issued separately some hours or days later. Potential consumers often ask if the item is worth their time and trouble downloading and will first seek a detailed description from other users, and these descriptions provide specific evidence of the material discussed. On the "Maestro" bulletin board, which was long a crucial information source for the subculture, a participant submitted a query as follows:

> I've been hearing great stuff about the Vicky movie on *abpep-t*. Can someone give me a quick content rundown so I know if they are worth my while? Thanx. [Godfather Corleone responded that it was] excellent material, basically a ten/eleven year old girl doing some handjobs, getting herself rubbed, doing some blowjob and gets a facial, pity not all series are filmed this way, this is already the new goddess after Helena (hel-lo), that's for sure.[23]

In such exchanges, misstatements or false claims are met with instant rebuttal and furious denunciation. If someone dared to recommend a putative child porn site that, on closer examination, proved to depict adult women in schoolgirl uniforms ("old hags," "toothless grandmas"), several other contributors would expose that fact within minutes. The original poster might be barred from contributing to that board again and might also suffer hacking and virus attacks. The quality control system is finely tuned.

Such exchanges provide abundant information about the photo sets and movies available on the boards, without the necessity to view them directly. The message boards devote extensive space to discussing pictures and individual subjects, some of whom have followings similar to those of adult supermodels or porn queens. Apart from the Helena already mentioned, examples include Vicky, Laika, Hayley, and "Louisiana." Observers comment on the date and place of particular picture runs and seek to date a picture through internal clues such as posters seen on the wall behind the subject or magazines on a table. One observer may speculate that a picture dates from the mid-1980s, while another will point out that a *Titanic* poster establishes the date as late 1990s. This kind of critical reaction leads me to believe that the remarks I will make about the nature of particular sites are accurate, though I recognize that I am falling far short of the kind of direct observation that would normally be demanded in reporting such a study. I can only say that I have used what I believe to be the best possible methodology in the particular situation, while remaining within the law.

Ethics

Some other ethical issues are peculiar to this thorny environment. One involves the reporting of illegal activity, a dilemma encountered by anyone using an ethnographic approach. What should a researcher do when asked by police about the gangs or drug dealers with whom he or she has been associating? Some academics might provide this information; others would not, even at the cost of forfeiting their own liberty. I face no such dilemma, as I do not know the names, e-mail addresses, or any identifying features of the individuals with whom I am concerned and cannot provide any information of that kind to the authorities.

Also, as I will explain, URL addresses themselves are all but useless to authorities. Most of the sites and message boards are well-established and long-running affairs, and these are already well known to both criminal justice agencies and to anti-pornography activists, who sometimes try to sabotage operations. Other sites, which contain the most seriously illegal material, last only for a few hours, and there would be no point in reporting these to the authorities. No information I could provide would be of any significant use in suppressing the child pornography trade or in causing more than a dent. When I first encountered child porn material, I naively tried to supply lists of URLs and related information to various agencies, originally to the child protection section of the U.S. Customs Service and later, via a European anti-porn pressure group, to the relevant department of Interpol; but I gave up trying when I realized the futility of reporting ephemeral sites.[24]

One other ethical issue relates to the citation of sources. Though I describe at length the boards and sites that I have used, I do not provide specific URLs that would allow other researchers to use them, and I refer to the active boards and newsgroups through pseudonyms (the Maestro board is one such). I am painfully aware that this is a prima facie violation of the rules of social science, as it prevents any kind of replication of the research, but my rationale is strong. The sites I have been using are exceedingly difficult to find and cannot be located simply by using a regular search engine such as Excite or Google. Using such an engine to locate "child pornography" or "lolitas" will produce hundreds of sites, including tirades against the porn trade and advice on how to report criminal activity as well as fraudulent sites targeted at the gullible. But supplying the URL of just one authentic site would potentially create a network effect that would bring the observer into the whole subculture. It would be wrong to publish material that could assist a person seeking such images or that could lead a person to discover within himself an interest in this kind of sexual activity. At its worst, these kind of images can serve as a kind of visual heroin, dangerously addictive. As a warning, I offer a frightening message posted on a child porn board by "Dad," in answer to the question "How did you become a loli-lover?" that is, a pedophile:

> I remember one day I done a search for teen girls on the net, I expected to find girls of 18+, ye know the usual. But this one time I found a girl-love site, . . . it was wonderful. One girl in particular, Laika, the 'Internet princess'. Then I started to search for loli on the various engines and got the usual rubbish, pay sites and misleading links, soon I found out about news [newsgroups] and went from there, that was three years ago. . . . If it wasn't for the Internet I would have never known. I think as the Internet grows, more people will find out their sexual desires just as I did.[25]

Perhaps they will, but I do not propose to help them. I will supply addresses to any law enforcement agency that requests them, together with any research notes, but will not publish identifying URLs.

With all the caveats mentioned, using the bulletin boards and newsgroups offers a remarkably rich body of material for understanding the child porn world, which can be observed in greater detail than perhaps any deviant culture. What other criminal fraternity produces thousands of lines of textual information each and every day, in which strikingly literate participants discuss techniques and legal issues, mores and ethical questions? However off-putting the legal environment may initially seem, the opportunities for research here are, in fact, very rich. But most important for legislators and policymakers is the fact that this material exists at all, despite a daunting array of statutes and an overwhelming popular consensus condemning it. If child porn cannot be suppressed on the Internet, then what can?

TWO

Child Pornography

Where were most of you twenty years ago? It was an excit-
ing time online.
                    —Kindred, Maestro board, March 18, 2000

For most observers, child pornography is not only repulsive but genuinely baffling, which may explain the reluctance to believe it is so
widespread on the Internet, except as a kind of sick joke. Surely so
many people cannot be so very disturbed as this phenomenon would
suggest? In fact, there is abundant evidence of adults being sexually interested in, even obsessed with, children, which accounts for an enduring market in pornographic materials. Though far removed from any
kind of social mainstream, a sexual interest in children is not confined
to a tiny segment of hard-core individuals who are demonized under
some such damning label as "perverts" or "pedophiles." Child pornography has a substantial, if murky, history, and in recent times individuals have always been able to find materials of this kind, often by re-
sorting to creative subterfuges and new technologies. The Internet
merely marks the latest phase in this story.

"Barely Legal"

The prohibition on sex between adults and minors is neither absolute
nor universal. A basic biological instinct mandates the protection of the
young, which explains the common taboo against intercourse with very
small children. Having said this, many societies both past and present are

far more tolerant of sexual play with children than modern Western standards would permit. In addition, the definition of *childhood* varies greatly according to time and location. "Minority" is a legal concept profoundly shaped by political pressures and interactions in any given society. While virtually all societies define a five-year-old as a child, only in relatively recent times would a fifteen-year-old be placed in a comparable category and subject to the same kind of legal restraints and protections. The concept of "adolescence" dates only to the early twentieth century.[1]

In most traditional societies, the transition from girlhood to womanhood is linked to puberty, and the assumption is that at this point the young woman is able to participate legally in sexual activity, subject to the moral codes of the community in question. Nor is even puberty necessarily a hard and fast dividing line. In the United States, the age of consent for girls stood at ten years from colonial times until the 1880s, when it was raised in response to heightened sensitivity to sexual dangers. Over the next century, the American age of legal consent rose steadily, commonly to sixteen or eighteen, while the physical age of sexual maturity fell equally dramatically, from fifteen to twelve or thirteen. During the twentieth century, therefore, young teenage girls were far more likely to be sexually active than their predecessors, though virtually all such behaviors were newly defined as seriously illegal. Only as recently as 1984 was the age at which individuals could legally be depicted in a sexual or pornographic context raised from sixteen to eighteen. The notion that a seventeen-year-old girl is legally a "child" has thus been legislated within very recent memory. The historically contingent nature of the notion of "childhood" was emphasized in a recent Canadian child pornography case, in which a senior judge took issue with that nation's current definition of the age of sexual majority:

> In this judgment, when I myself use the word "child" . . . I mean those below the age of puberty. At common law, these ages were deemed to be twelve for a girl and fourteen for a boy. As, however, fourteen is the age of consent in Canada and has been, for girls, for over one hundred years, I define a "child" as anyone under the age of fourteen years. I appreciate that in the latter part of this century, fifteen, sixteen and sev-

enteen-year-olds have been considered barely more than children. Our forebears thought no such thing. Boys were sent to sea at thirteen or fourteen and girls could be apprenticed to domestic service, with their consent, at twelve. Boys under eighteen, by lying about their age, fought in the forces in both wars.[2]

Rather than imagining a fundamental gulf dividing "child-lovers" from "normal" people, we should rather speak of a continuum, in which popular condemnation of behavior is inversely proportionate to the age of the subject. If an adult man is sexually interested in younger teenage girls, then he may well violate the moral codes of a particular society, but he cannot be said to contradict any universal or natural law, any biological imperative. This is a classic example of a *mala prohibita* offense, condemned in some communities but not others. If it is not "natural" or acceptable for a thirty-year-old man to be sexually excited by a fourteen-year-old girl, at least it requires less explanation than true pedophilia, an interest in smaller, pre-pubescent children. The same is true for a man collecting pictures of young teenage girls. Since sexual behavior with teenagers has been considered normal in most societies, we have no damning label for the man who experiences such temptations. How many people even know the arcane psychiatric label of "ephebophilia," which is applied to those attracted to younger teenagers?[3] And while sexual activity between men and teenage boys is less widely accepted than acts involving girls, this, too, has been tolerated, or nodded at, in many historical societies.

A sexual interest in younger teenage girls is exploited by a sizable legal market in the United States, which has such stringent laws against any erotica involving children. In 1993 there appeared the first number of a popular adult magazine titled *Barely Legal*, which depicts adult (over-eighteen) women masquerading as much younger teens, and the publication was widely imitated. A recent journalistic article on the "the flourishing imitation child-porn industry" notes:

> Though the *Barely Legal* video, a spinoff from the highly successful porn mag of the same name, is a popular rental . . . it's hardly alone in

the field. Scan the racks of your local porn parlor and the series titles read like a bobby-sox chaser's wet dream: *Virgin Stories, Cherries, Rookie Cookies, Cherry Poppers, Young and Anal, Cheerleader Confessions* and the memorable *Young, Dumb and Full of Cum. Adult Video News* even dedicated its September 1999 issue to the genre with a "Back to School" cover showing two "carnal cuties" in saddle shoes and plaid skirts.[4]

The popularity of such materials indicates a mass popular market for teen sexuality.

Adult-Child Sex

We are in very different territory when considering pedophilia, which is severely condemned in most communities. Incidentally, psychiatry here is in conflict with law and general usage, in that pedophilia properly defined refers only to the interest in children at or below the age of puberty and not in young teenagers. Also, actually being a pedophile is no more illegal than being an alcoholic. Pedophilia is a condition, a set of interests and obsessions, which does not of itself violate any law because it does not necessarily lead to any type of conduct. This should be emphasized in view of the news headlines we so often read about police "hunting for pedophiles."

In legal language, sex with prepubescent children can be considered as *mala in se*, "evil in itself," and contrary to nature. At first sight, it seems difficult to imagine how an adult might develop a sexual interest in small children, but that notion is itself wrongly phrased in the sense that, at some point, probably every individual on the planet has such an interest and often indulges in the exploration that accompanies it. For most individuals, though, interest in (say) six-year-olds of the opposite sex occurs when he or she is about that age, and any sexual behavior or fondling is likely dismissed as harmless play. In many cases, such exploration can occur with others of the same sex. Theories of pedophilia customarily assume that an individual fails to grow out of a quite normal early interest in fellow children, so that one's sexuality does not mature into the appropriate relationship with adults. Relations with adults of the opposite sex might produce fear or discomfort, which are not present with sexually immature subjects: children are seen as safe, unthreatening. In addition to seeking younger people as sexual partners, a pedophile might wish for the kinds of interaction that characterize infantile fantasy and play—for fondling, voyeurism, and exhibitionism rather than penetrative sex.[5]

Though pedophiles are often dismissed as a tiny, aberrant minority, their fascination with childhood sexual fantasies and experiences may be quite widely shared, though to a far milder degree than is found among the "perverts." As Freud had pronounced, "perverted sexuality is nothing but infantile sexuality magnified and separated into its component parts." The idea that many otherwise normal individuals seek a frisson from recalling childhood sexual fantasies is confirmed by observing the content of much so-called adult pornography, and particularly the remarkable volume of images and stories now available on the Internet.[6] Such, for instance, is much sadomasochistic material, in which men fantasize about being under the dominant control of a woman, who plays the role of a stern but loving mother. Other taboo subjects that have proliferated on so-called adult Web sites include "water sports," an interest in female urination, which perhaps relies on the recollection of boyhood fantasies. Also popular are voyeuristic sites, permitting men to share the experience of gazing up women's skirts or spying through windows. We might also see a kind of infantilism in another common type of pornographic image, namely, the "shemale," or transsexual, a man who through surgery and chemical treatments adopts many of the bodily features of a woman, including breasts and rounded hips, but who still retains male genitalia. The appeal of this type of image may be related to childish concepts of the opposite sex, since small boys without direct knowledge of female bodies often imagine that girls too must possess a penis, and the shemale might be seen as a confirmation of those immature concepts.

Many adult sites claim to offer "lolitas" or even "child porn," though as I remarked earlier, these are invariably bogus: even so, it is interesting that porn merchants might assume that a substantial audience would be interested in something that notionally lies so far beyond the pale. Countless "adult" images portray grown women as schoolgirls or with shaved pubic hair. While the patrons of adult magazines or Web sites would be appalled to be told they had anything in common with the loathed pedophiles, some of the psychological stimuli are related. These comments are not intended to excuse or justify pedophilia but rather to suggest that those interested in child pornography might not be so far removed from the "normal" population. The gulf with normality is all the narrower when the materials in question involve young teenagers.

Child Porn

As long as there is a sexual interest in a behavior or a type of person, that will lead to commodification and commercialization, in the form of prostitution and pornography. Occasionally, the process of selling youthful sex might appear in the mainstream, and when censorship restrictions weakened during the 1970s, images of pubescent sexuality proliferated in major films. Sexually precocious young girls were portrayed in popular films such as *Taxi Driver*, *Alice's Restaurant*, *Night Moves*, and *Pretty Baby*. More commonly, themes of adult-child sex are the preserve of the vice industry. Underage and pubescent prostitutes are found as a specialized and highly valued commodity in the vice scene in any big city, and the patchy historical records that we have suggest this has long been the case. In London, the traffic in pubescent prostitutes in the 1880s ignited one of that city's most damning vice scandals and caused British legislators to raise the age of consent. In Los Angeles in the 1930s, a devastating scandal exposed a flourishing vice trade in underage girls, some of whom were kidnapped from orphanages. Parallel to this heterosexual market was (and is) a widespread traffic in boys. At the end of the nineteenth century, moralists and social investigators in American cities found ample evidence of boy prostitutes, often pre-pubescent, and later social investigators would periodically rediscover such pederastic underworlds.[7]

The pornography trade represents another segment of commercialized vice. The history of pornography as such is difficult to write, given the illegal and surreptitious nature of the trade, but child pornography in particular is very difficult to observe.[8] Accounts of sex with very young boys and girls are commonplace in nineteenth-century erotic classics such as *The Pearl* and Walter's *My Secret Life*, and we know of nude photographs and prints of young teenagers and pre-pubescent children from the Victorian period. Often, these images sought a kind of respectability by portraying their subjects in classical and artistic poses, but the prominent display of the genitalia leaves little doubt about the erotic purpose of the works. It is a fair guess that the first such images appeared very shortly after the invention of photography: as in the case of the Internet, people rarely hesitate too long before exploring the erotic implications of any new form of technology. To take one celebrated instance, we know that from 1867 onward, Charles Dodgson (better known as Lewis Carroll) was regularly taking nude photographs of little girls, some as young as six. By the turn of the century, such images were acquiring more explicitly pornographic connotations. Even before the First World War, American police in child murder investigations were seizing collections of indecent photographs of children as indicators that the possessor might be a "fiend" or serial killer.[9]

The modern history of child porn dates from the general relaxation of censorship standards in the 1960s, when pornographic pictures and films of children became widely available in Europe and the United States. The changed attitude reflected the general sexual liberalization of those years, a shift supported by changes in professional opinion. European evidence seemed to show that greater availability of hard-core pornography was closely correlated with a decline in actual sex crimes, indicating that porn provided a beneficial safety valve for violent instincts. The year 1969 marked the beginning of a production boom in child pornography, particularly through the Danish firm of Rodox/Color Climax. Other Scandinavian nations and the Netherlands were also deeply involved in what journalist Tim Tate has described as "the ten year madness (1969–1979)." This era has achieved legendary status among devotees of this material, and particularly of the movies: as one aficionado writes on a child porn board, "I remember in the eighties seeing a whole bunch of them—some of them numbered in the hundreds, so there must be a load I never saw. . . . Some of the girls were probably about 13–14 from what I remember."[10] The magazines produced in these years offered a wide range of subjects, from girls in their mid-teens down to toddlers, and the activities portrayed varied from innocuous nudity on a beach or at a nudist camp to extreme sexual acts, showing children performing with each other and with adults. Some magazines, such as *Children-Love, Lolita, Lollitots, Nudist Moppets,* and *Bambina-Sex,* developed a powerful brand-name identity.

Many European films and magazines were imported into the United States, while other child pornography was manufactured domestically, often disguised as imports to evade the attentions of law enforcement agencies.[11] At least for a few years, it was easy to walk into a store in New York, Los Angeles, or London and purchase what was frankly advertised as child porn. This might include pictures of, say, young girls performing oral sex on adult men or women or men performing anal sex on young boys, as well as countless pictures of eight- or ten-year-old girls in *Penthouse*-type cheesecake poses. These images also developed a following outside the porn world strictly defined, as the post-hippie counterculture adopted free sexuality as a central tenet of belief. In the early 1970s, European and U.S. "underground" magazines notionally devoted to rock music and radical politics would also throw in occasional images of pubescent nudes, which thereby reached an unprecedented audience.

The Great Reaction

By the mid-1970s, this new openness provoked an intense reaction. Even in societies reluctant to tolerate censorship of sexual materials, the use of child subjects crossed the line. Suppression was made easier when decency campaigners and feminists successfully promoted the idea that pornographic material was directly linked with actual sexual misconduct.[12] In 1976 and 1977, the existence of child pornography provided the impetus for a ferocious morality campaign: this was the time when the phrase "child abuse" gained its present implication of sexual interference or molestation. Over the next few years, fears of child sexual exploitation became inextricably linked to other concerns of the age, including kidnapping, serial murder, and organized sex rings. Moral activists pressured the New York City police department to act decisively against the underage vice culture that had emerged around Times Square, which had become the symbolic center of child porn trafficking. The New York campaign was imitated in other cities, and claims-makers successfully presented their views on the national stage.[13] Much of the public outrage focused on the tiny pedophile organizations that had emerged in the early 1970s, which now became targets of official investigation. This campaign made pariahs of groups such as NAMBLA (North American Man-Boy Love Association) and the British PIE (Pedophile Information Exchange). By the early 1980s, both had largely been forced back into the shadows from which they had emerged so briefly.

The news media used extravagantly inflated statistics to present child porn as a pressing social menace. A 1977 report on NBC television news claimed, "It's been estimated that as many as two million American youngsters are involved in the fast-growing, multi-million-dollar child pornography business." The 1977 campaign began a pattern that would dominate accounts over the next decade, when moralistic critics competed to assert the most excessive claims about the size and profitability of the trade. In 1985, an exposé of "the shame of the nation" in a family magazine noted "a dramatic increase in child sexual abuse over the past five years in this country, at least half of them involving children compelled to participate in the making of pornography. According to one Los Angeles Police Department estimate, at least 300,000 children under the age of 16 are involved in the nationwide child pornography racket." The pornography problem was connected with "even more dramatic increases in the number of missing children." In 1986, anti-smut crusader Donald Wildmon claimed that "each year, fifty thousand missing children are victims of pornography. Most are kidnapped, raped, abused, filmed for porno magazines and movies and, more often than not, murdered." Critics asserted that the child porn industry earned annual revenues of $5 billion.[14]

In addition to its supposedly vast scale, the child porn trade was said to be extremely well organized, and conspiracy theories about pedophile sex rings ran rampant between about 1977 and 1986. In 1977, the *Chicago Tribune* suggested that kiddie porn was organized through "child sex rackets" that "operate on a national and international scale involving thousands of adult perverts often working with one another and exchanging child victims." In 1983, the FBI and other agencies formed a task force to investigate "the kidnapping and selling of children and their use in porn films, the murder of children and adolescents by kidnappers." These ideas were publicized by the special investigation of pornography sponsored by U.S. Attorney General Edwin Meese. The Meese Commission urged the creation of a national task force to examine "possible links between sex rings, child pornography and organized crime . . . [and] possible linkages between multi-victim, multi-perpetrator child sex rings throughout the United States." Conspiracy charges were further popularized in the fictional writings of Jonathan Kellerman and Andrew Vachss. Vachss's 1985 novel *Flood* featured a pedophile villain active in the manufacture and sale of child pornography, much of it depicting acts of violence.[15]

Virtually all the more extreme charges made in these years have been discredited. There never was the slightest basis for the statement that the number of children involved in the trade was three hundred thousand or a million, and all such figures can be traced back to the rhetoric of well-intentioned activists. Equally ludicrous were the multibillion-dollar estimates for the financial scale of the business. Even at its height in the mid-1970s, child pornography activity would more properly be characterized as multimillion-dollar at most, but the "billion" figure circulated through the next decade. As recently as 2000, one author remarked, "In the late 1980s, it was estimated that child pornography exploited some 1.2 million children and generated more than $2.4 billion annually. . . .

Those numbers have only increased with time." Claims about vast, tightly organized pedophile rings were equally ill supported: these conspiratorial ideas would ultimately evolve into the widespread panic over Satanic rings molesting children, a scare that is now commonly recognized to have no basis whatever. A concise evaluation of the various charges is found in the 1980 study of "Sexual Exploitation of Children" presented by a special investigative committee of the Illinois state legislature. This report deflated all current claims about a vast organized industry:

> The report did discover child pornography, most of it made for private use or circulation by "individual child molesters." According to the report, in 1980 the FBI completed a two and a half year porn sting operation. "None of the 60 raids resulted in any seizures of child pornography, even though the raids were comprehensive and nationwide." The longest lasting, biggest-selling underground child porn magazine of the 1970s, the *Broad Street Magazine*, . . . never sold to more than 800 individuals, nor grossed more than $30,000 a year.[16]

The Law

Despite these caveats, the legal campaign against child porn continued vigorously, ensuring that the legal availability of child porn material declined sharply. In 1978, a federal Sexual Exploitation of Children Act prohibited the manufacture or commercial distribution of obscene material involving subjects aged under sixteen years, and this measure virtually eliminated the open availability of child porn materials in adult stores. Later acts increased penalties and expanded police powers to seek out and suppress this material, eroding the distinction between obscenity and indecency where children were concerned. Contrary to public impression, "obscenity" is and always has been illegal in the United States, but in order to be prohibited, material has to be truly obscene rather than merely indecent, and this fact is difficult to prove in court. At least since the libertarian Supreme Court decisions of the 1950s, nudity per se rarely made a picture obscene where adult subjects were concerned, and by the 1970s, even hard-core depictions of sexual activity were generally covered under the lesser, non-prohibited, category of indecency. This distinction made prosecutions difficult, and even quite extreme adult material condemned by lower courts is usually vindicated at appeal level. This environment made police and prosecutors reluctant to enter into obscenity cases, particularly when they knew they would receive little support from media or the public at large. From 1977, however, it was obvious that the public would support the total suppression of child porn materials, and law enforcement agencies became much more active in seizures and prosecutions.

Federal laws increasingly placed all sexual depictions of children into the category of obscenity, whether or not the child was participating in sexual activity. The crucial measure in this process was the 1984 Child Protection Act, which virtually removed the whole category of child pornography from First Amendment protection. Any depiction of sex involving a minor was automatically obscene, making it child pornography and therefore illegal. The 1984 law also raised the age of a minor for these purposes from sixteen to eighteen, applying the label of "child" to millions of individuals old enough to marry. This move produced some bizarre and troubling consequences. In a 1999 Michigan case, a twenty-four-year-old man was federally convicted of taking and possessing nude images of his seventeen-year-old girlfriend, who consented to the photographs being taken: regardless, the man faced a five-year prison sentence.[17]

American courts upheld the progressive expansion of the child pornography label. In 1982, the key Supreme Court case of *New York v. Ferber* rejected constitutional challenges to the special standards of indecency applied in child pornography cases and agreed that the government had "compelling" and "surpassing" interests in the protection of children, with a broad definition of age limits: "The distribution of photographs and films depicting sexual activity by *juveniles* is intrinsically related to the sexual abuse of *children*" (my emphasis; "juveniles," of course, are not necessarily "children"). In 1986, a federal trial court in California devised the so-called *Dost* test as to whether visual depictions of young people were illegal and specified six factors that might make an image "lascivious." Among other elements, judges should determine whether the focal point of the visual depiction is on the child's pubic area; whether the setting of the visual depiction is sexually suggestive; whether the child is depicted in an unnatural pose or in inappropriate attire, considering the age of the child; whether the child is fully or partially clothed or nude; whether the visual depiction suggests sexual coyness or a willingness to engage in sexual activity; and whether the visual depiction is intended to elicit a sexual response in the viewer. Such subjective criteria gave courts huge latitude in assessing the legality of any given image.

By the 1990s, child pornography was defined as "visual depiction . . . of a minor engaging in sexually explicit conduct," including "lascivious exhibition of the genitals or pubic area of any person," a characterization that would be only indecent where adults were concerned. In the 1993 case of *U.S. v. Knox*, a man was imprisoned for possessing suggestive videotapes depicting scantily clad young girls, with the camera focusing on "lascivious exhibition" of their clothed genital areas. If the same standards were applied to adult subjects, many thousands of advertisements that appear in mainstream magazines every month would immediately be criminalized, to say nothing of the entire production of the adult porn industry. One rare example of judicial caution in this area occurred in 1999, when a federal court struck down a law against "virtual" child pornography, namely, the creation of any computer-generated image that "appears to be . . . of a minor" engaging in sexual activity.

The courts permitted sweeping police measures to assist the government in its "compelling" interest. Where adult materials were involved, police would act only against producers or distributors, and even then rarely, but a totally different standard applied in child porn cases. A crime is committed by anyone who "knowingly receives, or distributes," or "knowingly possesses" images, in addition to making or selling them. In the 1990 case of *Osborne v. Ohio*, the Supreme Court agreed that private possession in the home should be criminalized, namely, a photograph of a "nude male adolescent." Though precedent defended the private possession of obscene matter, conviction in this case was justified in order to protect "the victims of child pornography" and to destroy "a market for the exploitative use of children."[18] For American police and prosecutors, the new laws were a dream come true. Whereas once law enforcement had to prove complex obscenity cases to skeptical juries against the background of criticism by social liberals and mass media, now all that was required was to show that John Doe possessed a nude photograph and that any reasonable person could see that the subject was underage.

Other measures followed in later years, though given the extent of existing prohibitions, these were largely symbolic. The continued outpouring of legislation reflects politicians' recognition that no measure even theoretically connected with child porn could fail to attract public support, while such actions demonstrated a responsiveness to "kids' issues." In 1986, the U.S. Child Sexual Abuse and Pornography Act banned the production and use of advertisements for child pornography; in 1988, a Child Protection and Obscenity Enforcement Act made it unlawful to use a computer to transmit advertisements for or visual depictions of child pornography. These restrictions were further enhanced by the Protection of Children From Sexual Predators Act (1999). Meanwhile, states continued passing statutes intended to suppress child porn or cyberporn, however superfluous they may have appeared in light of the expanding federal code.[19]

Increasingly, a prohibitionist attitude to youthful sexuality affected images of children far removed from anything that could loosely be construed as pornography. This attitude was applied to artistic depictions of children. Often, parental pictures of small children are reported to police by the staff of photographic developing labs, who demonstrate a puritanical vigilante zeal, and the resulting prosecutions have often ventured into farce. Serious visual artists have also suffered. In 1998, jurisdictions in Alabama and Tennessee indicted the Barnes and Noble bookstore chain for stocking copies of art photography books by Jock Sturges and David Hamilton, both of whom included studies of nude children. Some campaigners, led by anti-abortion extremist Randall Terry, destroyed copies of the books in stores, as Terry himself declared that "we're de-

stroying the weapon. I mean, these are the tools of child molesters."
More recently, a California court decided that Hamilton's book *Twenty
Five Years of an Artist* is pornographic and cannot even be displayed in
public libraries, although the work has sold a million copies to the general public. The book is freely available through Amazon.com, as are parallel works by Sturges.[20] Concerns about legal action terrified U.S. film
distributors, who refused to support serious and well-reviewed movies
with plots revolving around pedophilia, such as *Happiness* and the 1998
remake of *Lolita*. Distributors are painfully aware of the 1997 Oklahoma
case in which a judge categorized as illicit child pornography the award-
winning film *The Tin Drum*. This judgment was ultimately overturned,
but few movie or video corporations wish to expend money and effort
solely to establish a legal principle. Even advertisements featuring naked
children, common enough in Europe and the Pacific Rim, are strictly
taboo in the United States. The new laws made childhood sexuality an
absolute taboo.[21]

And the public was likely to cheer, or at least to raise no objections.
The topic of child pornography rarely surfaced in popular culture, since
it was felt to be simply too ugly and distressing, but two treatments sum-
marize its thoroughly condemned status. In the 1997 film *Boogie Nights*,
which is set in the world of hard-core pornography, most of the charac-
ters are depicted highly sympathetically. One of the few exceptions is the
elderly financier of the group, whose interest in underage girls and child
porn makes him a far more sinister and exploitative character and leads
to his destruction. The following year, in the movie version of *The X-
Files*, the most effective tactic that a sinister global conspiracy can deploy
against a whistle-blower is to plant child pornography on his computer,
thereby evoking a massive police response. In both films, the common
theme is that child porn represents an ultimate evil that rightly brings
ruin to anyone who dabbles in it.

Although child pornography was severely criminalized, there remained a sizable number of individuals with a taste for this material,
who sought it out by any means possible, despite the closure of successive loopholes. When the adult stores went out of the business, there

were still private mail-order suppliers, who, by the 1980s, were increasingly moving into the new technology of videotaping. (The proportion of Americans owning a VCR grew from 1 percent in 1979 to 60 percent by 1988.) Yet this avenue, too, became ever more dangerous, because a customer never knew whether a particular operation might be a front for law enforcement, for agents of the FBI, postal inspectors, or the U.S. Customs Service. Sting operations became common. One typical example in the 1980s began when a man entering the United States from Mexico was arrested while carrying child pornography videos. When police broke up the firm organizing this venture, they seized its mailing list, which was then used by postal inspectors to send out solicitations offering videos featuring young children. Videos were ordered and delivered, and if delivery was accepted, authorities then obtained a warrant to search the premises for child pornography. This single investigation led to over forty arrests nationwide. By 1996, the Postal Inspection Service could announce that since 1984, "postal inspectors have conducted over 2,600 investigations, resulting in the arrests and conviction of more than 2,200 individuals for trafficking in child pornography through the U.S. Mail."[22]

Nor was there any longer a financial network manufacturing and distributing this material. Though some entrepreneurs had arisen in the 1970s and had been vilified by the media, all had bailed out of this dangerous area by the early 1980s. The end of the liberal era is epitomized by the 1982 arrest of Catherine Stubblefield Wilson, a Los Angeles woman whose thriving child porn business reputedly had a mailing list of tens of thousands of clients worldwide. Tim Tate—never one to underclaim the seriousness of real or alleged menaces against children—accurately describes her as "the last major commercial supplier [of child porn] to be based inside the United States." According to U.S. law enforcement agents, "by jailing her, they eliminated 80 percent of all non-directly imported child pornography dealing overnight."[23] Though moralists were complaining in the mid-1980s that "ever-widening child pornography distribution rings . . . are making unprecedented profits," in reality, the whole business appeared to be on the verge of extinction.

Bulletin Boards

By 1986, virtually all the traditional avenues for obtaining this kind of material had been firmly closed, raising the possibility of a thorough suppression of the whole child porn trade. Seeking out child porn almost automatically meant a confrontation with all the might of federal law enforcement. But it was precisely at that point that personal computers were becoming widely available, and with them, the burgeoning network of electronic databases. The chronology deserves emphasis. Perhaps ten years before the Internet became known to the general public, computer databases and bulletin boards were becoming the favored tools of child pornographers, a strikingly precocious use of computer technologies.

Though today we speak generally in terms of "Internet porn," in fact computerized pornography developed separately from the Net. Some history is in order here. Although the World Wide Web was a product of the 1990s, the notion of using interlinked computers to share information has a much longer pedigree. When computers were combined with modems, it became possible for ordinary users to access bulletin board systems (BBS's), the first of which dates from 1978. Home computing became somewhat more accessible with the introduction of the IBM PC in 1981 and the Macintosh in 1984: the first consumer modem also dates from 1981.[24]

In retrospect, the computer world of these former days seems a complex and forbidding place, with nothing like the ease of networking made possible by the Internet. The closest approximation of the later Net was in pay services such as Compuserve, which permitted users to "surf" around a wide range of sites and discussion groups. It also allowed postings in bulletin boards and, crucially for our present purposes, established chat rooms in which like-minded individuals could make private contact in real time. Otherwise, using online services and bulletin boards at this stage was a slow and clunky business that appealed chiefly to dedicated hobbyists. To understand just how different things were in what is, after all, not too distant a historical era, it is useful to look at one of the early best-selling guides to computer communication, Mike Cane's

Computer Phone Book Directory of Online Systems, originally published in 1983.[25] The book explains basic concepts like modems and how computers speak to each other and describes the various means required to contact online systems through the telephone. Except when dealing with a major provider such as Compuserve, the computer user needed to know not just the telephone number of each individual BBS but the appropriate settings and probably a password. The modem had to be set to the appropriate speed, in most cases either 300, 1,200, or 2,400 bauds. (Today, a speed of 56,000 is considered barely adequate.) Since several specific settings were needed in addition to baud rate, the scope for error was enormous. At the time, it seemed as if the future of computer communications would always necessitate guidebooks of this sort, presumably getting ever longer and more cumbersome.

Once online, the user could gain access to Compuserve, to local or community-based equivalents, and to specific BBS's. One made a call, posted a message, read messages by other like-minded souls, downloaded software, and logged off. Moving from one service to another meant hanging up the phone, resetting the modem, and redialing. Many services and BBS's charged fees in addition to the telephone charges incurred: phone costs made access to overseas BBS's intolerably expensive. Access was also limited by the comparatively slow and low-powered computer systems then available. Suggesting the extent to which this picture comes from another era, Cane's 1986 edition remarks, "BBS's can only handle one caller at a time because the system is running on a computer such as an Apple, a TRS-80, a PET or a Commodore-64."[26] Calls to BBS's were limited to ten or fifteen minutes at a time, and callers were limited to one visit per day. The reference to the Commodore-64 recalls a time when 64K of memory was considered adequate for most purposes, though computers with so relatively little memory cost at least as much as a modern machine with vastly more capacity. Most navigation involved dealing with text rather than images, so that "shopping" by means of a Compuserve session in the mid-1980s was entirely a matter of reading descriptions of items and pressing Y/N choices to make purchases. Viewing, pointing, and clicking were all remote dreams.

Running BBS's involved a good deal of effort. Computer guides at the time warned potential BBS system operators *(sysops)* of the high investment required in terms of equipment, money, and time. One needed a personal computer dedicated to this purpose, as well as a BBS program and a second phone line. Mike Cane's book also raises the specter that the sysop might have to buy "a second disk drive (or even a hard disk)." There was a time when hard drives were a luxury. The operator was advised to spend at least two hours a day running the system: "You'll have to check the disk drives, the userlog and the message base; reply to messages and questions from callers; issue passwords; compress files; delete old messages; make sure that uploads are in the public domain; and read every message to make sure that you're not open to lawsuits for slander, libel, invasion of privacy or violation of any criminal statutes."[27] Even when running, the facilities they could offer users seem pathetically limited by today's standards.

But for anyone prepared to run a BBS, its potential was enormous. Messages could deal with any subject under the sun; but BBS's offered an ideal means of private communication for deviant or unpopular groups that could not make their views heard through conventional channels. Neo-Nazi activists had already created their Aryan Liberty Net by 1984, where enthusiasts could post hit lists of enemies marked for assassination. Pornographers could likewise post information or arrange contacts, but the same technology that permitted the posting of text also allowed images to be uploaded in binary form, and computer pornography was born.

Even the problems in accessing and publicizing BBS's were an advantage for the pornographers. Given the difficulties of the technology, the main danger at this point was not so much in having unwanted visitors stumbling into a private site but rather in attracting business: Cane advises methods of advertising a new BBS, perhaps through flyers or business cards. For pornographers, though, publicity was undesirable and counterproductive. Obscurity was a boon, since one's doings were more likely to remain clandestine, as only true specialists likely had the technical knowledge to deduce what was happening. Moreover, taking child porn activities to the electronic world immediately removed most participants beyond the territory law enforcement agencies had come to dominate so thoroughly. Even if police suspected the scale of computerized operations, few had the knowledge to pursue these criminal activities online, while the legal environment was fuzzy. The move to computers effectively ruined any effort at proactive policing, reducing law enforcement to merely reacting to ostentatious violations of law. At best, police might confiscate materials discovered while arresting an individual for non-computer-related crimes.

No later than 1982, child pornographers had established their own BBS's; we have no idea of exactly when or how many were in operation at any given time. By 1983, investigations of NAMBLA alleged that abusers were using computers to circulate details of potential victims as well as pornographic images and fantasies. The next year, media reports were claiming, "Scores of child molesters using computers to swap the names and addresses of their child victims have been arrested in the Chicago area in recent months." FBI agent Kenneth Lanning, a specialist in child abuse investigations, remarked at this time, "Like advertisements in swinger magazines, pedophiles use electronic bulletin boards to find each other. They swap pornographic photographs the way boys swap baseball cards." In 1985, a major exposé in the *Los Angeles Times* claimed, "Newest industry innovations include computerized sex bulletin boards that list children for sale." Based on such cases, in 1986 the Meese Commission noted, "Recently, pedophile offenders and child pornographers have begun to use computers for communications. A person may now subscribe to an information service whereby he or she can contact other subscribers. The services are private commercial enterprises which sell access codes to subscribing members." The commission placed special emphasis on the need to control the exchange of child pornography through computer networks, including both BBS's and chat rooms on Compuserve and like networks. In 1987, the pioneering British adult BBS known as PBB was pressured into closing after one of its interest groups was reportedly active in "pedophilic porn solicitation."[28]

In retrospect, it is curious to read all the accounts of pedophiles using bulletin boards to circulate information about children as possible victims, to "list children for sale," and so on. This activity did occur, but it was dwarfed by the massive growth of trafficking in pornographic images. One reason for this misleading emphasis may well have been that, through the 1980s and beyond, many laypeople were skeptical that computers really could transmit visual images. Hence, police and media focused on aspects of electronic technology they could understand and presumed that pedophiles were using computers solely to disseminate information by means of text. What else could they be doing?

The Internet

But where, in this story, is the Internet? In the mid-1980s, it still remained largely a specialized professional preserve, and only gradually did it become accessible beyond the ranks of government, the military, and the research universities. The early origins of the Internet can be traced to 1969 and the creation of the Arpanet, a group of interconnected computers under the Advanced Research Projects Agency (ARPA) of the Department of Defense. The new system's potential as a communication tool soon became apparent:

> Two years after the first transmission, the number of host computers grew to 23. The @ symbol was invented in 1972, and a year later 75 percent of the ARPAnet traffic was E-mail. It was starting to look like the Net. . . . By the late 1970's, [designers] were putting the finishing touches on the lingua franca, inelegantly called TCP/IP, that would weave the patches into the electronic quilt called the Internet.

Originally, the system's functions were strictly military and defense related, but the growing number of academic computers involved in the system gradually led to a split between the military network *(milnet)* and the remaining sites. The two still communicated because both used a common Internet protocol, IP, which would be a familiar acronym: every networked computer has its individual IP address. In fact, the introduction of the Internet protocol in 1982 popularized the term *Internet*.

Several developments in the mid-1980s contributed vastly to making the Internet more accessible for ordinary users. For much of its history, using the Internet meant using programs on UNIX computers, which thus excluded both standard PCs and MACs. This changed with the introduction of SLIP software (serial line Internet protocol) and faster modems, which permitted home- or office-based computer users to access the major networks. By 1984, "the domain name system was established that lets *amazon.com* be *amazon.com* and not 208.216.182.15."[29] From 1984, too, the Arpanet passed into the hands of the National Science Foundation and soon became part of a series of interconnected networks running common protocols: the Internet was in full operation.

Already by the early 1980s, some creative writers were envisioning the future directions of the Net in extraordinarily ambitious terms. In 1982, William Gibson's story "Burning Chrome" coined the term *cyberspace*, and in 1984, his novel *Neuromancer* presented an intoxicating vision of a worldwide web of interlinked databases and the cyberpirates who break into them in order to purloin data.[30] By 1990, something like the Web we know today took shape through the efforts of CERN, the European Center for Particle Physics, based in Switzerland, which distributed information by means of hotlinks between sites. Soon afterwards the first graphical browsers vastly enhanced the kinds of information the Web could handle. This opened the way to a hyperlinked database that combines text with sound and pictures, in which easy navigation is undertaken by means of clicks on a mouse. We are still a long way from Gibson's world, in which the Web is navigated not through clumsy keyboards but through devices permitting direct interfaces with the human brain. If that day ever arrives, we can be sure that pornographers will be among the pioneers in finding uses for the new technology.

The greatest single breakthrough in popularizing Web technology was the introduction in 1993 of the Mosaic graphical browser software, which allowed the display of more than one type of information on a screen at one time. This event really opened up the Internet to general users, permitting them to surf rather than rely on endless separate telephone calls. Mosaic was superseded by Netscape's Navigator technology, which followed in 1994. It was at this point that many non-specialists first encountered the alphabet soup of acronyms that would become household words during the 1990s, such as *html, http, URL,* and of course *www,* the World Wide Web itself.

An astonishing boom in Net use now got under way. In 1981, fewer than three hundred computers were linked to the Internet, and by 1989, the number stood at ninety thousand; by 1993, there were over a million. The number of host computers grew to more than 36.7 million in mid-1998. When Bill Clinton took office as U.S. president in early 1993, there were fifty Web sites in the whole world. By 1998, the number of Web sites had grown to 1.3 million, and the number was doubling every few months, to exceed 50 million by early 2000. And as the sites proliferated, so did the Internet service providers (ISPs) offering access to them, particularly rapidly expanding goliaths such as America Online. Taken together, this was nothing short of a social revolution.

Seeking and Finding

Already by the late 1980s, pedophiles and child pornography enthusiasts were among the most experienced and knowledgeable members of the computerized communication world, so they were magnificently placed to benefit from the many technological leaps of the next few years. Operating Web sites was a vastly easier matter than the chore of running traditional BBS's and offered the virtues (and the dangers) of a much wider audience. Instead of trading between a few dozen enthusiasts in a particular city or region, it was now feasible to gain instant access to materials emanating from other continents, and from countries with very different legal environments. Moreover, as computers themselves became faster, with far larger memories and faster processors, it became possible to store and transmit much more complex information, including large numbers of high-resolution color images and movies. The child porn subculture on the Internet now began a boom that shows no sign of waning.

There are today veterans whose careers in circulating electronic child porn span twenty years or more. These dinosaurs occasionally reminisce about the primitive ages: "Hey, I remember things before there was *abpep-t*. Zmodem 8088 PC, 20 Meg hard drive with RGB monitor, when there wasn't even jpeg's, only gif's. . . . Its just amazing how things have changed." Another veteran recalls, "Twenty years ago I had a 300 baud modem, 16k memory and a 180k floppy drive. Didn't even consider a picture. My first HD cost about 500$US for 20megs in about 1984. It was about '87 before I had pictures with a 1 meg video card and SVGA." "Master Blaster," a venerated name on the child porn boards, wrote in 2000 that "I have been using it before most of you even knew the Net existed. I was online using a PDP-11 mainframe in 1980. We were hooked up to the **** intranet and in turn they were connected to the world via government and schools." Attacking a rival who was trying to appropriate his nickname, "Zapper" declared in 2000 that "I have had this nic since 1987 and will continue to use it."[31] We must be struck by the difficulty of tracking down people who have remained at liberty in such a dangerous environment for so many years. Sending police officers on intensive two- or three-week courses to learn about the Internet is simply not going to equip investigators adequately to confront such accumulated expertise.

Surprisingly, perhaps, the widespread presence of child-oriented material on the Net aroused only sporadic concern after the initial burst of interest in the mid-1980s, and even then very little of the attention focused on the major aspects of the subculture, rather than on incidental manifestations. This was apparent between 1993 and 1995, when the existence of child porn on the Net attracted some national attention but only as a subset of larger stories, which culminated in the debate over the Communications Decency Act.

In the mid-1990s, threats posed to children on the Internet made frequent headlines, so that any database search on this era will yield countless references to the topics of "children," "Internet," and "pornography." The media featured regular stories about children being seduced or abducted by friendly-seeming strangers they encountered online, particularly in chat rooms, and this occasionally drew attention to the use of such rooms for trading obscene photographs. America Online was a principal target for such complaints, and it is in one of the jeremiads against AOL that we find one of the few efforts to describe the impact of the new technology on the availability of child porn. In 1995, child protection activist Barry Crimmins told a congressional committee that AOL offered "numerous atrocious rooms" devoted to incest, pedophilia, and perversion. Crimmins argued, "There is a major crime wave taking place on America's computers. The proliferation of child pornography trafficking has created an anonymous 'Pedophile Superstore.' . . . The on-line service America OnLine has become an integral link in a network of child pornography traffickers. . . . AOL is the key link in a network of child pornography traffickers that has grown exponentially over the last several months."[32] These charges were not exactly true: AOL users certainly could find chat rooms with titles like "Dads'n'Daughters," though obviously these were not created with the provider's knowledge or consent. All AOL did was to offer users the ability to establish rooms devoted to their own interests, and some responded by creating perverse areas such as those which Crimmins was complaining about. Still, though his emphasis on AOL was misleading, Crimmins's account of the child porn boom stands in marked isolation amid the other commentaries at this time.

Child porn remained on the sidelines of the national clamor over what became known as "cyberporn," the problem of young people gaining access to adult material, which provoked Congress to try to limit the availability of online sex through its proposed CDA. Paradoxically, the cyberporn debate helped divert attention from the graver dangers of the Internet, particularly from child porn. By focusing public attention on the supposed threat posed by mainstream adult sites, anti-smut campaigners framed the debate in terms of depriving adults as well as children of the right to view nudity and "mainstream" porn sites. It seemed as if, in the name of child protection, conservative activists were seeking to reduce all Internet material to the level of what could be uncontroversially viewed by a ten-year-old girl. This puritanical rhetoric not only alienated moderate supporters (and provoked judicial skepticism); it also discredited future charges about the existence of a serious child porn problem. Equally, focusing on cyberporn meant that the discussion of solutions revolved entirely around ways of controlling children's access to sexual material, by means of filters and age-verification measures.

Further, CDA supporters suffered from charges that they were deploying distorted evidence, which raised suspicions about other claims concerning Net obscenity. In support of the political campaign against cyberporn, much publicity was given to a study of BBS materials by a Carnegie-Mellon student named Marty Rimm, who argued that the Internet offered "an unprecedented availability and demand of material like sadomasochism, bestiality, vaginal and rectal fisting, eroticized urination . . . and pedophilia." Moralist leaders enthusiastically adopted Rimm's sensational study in support of the cause of regulation, particularly his claims about pedophilia. Christian Coalition leader Ralph Reed stressed the dangers on the Internet: "this is bestiality, pedophilia, child molestation." The Rimm study became a major news event. *Time* magazine remarked that online erotica was "popular, pervasive and surprisingly perverse," citing Rimm's finding that "on those Usenet newsgroups where digitized images are stored, 83.5 percent of the pictures were pornographic." In retellings of the story, this figure was distorted to suggest that over 80 percent of Internet traffic was sexual or featured extreme perversions.[33]

The Rimm study was swiftly attacked, as its figures were wildly misleading if considered as a sample of Internet traffic as such. Most of the images surveyed were taken not from the Internet as a whole but from certain pay-service adult BBS's that catered to a specific market who chose to receive pornographic materials. Overall, the volume of pornography on the Internet was perhaps a fraction of 1 percent, rather than the huge proportion alleged, and the proportion of extreme perversion was correspondingly less. These problems helped undermine the case for the CDA and assisted liberals who strenuously opposed Internet regulation as a threat to the free development of the medium. The furor over Rimm's work also inoculated the public against future claims about perverse materials on the Net and ensured that the media would not risk a repetition of this embarrassing affair.

But the attack on Rimm and other moralists ignored the quite authentic material that they were reporting. The debate over the CDA tended to become polarized between two extreme stances: conservatives held that a vast amount of Internet business involved the most horrifying pornography, while liberals all but denied that such material existed and underplayed the existence of pedophile newsgroups and BBS's. But a third and less publicized position was possible, namely, that although pedophile interests and images account for only a small proportion of life on the Web, this was still a substantial volume, maintained by a small but very active underworld. Moreover, this subculture had evolved some remarkably imaginative means for surviving any potential assault by law enforcement.

THREE

Into the Net

Didn't any of you see the counter at the old new board,
the one that got shut down? If that is true, then there
were hundreds of thousands of visitors in a few days.
Was that counter real? If it was, there sure are a hell of a
lot of pedos out there.

—Dad, Maestro board, May 1, 2000

So how does child pornography work on the Internet? While a distinguished literature describes the organizational patterns found among various kinds of deviants, social, political, and sexual, perhaps no structure thus far examined rivals the child porn world for sheer complexity and creativity and for its global reach. Equally, the devices and subterfuges that make the trade possible are still startling even to people with a reasonable working familiarity with the Net. The subculture survives by exploiting the international character of the Internet but also by avoiding fixed and permanent "homes" in cyberspace that can be raided by officialdom.

The Internet is, of course, a rapidly developing technology, in which matters can change dramatically over the space of few months and something that lasts a year can acquire the air of a timeless institution. I believe that the picture offered here is an accurate description of the situation as it existed in the period 1999–2000, though already by early 2001, some of the cherished landmarks of the subculture were in disarray. In particular, the freewheeling chat that had hitherto flourished on the boards showed signs of fading away, leaving mainly technical information available—in addition to many, many, pictures and videos. My account should be seen as a snapshot of a particular historical moment, rather than claiming any lasting truth.

For most users, surfing the Web generally means typing a URL address or following a link that leads to a particular fixed site: most mornings, for instance, I visit the site of the *New York Times* at the URL, *www.nyt.com.* Such an approach would not work for posting child pornography, since a fixed open-access site located on a particular server could too easily be tracked down and suppressed. Just as guerrillas must avoid having known or public bases or headquarters, so child porn enthusiasts cannot remain exposed in fixed sites. A good rule of thumb is that an address featuring the term *childporn* or its ilk will feature anything under the sun except genuine child pornography. Although *www.childporn.com* is an authentic working Web address, it just leads to a conventional, legal, adult sex site, which is why I can list it here. An authentic *lolitasex.com* site claims to offer "steaming hot lolitas . . . innocent but horny," "young, tight and unexperienced," but the first page declares frankly enough, "All models on this site are 18+ years of age." Another URL, which includes the potent-sounding phrase "lolitaincest," offers an ingenious and non-sexual anti-Microsoft parody, depicting Bill Gates as Hitler under flags in which his company's logo has replaced the swastika.

In the absence of fixed sites, the subculture has to use a variety of alternatives and an ingenious array of connected Internet locations. The child porn underworld operates on the principle imagined for the original Internet of the late 1960s, which was reputedly intended to survive the destruction of many individual mainframe computers during a nuclear strike. Removing one server or site thus has no impact on the integrity of the whole system. Equally, destroying one bulletin board or Web site leaves the child porn subculture intact.

The institutions of this world can be described under four main headings, namely, newsgroups (Usenet); corporate-linked "communities"; Web-based bulletin boards; and closed groups.

Newsgroups

A major portion of the computerized universe consists of the ninety thousand or so newsgroups, the linear descendants of the electronic bulletin boards that were so popular in the 1980s. Together, these groups make up the Usenet: though often discussed as part of the Internet, Usenet is technically a separate entity and, indeed, the precursor to the Internet. The newsgroups are wide open in that, in most cases, anyone can submit a comment or opinion, raise an issue, or establish a wholly new group. Groups deal with every conceivable area of interest, every hobby and professional activity, and many of the most vigorous are found under headings such as "rec" (recreational), "soc" (social), and "alt" (alternative). The last is a bewilderingly vast grab bag of subjects that will not fit under other headings. From the several thousand *alt.* groups that I can access through my university's server, I find, for example, *alt.agriculture*, *alt.aquaria*, and *alt.archaeology*. There are also groups that exist in little more than name, created because someone thought the names would be funny: such, presumably, are *alt.buddha .short.fat.guy* and *alt.commercial-hit-radio.must.die*.

Naturally enough, a good number of groups deal with sexual issues, covering every conceivable taste and perversion, and some of these are binary groups, which permit the posting of photographs and images. At least five hundred such groups offering visual imagery begin with the title *alt.binaries.pictures.erotica*, such as *alt.binaries.pictures.erotica.high-heels*. The areas of interest denoted by the final word or phrase are extraordinarily diverse, including such topics as *redheads*, *female.ejaculation*, *fetish.diapers*, and *garters-and-heels*. The vast majority of binary sites cater to legitimate (or at least legal) adult interests, but some do provide child pornography. Among these are the legendary *alt.binaries.pictures.erotica.pre-teen* (*abpep-t*) and the less notorious *alt.binaries.pictures.erotica.ll-series* (*abpell*), the latter of which features "older lolitas," girls in their mid-teens. A current list of major underage-oriented groups includes the following:

alt.binaries.pictures.bc-series
alt.binaries.adolescents
alt.binaries.pictures.boys
alt.binaries.pictures.erotica.children
alt.binaries.pictures.erotica.age.13-17
alt.binaries.pictures.erotica.pre-teen
alt.binaries.pictures.erotica.early-teen
alt.binaries.pictures.erotica.ll-series
alt.binaries.pictures.erotica.mclt
alt.binaries.pictures.rika-nishimura
alt.binaries.pictures.youth-and-beauty
alt.fan.prettyboy
alt.binaries.pictures.asparagus
alt.freedom.jbpel (that is, *japan.binaries.pictures.erotica.lolita*)

For current purposes, though, by far the most important of these is *abpep-t*. As Godfather Corleone advised a novice, "Trading thru e-mail is a rather un-efficient way to get pics. Learn about using newsgroups instead, that way you will be able to fill a few CD's every week ;)."[1] As is suggested by the emoticon, the winking punctuation mark, that is hyperbole, since a single CD can store ten or fifteen thousand images. The point about the sheer quantity of material available on the newsgroups is nevertheless well taken. Another, more precise comment on the boards notes:

> Right now *abpep-t* contains tons of new mpeg's. Normally *abpep-t* gets approx 5000-7000 new posts every week, and the latest 14,000 posts are available right now at one pay-server [address deleted]. You will find that *abpep-t* is the best source in terms of finding on-topic (under thirteen y.o.) material, as 99% of the stuff at sites were taken from there, and that other 1% will surely turn up at *abpep-t*.[2]

The material on *abpep-t* is astonishingly diverse, from hard-core child porn through naked images to winsome pictures of fully clothed children and even twenty-five-year-old bogus "lolitas." Restrictions are minimal. To quote the *abpep-t* FAQ:

> The name of this group says . . . pictures.erotica.pre-teen. This means we want to share pictures of *pre-teens*, that is, under thirteen. Pre-teen means just that, younger than thirteen, we don't want to see teens or grandma, so please keep it on-topic (or at least close). Both boys and girls are considered on-topic.

The child pornographer's course of action therefore seems simple: just access *abpep-t* and download whatever pictures appeal. But matters are not that simple, which is why I can discuss these groups here under their actual names. Using a standard Web search engine under the name *abpep-t* will produce only a handful of articles, mainly concerning legal efforts to suppress these groups. The portions of the Usenet to which you have access are determined by the server on which you rely, and most servers exercise at least some degree of censorship. My own server at Penn State University carries virtually none of the *alt.sex* groups, including the relatively "straight" adult discussion and fantasy ones, to the point of having the search engine deny that they exist, anywhere. Nor do major commercial organizations like America Online permit access to groups such as *abpep-t*, the content of which is blatantly illegal in most advanced nations. There are servers that carry all the sexually oriented groups, but most require payment, a moderate ten dollars a month or so, which usually means use of a check or credit card, as well as an e-mail address. Most members of the child porn subculture are understandably leery of giving names or other identifiers, so this avenue is not open to everybody. In the United States and most West European nations, anyone giving credit card information prior to entering *abpep-t* is inviting a police raid. Concerns about security also explain why so many surfers are chary about using Web sites that offer child porn material for a fee. These sites operate within the law within their particular countries, though using them is strictly prohibited for visitors from the United States, who are taking a grave risk if they provide credit card numbers. Nevertheless, enough individuals feel confident enough to do this to sustain the existence of a number of lucrative pay sites.

There are means of avoiding these traps, but all require some expertise and complex methods of securing truly anonymous e-mail addresses. Some users succeed in hacking into a pay news server, altogether avoiding security issues, but this route is only for the truly ingenious. One of the commonest pleas posted on the child porn bulletin board is for information about servers offering relevant newsgroups:

> I had a hacked pw [password] for ****news, but now the guy hasn't paid his bills, so the account is disconnected. Do anybody know of any free newsserver that caries *abpep-t?* Or maybe a new pw for ****news?[3]

A handful of news servers do offer *abpep-t* and the like free, though for obvious reasons they are a shrinking minority. Whenever the word is passed of their existence, these sites are flooded by child porn enthusiasts, usually causing the servers to drop access immediately. For child porn users, matters are made still more perilous by the technology that permits sites to read the individualized IP address of any home computer used to access them. One never knows when police might gain access to the logs of a server and retrieve the identities of every computer ever used to access an illegal newsgroup. Still, *abpep-t* is widely used by those with the technical ability to conceal their true identity by means of proxies, "false flag" addresses, the use of which means that the host site will not be able to identify a visitor's true IP.

Story Boards

In addition to the traffic in visual images, many Usenet sites cater to pedophile interests through stories and written fantasies, which are entirely supplied by amateurs catering to other enthusiasts. In the language of the dissident underground of the old USSR, they are purely *samizdat*, "self-published." These stories are originally posted in Usenet groups and subsequently collected in open Web sites. These written works are almost certainly legal, protected speech within the United States, which is paradoxical since these stories are often grossly violent or even homicidal in their content. To put the paradox at its simplest, a photograph of a naked five-year-old girl happily eating an ice cream on the beach is strictly criminalized, even if the child is shown accompanied by doting parents, but it is quite legal to publish a detailed fantasy about the rape, torture, and murder of the same child. To give an idea of the content of some of these tales, the following represents a selection of the new stories listed on one extreme-content site in 2000, together with the editor's summaries of the themes offered in each case ("NC" means nonconsensual, "Scat" means scatological, "WS" means water sports or urination, "Snuff" means killing):

14 Year Old Avenger by brisko65 (Pedo, Bi sex, Scat, WS, Vomit, Animal, Torture, Spanking, Snuff, Incest)

*A Hunt by ***** (Rape, Torture, Cannibalism, Snuff)*

A Little Inheritance by S.o.S. (Incest-daddy/daughter, Pedo, Oral)

A Night in the Kids Room by S.o.S. (Pedo/toddler, Incest-brothers/sisters, Oral, Anal, Gangbang)

Amanda the Slut Episode 1 by sex freak (Preteen, NC, S/M, Suggested snuff)

Anne by Kinnik (Rape, Pedo, Torture, Snuff)

B&B 2-Dad visits Kids by Chucketal (Incest-father/son, Pedo)

Baby in the Arcade by S.o.S. (Drug use, Pedo, Toddler rape)

Baby Sex is the Best—Part II by Evil Dad (Child rape & abuse, Pedo, Scat, WS)

Children's Ward by xtight (Pedo, Anal)

Do You like my Bottom Daddy? by UK Snowy (Oral incest-father/daughter, Pedo)

Fucking in the Family—The Tradition Continues by Lund Pasand (Incest-whole family, Pedo, First time)

Nigger Lust by N-lover (Hetero sex, Pedo, Racist, Interracial, Scat, WS)

*The Most Perfect 10 by ***** (Bi sex, Pedo, Fisting)*

By no means are all story groups anything like this bizarre or repulsive in their content, and this is avowedly an extreme site. Nevertheless, the predominance of underage themes is notable. Of forty-four new stories listed at this site in April 2000, no fewer than twenty included "Pedo" (pedophile) or "Preteen" as one of their subject keywords.

Hiding in Plain Sight

Another recently popular technique of child porn distribution avoids the need for a news server, as the system operates on the principle of hiding in plain sight. A number of aboveboard Internet servers now permit individuals to establish interest groups, to which people can post images or messages. Basically, this development opens something like the Usenet to everyone with access to the Web, and since sites can be accessed without payment or subscription, users are largely anonymous.

Some of the most popular and easily accessible such servers are operated by the corporate giants of the Web world, including MSN (the Microsoft Network) and Yahoo. Yahoo owns *egroups.com*, a collection of many thousands of groups on virtually every topic imaginable—business and computers, shopping, health and fitness, and so on. Opening a new group is free and quite simple, so not surprisingly we find thousands of sexually oriented groups, the vast majority dedicated to legal adult topics. In addition to permitting posting, many such groups also run chat rooms in which private contacts can be made and photos traded. Providers operate a rigorous policy of excluding child porn, and virtually all the sexual groups reinforce this in their introductory messages, but nevertheless, some popular groups have acquired a blatant child-oriented strand. In 2000, some of the most active e-groups bore names such as *justyoungnudists, nudist-preteens, sixteen_years_naturist_teens, onlypreteenboy,* and *young_naturist_girls.* Most counted members in the range of two or three thousand, but a few ran much higher, placing them on a par with the most popular sex-oriented adult groups. The volume of activity on these groups was impressive. In one case, a group called *yourdaughter* was formed in September 2000 as an outlet for "pictures of 'real' girls . . . nude or topless is ok, even preferred"; within just four days, membership had soared to eight hundred. Another group, frankly called *sweet-preteen-lolita-pics,* gained over four thousand members within its two brief weeks of operation.

Other groups were rather more discreet, since they incorporated child porn content alongside adult material. One group, notionally concerned with soft-core photos of young women in underwear, developed a strong child porn undercurrent in late 1999, despite administrators' efforts to purge the worst offenders. At this point, the group claimed nearly three thousand members. I do not know whether child pornographers were using this site as a clever means of putting material out surreptitiously, or whether posters genuinely believed that soft-core pictures of nude or semi-nude youngsters did not constitute illegal child porn. Perhaps they lived in countries where such images were legal. The international diversity of standards is suggested by the furious response of one administrator when a group member offered to trade "young pictures, wink wink":

> If by "young photos, wink wink" you mean underage models, then *get off this list* before I kick you off and report you to the proper authorities. If, by some chance, you mean teens over sixteen, then accept my apologies and swap away. The insinuation is clear—I will not accept pedophiles on this list.

In psychological terms, the administrator is quite accurate in that a sexual interest in girls of sixteen and seventeen is quite distinct from pedophilia; but by American standards, at least, images of girls of this age are still highly criminal and technically constitute child porn.

It is a matter of debate how far such groups and their founders self-consciously offer pornographic material, and where exactly they draw the boundaries against child porn. The group *sixteen_years_naturist_teens* offered this self-description:

> Please send photos . . . naturist and nude teens girl 16, 17, 18 years old, not under this age please!! Naturist photos not sexual act please!! . . . remember . . . not post sex, masturbate, or child, no girls without hair between legs, *no child* please or you are *banned immediately*!!!!!

Again, the list owner is banning images that would qualify as child porn by European standards, but the materials are still intended to be sexually stimulating. Naturism may be a serious topic worthy of weighty discussion, but it is not easy to see what contribution could be made by a photograph labeled "15 y.o., nice tits." This group too has its standards and limits, but again, by American standards, *every* single image on this group is criminal, and every American member who views pictures here is in violation of federal law. The same applies to the site that offered this description: "This Group is for the lovers of black female teens. Feel free to post pics of black girls between 13 and 17 years, but don't post any pornographical things!" One naturist site declared itself "A place for nudist of all ages to meet and exchange photos. We have photos of nude children posted. If you don't care for that don't join." On the extreme margins of the law, we find a group "dedicated to a little girls bedtime. This includes everything from bathtime to storytime to bedtime. Photos and stories wanted. Share your photos and stories of your little one getting ready for bed. Nude photos OK if they are of innocent nature."

In other cases, posters seem to be well aware that they are dealing with child pornography and not merely with images that might be ambiguous under the laws of different countries. Some were outrageously blatant: one urged, "Send Pics or Movies—sperm-filled pussy from underaged girls"; another asked members, "Post and share your preteen Lolita Pix (10–16 yrs) Latin, Russian, Asian and others." One group offered an introductory message that began with a deliberate reference to *hel-lo*, presumably as a wink to other child porn fans: "Hel-lo, this is a place to post pic's and Mpegs of incest or similar . . . this is a free and unrestricted group . . . enjoy—hel-lo, ll-series, lolita young teen." One e-group declares its goals thus: "This is a place to post your high quality, high resolution pics and vids of beautiful *young* ladies. . . . The only other firm rule is don't post any *obvious* child porn!" (my emphasis). This qualification surely implies that discreet child-oriented materials are acceptable.

Some of the worst offenders are highly temporary groups, which exist just long enough for collectors to gather "fills" for their collections. In one instance, a short note on a soft-core group announced the existence of a new board dedicated to "Tiny Americans," the board bearing a non-sense name with no sexual connotation. Only those with a previous acquaintance with the child porn world would know that Tiny Americans is the brand name of a large and popular series of preteen soft-core nudes, containing perhaps two thousand images. (The pictures were reputedly taken in Paraguay.) Within just two weeks of its founding, the new group had twelve hundred members and was expanding at the rate of a couple of hundred a day. Noting the suppression of another short-lived "lolita" group, one member crowed about his own group's farsightedness:

> It must have had to do with the name of the group. I mean, if you're searching for keywords of groups to shut down, *lolita* has got to be one of the words you'd use. The content of the group is no worse than what is shown here, but who'd think to look at a group called *****
> for young nude girls? They should, and will I hope, start up the group under a more covert name.

The sheer scale of the child porn presence on *egroups.com* is daunting. In early 2001, at least a hundred active groups catered to this interest on any given day, and when five or ten were suppressed, they were replaced almost immediately. Some of these groups offered very hard-core fare indeed, including hel-lo, the Vicky series, and even KX.

Egroups.com is not the only corporate site to host child porn, however unwittingly, since the "communities" run by MSN are at least as blatant. In late 2000, I ran a simple name search under the keyword *pre-teen*, and found over a hundred MSN groups with this word in their title or description. The great majority were innocent and even praiseworthy sites that permitted children and young teenagers to chat with friends about music, computers, and dating, but the descriptions of at least twenty others were harrowing. Titles of some such communities included: "Pre-teen Lesbians"; "Pre Teen Sex" ("Here you can swap pics and share stories!"); "Young Pre-teen Sex Pics" ("Sex for kids 10-12"); "Preteen gays"; "Pre-teen Pic Trade" ("If you are looking for the best nude preteens or kids then come in. But to be a member for long you must post pics"); "Upclose Pre-teen Pics" ("This is probably the hottest pre-teen close up pics. . . . Non-pornographic pics and pornographic pictures accepted"); and "Nude Pre-teens and teens, ages 8-16 only." I stress that these are only the sites found with the keyword *pre-teen*, and many other possible search terms suggest themselves. Some, at least, of these suspicious sites might well be honey traps established by law enforcement to entice unwary pedophiles, but a plethora of MSN communities genuinely do serve the child porn world. Among the ranks of *Yahoo Clubs* (a distinct enterprise from *egroups*), we find such interesting gathering places as "Teen/Preteen Steam" ("a place to view the best in Teen/Preteen Pix!"); "preteen poontang pie"; and "preteen boys nude." When a new site appears, it is blazoned through all the related groups with a headline like "msn goood pthc club!!!"—the acronym signifies "preteen hardcore."

The managements of Yahoo and MSN are well aware of the problem they face and have a justified reputation of responding instantly and severely to any such violations. Offending groups are closed swiftly when a user informs them of child porn activity, sometimes within hours. I can confirm this from witnessing the speedy response after I alerted *egroups.com* to several such egregious sites. It is because they are now defunct that I can refer here to groups such as *sixteen_years_naturist_teens*, *sweet-preteen-lolita-pics*, and *nudist-preteens*. Another effective tactic has been adjusting the *egroups* search engine so that it denies all knowledge of groups that feature keywords such as *preteen* or *lolita*, an omission that makes it all but impossible to find groups by casual surfing. The firm is well known for its willingness to turn offenders over to the criminal justice system. In one major arrest in 2000, a man was convicted of operating a blatant site, "dedicated to nude male teen and twink [i.e., young boys] pix."

Nevertheless, the difficulties even for the best-intentioned provider are enormous. Despite the flagrant examples I have quoted here, in many cases there is nothing in the titles or messages that indicates the CP theme, nothing for a search robot to detect, and the problem will not be detected unless and until some user launches a protest. And since most group members are there to enjoy the pictures, they are not likely to report the activity to police. In the case of the Tiny Americans group, nothing in that phrase or any language used in the description necessarily sounded suspicious. A group so named might conceivably be offering serious discussion about child rearing or perhaps youth gymnastics. If a pornographer gives a group an innocuous sounding code-name such as "volleyball" or "hel-lo," why should the provider be expected to identify it as suspect? On the consumer's side, surveillance of Web use will not detect improper surfing, since an *egroups* user could claim to be visiting only sites dealing with, say, personal finance or even a legal adult site. In a sense, the child porn images are camouflaged by the legal porn on the site. If a group is closed down for malfeasance, then it takes only a few minutes to initiate another innocuous-sounding group, which can develop its own stream of kiddie porn traffic. Such Web-friendly newsgroups represent one of the more worrying developments of the child porn world.

Bulletin Boards: The World of the Maestro

Distinct from the newsgroups are the Web-based bulletin boards, which exist as open sites and which effectively serve as command centers for the whole traffic in child porn. Typically, a board may allow a person to post a brief note, usually containing the URL of what is purported to be a child porn site, though a fair number of these addresses are either not what they claim to be or are extinct by the time the user gets there: the boards offer a very high proportion of chaff. A characteristic index page includes several columns, respectively giving the item number, a brief description, the poster, date, and the number of hits or visitors. Each major item may be followed by one or more follow-up comments by users, often denouncing the original posting as fraudulent or spam.

Though several hundred boards cater to this interest, a few in particular achieved prominence in the late 1990s—above all, twenty or so sites or groups of sites operating from Japanese servers, while a dozen or so others run from South Korea, Russia, and assorted other nations. Of the nature of the Web, all such boards are ephemeral, and just between 1998 and 2000, dozens perished and new ones were born. I would hesitate to say whether the rate of attrition was any higher than that for conventional Web pages devoted to, say, rock music or fashion.

The Japanese-based boards were pivotal to the child porn subculture worldwide. Among the most important and enduring network operating in the late 1990s was a group of several boards theoretically run by an individual known as the "Maestro," with the cooperation of four or five other regular administrators. Though not necessarily the most important sites, they were in these years the settings for the most intense activity, and these are the ones I monitored most closely. Each of the Maestro boards performed a different function, allowing discussion at greater or lesser length and in a variety of languages, though mainly English. Since some of the Maestro boards permitted extensive discussion in addition to simple URLs, these sites offered extraordinarily rich resources for members of the child porn subculture. For all the blatant illegalities discussed in these pages, the owners and organizers of the boards were committing no crime, either under U.S. law or that of any other country: they were merely facilitating verbal exchanges, which represent protected speech.

Sites like the Maestro's operate like any board or newsgroup, in that individuals place comments and queries, which are united by topic in common "threads" of discussion. Matters of interest might include technical queries, but debates range widely and almost limitlessly over practical, political, and ethical issues, all relating to the general topics of child pornography and pedophilia. A typical sequence might proceed as follows:

NAME: DaughterLover   DATE: 09.Jan 2000
My First Post !!!—http://********
* **Death** > Thanks I Never seen These Before. WOW!!!
* **huh** > pay site !!! try this backdoor..!!http://*********
* **moose** > tried 3 times to get in, no luck.

In other words, "DaughterLover" posts a Web site featuring pornographic images of children, and other participants respond critically.

"Death" is enthusiastic; "huh" complains that it is a pay site but points out that users can avoid payment by using an alternative backdoor for free access. This exchange is atypical only in its brevity: a query can ignite a discussion running over several days and a thousand lines of text. As we will see in a later chapter, the discussions that run to greatest length are those that raise ethical questions about the nature of the traffic.

One reason the major boards are so popular and enduring is that they are strictly regulated by their administrators. They are not moderated in the sense that incoming messages are reviewed and approved in detail prior to posting, but system administrators take care to delete any messages that are disruptive or blatantly irrelevant, so the boards are thoroughly weeded on a frequent basis. This is important because the whole area of child porn and pedophilia is deeply controversial and the "pedo boards" attract so many hostile messages from critics, the so-called anti-pedos. Some enemies are content to denounce the boards and their participants, perhaps by proclaiming biblical messages warning of hell and damnation, but more sophisticated critics sow dissent by planting controversial or provocative messages, trying to encourage paranoia. Others sabotage the boards by overwhelming them with endlessly repetitive material, such as extracts from articles about sex crimes against children. On occasion, such means have succeeded in shutting down boards for days at a time, but most of the Maestro "family" long managed to resist such attacks, because they were so well defended by the expertise of the administrators.

Equally damaging to any sexually oriented board is the threat of "spam," lurid advertisements intended to persuade a gullible surfer to visit a site that in practice offers nothing of value, or at least not for free. Commonly, these spurious sites show titillating photos, and some fraudulently offer illicit material for a fee. Apart from attracting potential customers, spammers profit by generating a small payment from advertisers for each hit recorded on their site, usually a few cents per hit, so it is very much in their interest to put out a great deal of bait. This is a typical advertisement inviting Web users to enter a career as a spammer:

******.com will pay for each and every click generated by you to our site. You can use Text Links, Thumbnails, Enter / Exit Buttons, redirects from Toplists, Consoles and even New Windows opening. We will accept all your traffic. As long as it is a live user clicking and seeing our link we will pay for it.

What this means is that the company will pay for any traffic to its site, even if obtained by deceptive means. If not weeded regularly, which means every hour or two, a board can be overwhelmed by the deluge of spam, making it impossible for users to find any genuine postings. Several child porn boards have been shut down by such means, and the capacity to resist spam is one of the most important features of a successful board. Once again, the Maestro boards were vigilant in deleting such items. When bogus sites are posted, they are immediately denounced and rapidly pulled. This is a typical protest against a well-known bogus porn site: "100% 70 year old ladies for payment. Spam for everyone. 100% legal and useless."[4] The women in question are presumably closer to twenty-five than to seventy, but the basic point is made: the site is for profit, and worse, it is "legal and useless."

The Global Game

The effort taken to defend the Maestro network indicates its significance in the subculture. Though the boards never permit the posting of visual materials, they nevertheless act as guideposts to actual images, operating on a wholly global scale and freely crossing international boundaries and jurisdictions. The reasons why the boards act as they do can be understood if we take the posting cited above by DaughterLover, who advertised child porn materials at a particular Web site. For anyone unacquainted with the subculture, the official response to this would seem obvious. Law enforcement agencies should keep these boards under constant surveillance, and when a site like this is posted, police could promptly shut it down and then find the culprit who established it, eliminating both the pornographer and his sordid materials. The difficulty is that the bulletin boards permit porn sites to exist and be used on a purely transient and anonymous basis.

The best way to illustrate the workings of this world is to describe a typical example, of the sort that is repeated hundreds of time each day. A man in California might possess a collection of several thousand child porn images, and one day he decides to show off part of his collection. First, he obtains a proxy that conceals his name and location and acquires a new e-mail account under a false name from an anonymous provider, likely in a third world nation: both are easy to do. With these bogus credentials, he opens an account that permits him to set up a home page on an innocent and aboveboard public server such as *angelfire.com*, which usually functions for the display of personal information or private hobbies, many of which are sexually oriented. Another popular venue was, for a while, *sexhound.net*, which permits the display of amateur adult photographs. I specifically mention *angelfire* and *sexhound* since both have succeeded in determined campaigns to evict child pornographers, and both can be cited as free of illicit material.

Unknown to the provider, the Californian now loads ten or twenty or five hundred photographs or videos featuring illegal child porn materials, perhaps even depicting acts of molestation by the poster himself. Some are taken from newsgroups such as *abpep-t*, making these images available to the many without the means to access that source. Still, the site is of no use to anyone as yet, in that nobody is likely to stumble across it by accident, and it is here that the "pedo boards" come in. The hypothetical individual now announces the posting of the series on the Maestro board or one of its counterparts, where the message is read and acknowledged gratefully by other "loli fans," who might be located in the next town to him or in Budapest or in Singapore—there is no way of knowing. And because of the board's location, U.S. or European law enforcement agencies would probably need the cooperation of the Japanese server to obtain logs of IP addresses.

Duly alerted, consumers then flock to the site advertised, which may be based in any of twenty countries, and they download the pictures. The images will exist at that site only for a few hours before they are removed and the site ceases to exist. There is a continuing battle of wits between the posters and the administrators of the server, who are sincerely anxious to avoid any illicit material appearing under their name. Not every new Web page can be checked instantly, and server administrators rely heavily on search robots to scan the titles of home pages for any keywords that indicate the presence of child pornography. Apart from the obvious *childporn,* loaded words might include *lolita, nudists, cp, kinder,* or perhaps the names of famous series like hel-lo or KG. The subculture has had some success in evading this surveillance by giving Web sites codeword titles relating to sport, such as *soccer, volleyball,* and so on, though the robots are becoming familiar with this ruse. The best indication that a home page is offering improper material is when a new site suddenly attracts thousands of hits within a few hours, and this is usually sufficient for server administrators to examine its contents and suppress it.

The transient nature of sites massively complicates any chance of effective surveillance of illegal materials on the Internet, since logs of sites visited by a given user will only show that on, say, June 1, 2000, the computer in question was employed to access a URL with a neutral-sounding title such as *www.angelfire.com/volleyball/123.* Elaborate retrospective cross-checking would be needed to show that for a few hours on this exact day, that particular site was used to display a hundred hard-core child porn images. Other URLs might be more suspect, for instance, if they used a term such as *sexhound,* but only a tiny proportion of visitors to a site bearing this name would be there to download illegal material, as opposed to conventional adult images.

The need to deceive search robots explains one of the odder features of the pedo boards, namely, the very thin disguise invariably provided for URL addresses, which might refer to a site in a form such as *h##p:// a#gelfire.com.* To give an analogy from a strictly legitimate site, it is almost as if the *New York Times* address were cited as *h**p://www.ny*.com* (* = t). A glance at this transparent code will reveal what the actual address is, so why it is not cited fully as *http://www.nyt.com?* There are two reasons, both connected with the need to prevent detection by search engines. First, if the full address of a porn site appeared on the page, a user could simply hit that link and be transported to the relevant page, and the server's robots would rapidly note an influx of hits linked directly from a well-known pedo board. When the address is given in mildly disguised form, the user is forced to type it in himself, so that there is no evidence of a direct linkage. For similar reasons, those who frequent the boards generally avoid entire phrases that might be picked up by surveillance engines, so that messages might refer to "ch*ld p*rn," "p$dophiles," or "s#x with ch#ldren" and to "on-topic" material, the most common euphemism for child pornography. Another reason for disguise involves defense against spam: "When the board was new, spammers would use software to post links on this page often. The Maestro added banned words to make their links return error messages."[5]

Games like this succeed in keeping the temporary porn site alive for a few minutes or hours longer than might be expected naturally, but sooner or later it will be detected and destroyed. This is why there is no point in reporting such addresses to authorities; the site was active only for a few hours, and once it is gone, it will never be reused for illicit purposes. Nevertheless, anti-porn activists persist in citing long lists of such sites as if they were permanent institutions. One of the individuals most quoted in the media on this subject is attorney Parry Aftab, executive director of the vigilante group Cyber Angels, who "says that there are literally thousands of Web sites devoted to the topic of pedophilia"; others place the number at a surprisingly specific "23,000." If there were indeed thousands of Web sites with known, fixed URLs, they could all be shut down in a matter of days.[6]

The images in question have been posted and the site visited. In a minority of cases, the photographs or videos are displayed in a form accessible to any user, who can simply download them and perhaps save them to a hard drive. These are known as "Web-friendly" postings and are offered as a gesture of goodwill to novices. More commonly, though, another stage intervenes, since the images are presented in Zip form, coded, and unintelligible to anyone lacking the necessary password. Only some hours or days after the original posting has been removed or suppressed, the Californian supplier will provide the codewords that will allow consumers to decode what they have obtained. The reasons for this delay are ingenious:

> If you ran a server where people could create sites, and you wanted to see if anyone had uploaded any illegal stuff, you could easily do so by simply having a look at the site, right? Well, if all you found were PW protected zips, all you could do is try cracking those in order to find out the content. The poster usually gives the PW for all to have after a certain amount of time, usually after 48 hours, and usually after he has killed his own zips. This of course in order to avoid having the admin of the server he uploaded his site at, knowing he posted on-topic material. Let's say the admin of that server cared to bother trying to crack the zips, or that someone gave him the PW, all he could say is 'hey, you posted illegal material at my server!' The poster could of course respond, 'Well, I know, and it's awful! I found these zips myself at another site, and when I found out the content deleted the zips of course, didn't you notice?' ;)[7]

The poster might supply these codewords directly on a board such as the Maestro's or might cross-reference to yet another popular password board that is notionally based in the South Pacific states of Nauru (.nu) or Tonga (.to), though it actually exists on a server anywhere in the world: it could even be in the street next to him. Once a consumer obtains the passwords and decodes the pictures, he might offer a report on them on a board, expressing a desire for other images he would like to view. In gratitude, he might present some of his own collection. Through such devious means, a child porn enthusiast can acquire dozens or hundreds of images or movies every day, though only a tiny proportion is likely to represent wholly new material for the aficionado.

How Large an Underworld?

In the countless board discussions on security, one recurrent theme is that of "safety in numbers," in other words, that porn users could in theory be tracked down, but the sheer volume of traffic makes this next to impossible. In a discussion of the wisdom of using *abpep-t*, Godfather Corleone advised:

> There are millions of people using newsgroups, and tens of thousands of them do visit *abpep-t* on a very regular basis. Therefore the likelihood the server would want to spend time tracking someone down for visiting a newsgroup they are responsible for providing people with, is rather small.

Such comments raise the difficult but inevitable question of just how large a community we are dealing with, and the Godfather's remark about "tens of thousands" is not only plausible but perhaps modest.

The exact amount of traffic on the boards is difficult to assess, because all users employ pseudonyms, and one individual might use several over time. In one unusual instance, an active participant on the Maestro boards described the names he had used in recent years:

> Hello everyone—this is Pirra8. For the last time, I come to you as the number 8 Pirate. But, because of an error in judgment, I can no longer use the nickname. It is because someone has found out my old nickname of Atom. Yes, I also was Klowne of the Dark Karnival and Nat King Hole. But Atom is pretty well known, and I can no longer live up to that reputation. I have a hard time living up to the Pirra8 nickname. So, look for a newbie nickname that may be around a little longer.[8]

It is conceivable, if unlikely, that five (or fifty) of the notes appearing at a site on a particular day derive from one individual using multiple nicknames.

With that difficulty in mind, we can say that at a given moment on an average day, the main Maestro discussion board contained contributions from about sixty or so pseudonymous contributors, though that is only a snapshot, and the total contributing during a whole day is considerably larger. Given the delicate subject matter, the figure for "lurkers" (people who observe but do not contribute) is likely to be far larger than for typical Usenet groups. At a minimum, the Maestro community certainly ran to several thousand. A useful analogy may be provided by other, less popular child porn sites that record the number of hits for each posting. The volume of hits largely depends on the plausibility that the original message does, in fact, lead to a genuine CP site; but where the poster is well known and trusted, the number of hits is usually between two and four thousand and may well approach ten thousand. Of course, a person might visit a particular site only sporadically or concentrate only on one board to the exclusion of others. Still, that provides an absolute minimum for the size of the core CP community on the Internet, those who frequent at least one of the various boards on a regular basis: we have already seen that *egroups* sites with child porn content can run to several thousand members. Confirming this scale, G-Man, one of the most experienced contributors to the Maestro board, wrote, "To each of my posts I get approx 1,000 to 5,000 visitors to my site (nearly 90,000 in the past five weeks!)"[9]

Gauging the scale of the pedophile audience is a frequent talking point on the boards. One recent posting ran as follows:

> When you think about it, just how many lola lovers do we have here, maybe? 10,000 15,000 visit this board, what about other boards, and what of the others that can not find this and other boards? I have seen some of the log files from some of the net's search engines, and the top search is childporn and all the Lola lovers that don't have a computer, there must be millions out there some where ;).

Others agreed:

> * **Tomcat** > I had a site posted here with a counter that showed approx. 3,000 access after 4 hours, before the site was shut down. Extrapolate this to a whole day could be 18,000 only from this board at one day. And there are many more surfing in news (probable ratio 1:10 or more) and other boards. The number is constantly increasing as more people get access to the net. There was about half of them about half a year ago, and the increase itself is increasing. So no need to feel alone. I guess the ratio of posters and lookers on this board is about

1:100 or more. . . . That's the reason why I'm always stating that busting them all would hurt national economics.

* **Zep** > 12 months ago ***'s site, which had links to BBS's on its front page, was getting over 30,000 hits a day before the counter was taken off. *** BBS in its 'finest hour' (when this BBS went down for about 3 days about 6 months ago), was getting over 50,000 hits a day over this period. No, we are not alone in this world.

Confirming the general scale suggested here, Interpol, the international police agency, has suggested "that over 30,000 pedophiles are involved in organized child pornography rings in Europe, which began forming through the Internet." I stress, though, that we are dealing with core activists, since casual browsers may be much more numerous. Recently, U.S. Customs authorities claimed to have found child porn sites that scored literally millions of hits in a given month.[10]

Putting the different boards together, I would guess that the core population as of 2001 should be counted somewhere in the range of fifty to a hundred thousand individuals, though that is a very loose figure. It is also a global number: perhaps a third of these are located in the United States. Given the phenomenal expansion of the Internet since the mid-1990s, we can assume that this figure is changing very rapidly, and certainly expanding. While some old hands send farewell messages explaining that their interests have moved on to other things, almost every day on the boards we find first postings by recently arrived "newbies."

It is even more difficult to assess the demographics of the audience for the Maestro (or any) board. In many situations on the Internet, people tend to assume personas that are not necessarily their own, and in an illegal setting such as this there are powerful reasons to affect a different identity. A general impression, though, suggests that the vast majority of contributors to the board fall into the category of males, aged between perhaps twenty-five and fifty-five, mainly white but with a sizable Asian minority. This profile would certainly account for the vast majority of recorded arrests. My impression may be false in a number of ways, as several major users at least claim to be much younger than this would suggest, aged in their late teens. Given the distribution of computer skills across the population, a large cohort of teens and young adults would be quite predictable.

Nor can we say much about participants' regional or occupational backgrounds, except that both are highly diverse. This is indicated by the membership of the Wonderland Club, which, as we will see, was a closed network of elite traffickers broken up in 1998. The Wonderland group included some two hundred members in over forty countries, including the United States, Great Britain, Australia, Italy, France, Norway, Sweden, Germany, Austria, Belgium, Finland, and Portugal. American members included "an engineer from Portland, Maine, a scientist in New Britain, Conn. Other suspected members lived in sleepy towns like Broken Arrow, Oklahoma; Lawrence, Kansas; and Kennebunk, Maine. . . . A suspect living in a trailer park in St. Charles, Mo., was arrested after agents found, along with child porn, firearms and a stash of the black powder used to make bombs. According to Customs agents, a law student in New York City threw his hard drive into a neighbor's yard." Of the first eight members charged in the United Kingdom, we find three computer consultants—unsurprising in view of the level of expertise required for this world—but also two taxi drivers and three men who were described as unemployed.[11]

Gender represents another controversial point. Messages are often posted by individuals identifying themselves as women, and these claim that far more adult women are sexually interested in young girls than is commonly realized. One of the major posters on the boards over the last year or two bears the handle "Goddess." Goddess's real identity is controversial. Asked to speculate on the appearance of contributors, one poster wrote that he saw "Goddess as a rebellious schoolgirl with holes in her jeans (probably she is a he and 50 years old)." Still, lending credibility to claims of female involvement, there are documented cases of girls and women being involved in making and distributing electronic child porn, although they represent a small minority of activity.[12] Generally, we can safely assume that the bulk of board traffic is the work of white men in their thirties and forties.

Closed Groups

Apart from the newsgroups and the BBS's is yet another type of structure, which is the closed group or private electronic network, the closest parallel to the old private BBS. Of its nature, this part of the subculture is exceedingly difficult to penetrate, even by law enforcement, and activity here is confined to the hardest-core users, usually individuals with highly developed technical abilities. Essentially, these groups are an outgrowth of the kind of individual trading that has long existed on the Internet. A person in a chat room might announce that he has a video of his young niece and will trade a copy for a comparable item from a like-minded "hobbyist." At least since the late 1980s, such transactions have been exceedingly dangerous, given the high likelihood that the person ostensibly taking up the invitation is an undercover police officer. Within the subculture, the first and most frequently emphasized rule is "Never trade with anyone." That rule, however, does not apply within a closed circle of individuals well known to one another, who have all established their bona fides over a period of several years. If a person has been distributing hard-core child pornography since the late 1980s, the odds that he is a police mole or provocateur are very slim, though not non-existent.

The need for such a closed group is suggested by a comment from G-Man, writing in 1999:

> * **G-MAN** > O.K.—only 0.0001% of the material out there is getting to the public parts of the web (like *abpep-t*). Most people with new stuff know each other from the early days of 'net' (5 or 6 years ago) or before, and are not very eager to make new contacts. We all know that the public parts of the net are full of cops, wankers and other deadbeats. . . . Fortunately it seems like some of the people that have been active for so many years show up from time to time with a little material for the 99.9% (most of us) that don't have s#x with our children and are willing to give away pics of that. . . . It used to be so easy. Go to a shop where on-topic material was sold and look for the guy next to you—you had a new contact! Now we have to be a lot more care-

ful so no new contacts are being made other than people from the old groups introducing close personal friends.[13]

Within this tight circle, material of the very highest quality could be shared and traded. As "AnonAmos" commented in 2000:

Some people may wonder why the h/c pics and other vids are not re-leased. After about one year, you collect just about all that's out there. Believe me, there is only 30% that is released. A select group, called "elite," make the pics and vids. They hold it for various trades, usually from other groups. So, kg's, kx's, and other things (Lucy, Vicky, Helen) exist in large quantities, but the elite *do not* let them go. . . . Most material exists on CD or video tape. Like an iceberg, there's a lot going on under the surface, and eventually it disappears anyway.

Shortly afterward, "Jethro Tull" made a similar observation:

Yes, it's true that only a very small amount of pics from the Kata series have ever been posted, but I know for a fact there's many, many more of her available. But as I'm sure you know, these are only available to the traders and collectors, much like the infamous KG/X series. Only time will tell when all these wonderful goodies will come out, but lets all hope it's very soon![14]

The suggestion that even the vast quantity of images that are now pub-licly available represents only a fraction of the true repertoire is alarming.

Despite the obvious advantages of a tight network of intimates, there are serious dangers. Responding to a new "ring" created at about this time, one board user wrote that it was

a bad, bad thing. Why? Because it creates *personal* contact (at least, more personal than this board). The closer the contact, the more in-formation that can be gathered about you. In order for these people to get the password to the site, they had to use e-mail, ergo, they have supplied a complete *stranger* information that he/she did not have before. It's a numbers game that will, sadly, unstick some potentially great people.

Alternatively, "how do you stop bubba becoming a reg???"—that is, how do you prevent law enforcement infiltrators becoming regulars? "How do you check, because a private bbs is a sure way of people dropping their guard."[15]

Several such closed groups have appeared in the official record from time to time, confirming fears of police infiltration. One such was the San Jose–based Orchid Club, the investigation of which led to a far larger international ring, the Wonderland network discussed earlier. Access to this latter group was tightly controlled. Images were traded freely within the group, and some found their way into the wider child porn world. Indeed, the story of the hel-lo series provides a useful case study of the means by which such material disseminates. In response to a question about the origins of this "starlet," "PussyPig" wrote:

> She is English and her stepfather gave the original files to a few of us on Wonderland. Someone posted most of the series on a news server. The cops knew about the Hel-lo series but were unable to figure out who he was until the other girl blabbed to her mother and she went to the cops. They raided his house and found his log files of his involvement with Wonderland. I assume they traced many other collectors.[16]

Even though the Wonderland club is defunct, the hel-lo series has since entered general currency and is now so widely available that suppression is impossible.

Police alleged that cooperation between Wonderland members went further than merely sharing images. According to a report in *Time* magazine,

> members include computer programmers and hardware specialists, deployed an imposing system of codes and encryption. . . . Some club members in the U.S., Canada, Europe and Australia, . . . owned production facilities and transmitted live child-sex shows over the Web. Club members directed the sex acts by sending instructions to the producers via Wonderland chat rooms.[17]

Such live child-sex shows are never mentioned elsewhere in Net discussions, but the concept is not inherently impossible. Absence of evidence is not evidence of absence.

Though Wonderland ended, many of its members remained in operation, and PussyPig noted, "There are many still around (I have seen a couple here and a few other bbs's.)"[18] In early 2000, some of the mainstays of the Maestro board withdrew to establish a new password-protected board, allegedly a revived Wonderland Club, to the dismay of rank-and-file enthusiasts:

> If you have some hc cp [hard core child porn] mail Godfather Corleone your e-mail and public keys fast so you can get a pw. This will allow you to post. It's to be a new Wonderland-style setup. Once they swap we will get any new stuff left over that they feel like posting whenever they decide to drop by.[19]

To the best of my knowledge, this newer network still exists, as a deeply hidden conduit for the hardest and most current child porn—unless, of course, it is a well-concealed snare prepared by some law enforcement agency to flush out major figures in the trade.

In addition to these various methods of clandestine distribution, the subculture watches keenly for new technologies that might enhance security and secrecy. "Darkstar," for instance, has suggested: "Just as we have a BBS like this, it's inevitable that software will be developed that allows pedos to d/l pics and movies between themselves, similar to ICQ but private and virtual anon and locks out passing surfers, it will arrive." In this view, perhaps the most promising development on the horizon is Freenet software. A file-sharing system, Freenet represents a sizable advance over existing technologies like Gnutella or Napster, which allow people to download free music.

> [Freenet] promotes unfettered distribution and replication of digital information on the Internet . . . data is constantly shuffled from one user to another, and a computer owner doesn't know what's stored on

his hard drive at any given time. Once a piece of information enters the Freenet maw, it can't be expunged. . . . Information can be distributed throughout the Freenet network in such a way that it's effectively impossible to determine its location.

The total anonymity of a distributed or peer-to-peer system offers the prospect of "near-perfect anarchy," and advocates extol its virtues for dissidents fighting repressive regimes. In contrast, to quote a recent study in *Time*,

critics say it will be a boon to drug dealers, terrorists and child pornographers. And it poses a new threat to intellectual-property rights. With Napster, at least there's a company to sue and a way to trace individuals who have downloaded CDs. If Freenet catches on, it may be impossible to find anyone to punish. We may already be looking at the next generation of outlaw technology.[20]

The Content

What exactly are the images that require so much time and effort to circulate and collect? What does the label "child pornography" cover in practice? It may seem an obvious question, in the sense that most people know that the term *pornography* implies representations of sexual acts, and by extension, *child pornography* simply implies that these acts would be carried out by children. In fact, the topic is more complicated than this analogy would suggest, since so much of the content of "child porn" sites depicts poses and behaviors that would not be considered pornographic were the subjects adult. While I cannot attempt any kind of formal analysis, either quantitative or content based, some general points can be made.

I focus throughout on images of girls, since the pedo boards I have observed seldom traffic in images of young boys. Specialized boy-related boards certainly exist, though these seem to be fewer than those offering pictures of young girls. This may mean that the pederast subculture on the Web is smaller than that focused on young girls or, more likely, that it is so distinct that I have not succeeded in locating it. I do not know, for instance, of a pederastic equivalent of the Maestro board. One factor conditioning availability is that in major host nations for pedo boards, especially Japan, officialdom treats images of boys far less sympathetically than those of girls. Certainly the market for boy-related films and magazines has always been large, and European publications such as *Piccolo* had the same legendary status among collectors as the famous pedophile productions of the 1970s. Also, pictures of boys have featured heavily in reports of child porn arrests over the last few years, so the pictures are clearly out there. At any given time, *egroups* offers fifty or more sites devoted to "twinks," mainly teenage boys above the legal age but with a fair scattering of underage pictures.

In terms of young girls, the photographs and movies available on the Web fall broadly into two categories, namely, soft and hard core, and the two types should be discussed separately. Basically, the difference is that soft-core content features nudity but no sexual activity, while hard-core images depict actual sex or show the subjects in lewd poses. In an adult context, the numerous soft-core images would be given a gentler term, such as naughty, spicy, or what used to be called glamour photos. If the subjects were adults, the images would be far milder than the nudity commonly seen on cable television or in most underwear advertisements in newspapers or women's magazines. A good number of child images consist of fully clothed girls in party dresses or ballet clothes, and these cater to an audience genuinely fascinated by the young female form, without any overt sexual implications. Some popular sites even reproduce decades of Sears ads for panties and swimsuits or show publicity photos of young gymnasts. They become "pornographic" only through their setting and their juxtaposition to masturbatory images.

Probably the most common type of soft-core photographs involves nude young girls in innocent and non-sexual settings: these are the staples of the *egroups* trade. Many of these images have been taken in nudist camps or on nude beaches, and they generally picture children in groups or with their families, playing sports, or using playgrounds. If not for the context, the scenes would seem remarkably wholesome. In the whole range of images these are the least harmful, since the photographs were taken without causing any harm to the subjects. This material does raise sensitive questions, however, about the nudist/naturist subculture and its alleged relationship to child pornography. Particularly in North America, naturists have long been regarded as amiable cranks, but various activists and pressure groups have suggested that the movement has attracted more than its share of pedophiles and pornographers, and substantial evidence of misbehavior comes from criminal investigations and convictions over the years. Without having to accept extreme charges about mass perversion in the nudist world, the volume of nudist photography, particularly involving small children and toddlers, does indicate that the naturist movement has been exploited for pornographic purposes.[21]

Another common type of nude image is taken from the serious and non-pornographic work of art photographers like David Hamilton. A very large series in this tradition is identified by the letters MCLT, "my collection of lolitas and teens" which runs to several thousand images. Many cheesecake images are taken from the child porn magazines that circulated openly in Europe and North America during the 1970s. Most of these pictures have now been scanned into the Web and still circulate decades after they were produced. It is curious to think that subjects who were nine or ten at the time would now be approaching forty.

Hard-core material also exists in abundance, some from the magazines of the 1970s but a striking amount from very recent times, right up to the present day. If the ubiquitous images of naked children playing volleyball on a beach are the most innocuous items in this curious world, then modern-day series of homemade hard core are the worst of the breed, because they depict ongoing acts of rape and molestation by culprits who are still active and presumably still exploiting victims. A few images are the work of professional photographers but many were taken in domestic contexts, recording individual acts of molestation committed against young neighbors or family members. Most of the girl subjects are aged between perhaps eight and thirteen, but others involve much smaller children, down to toddlers. Because of the age of the subjects, most of the sex acts involved do not involve penetration but show the girls performing oral sex or mutual masturbation. Some images, however, do depict genital and anal penetration, as well as vibrators and other masturbatory devices. The hel-lo series already mentioned shows actual penetration. In addition, hard-core videos and photo series continue to be produced in fair abundance, seemingly using underage prostitutes in Asia or Latin America.

Just how much of the available material is new, and how much is "classic," from the 1970s or before? In answer to complaints about "nothing new on the boards," one of the Maestro board admins discussed this question:

> I took the time counting the amount of new series posted the last year (with new series, it's understood a series never posted in public before) and I came up with a couple of hundred series, none from the 60's or 70's. Looking at the amount of filmclip-series that has been posted (that is, snapshots from VHS tapes) the amount is also quite large, although of course not as large as the picture series. Generally what happens is a person shoots a series, that series is then being sold as VHS tapes to X amount of people. During that time, fragments of those series might pop up at IRC and finally at newsgroups (even though they perhaps weren't meant to, but most likely because they are being used to advertise the series in order to make people want to buy the tapes). When the tapes have been sold and the person (or persons) have received what they consider enough money, the material usually pops up more often, especially at various newsgroups. Still, the best parts are usually left only for trading within a small ring.[22]

Though it is a mild blessing in the context, violence or sadomasochistic themes virtually never feature, at least in the images in general circulation. Evidence to the contrary is limited and largely anecdotal. According to one report of the Wonderland group, for instance, members "'had standards. . . . The only thing they banned was snuff pictures, the actual killing of somebody.' According to Nick, a couple of members were barred because they trafficked in those pictures." The rarity of references to violent materials does not mean they do not exist, but the evidence is tenuous.[23]

Images are conveyed in various forms, commonly as stills (jpgs or gifs) but preferably as movies, in mpg format. Movies are easily uploaded and downloaded, a point that needs emphasis because of the common misapprehension that much of the illicit traffic involves pedophiles using the Web to sell and trade actual videos. As suggested by the quote above, videos certainly exist and are passed along in a small circle, before finding their way onto the newsgroups or Web sites. Darkstar boasts that "USA has the world's largest porn industry operating out of California, and probably the largest underground loli video network." Even so, these items are rarely advertised or traded online. Buying or trading items in this way is commonly known to be a suicidally dangerous practice; as the boards constantly reiterate:

> Anyone who says they have vids of on-topic material is to be avoided at all costs. If you spot someone trading or offering vids of on-topic material, these people have connections with LEAs. . . . The best way is to wait for the people to put up the actual film. It takes patience and watching news a lot, but they will eventually upload them for downloading.[24]

Why sell or own an actual video when all the material on it can simply be downloaded, to be viewed at leisure on your own computer screen? Why stockpile evidence against yourself? The continuing media and law enforcement emphasis on trading actual videos is reminiscent of the 1980s, when police and media refused to believe that computers could be used for visual images and so assumed that pedophiles must be swapping information about potential targets. At least until recently, many people have not grasped the capacity of the Internet to receive and broadcast movies and sound.

Supply and Demand

The relative value placed on the items available within the subculture is closely related to issues of supply. Both "oldies" and sex tourist images are so abundant as to be considered boring. In contrast, by far the most heavily sought-after images are the modern-day pictures record-ing sex acts involving children in North America or Europe, pictures taken after the imposition of strict laws against manufacturing or dis-tributing child porn. The special premium placed on this content may be augmented by the knowledge of the specially dangerous and illegal circumstances of manufacture. Also, some may find such contempo-rary images better for purposes of sexual fantasy, because the children depicted so closely resemble anyone who might be encountered on a street or playground and do not have the features of dress or hairstyle that so blatantly proclaim an older image as a product of the mid-1970s. By contrast, other fans prefer the older pictures precisely be-cause they remind users of the general style and appearance of the girls who were their contemporaries in youth, and about whom they might have had their earliest fantasies.

A common theme on the pedo boards is requests for material that is not readily available. This indicates the interests of the subculture and also suggests the sort of material that will come onto the market in a few months or years, once pornographers know there is a market for such items. The range of requests is bewilderingly perverse. A few themes recur often and arouse real enthusiasm. By far the most common include calls for "Black loli," African or African American subjects, of the sort now very rarely represented in the repertoire. Also in demand are incest pictures:

> Since I know that I'm loving l*li hc [lolita hard-core] pics, I'm after a special series. The pictures show an older women having s*x with an underage boy! So my question to you is if you could post this Series or another Mom & Son Series as a .zip file.
> * **moi** > Yeah, would be nice if someone posted that
> * **Born** > Yeah! He's right! That would be the best post of the last 2 months! Come on! Everybody with mom&son Pics! PLZ Post!
> * **demon** > Yeah right, I love mom&son pics too. Please post anyone.[25]

Other requests that appeared on the boards in early 2000 included the following:

* Does any-one know where I can get movies of 8 to 12yr girls being raped? Not hurt, just being forcefully de-flowered.
* We're looking desperately for girls or preteens making love to their teddybears, also sitting/lying on them. Anyone with sites/photos/clips??
* Please . . . can anyone tell me where can I find blowup dolls of underage little girls?
* Hi, boys and girls, I have a very special request, I'm searching for pics or videos from little boys and girls when they wash or get washed their hair. Does anybody know, where I can find something, it'll be great!
* I don't normally say anything but a preggy [pregnant] preteen is what I've been looking for over five years plezzz!
* Does anyone have any pre [-teen] pics of girls in lingerie or stockings? Or does anyone know of a page or address to download pics? I have one of a girl in B&W and I am sure there is a series.
* Please tell me where can I find Catholic-schoolgirls pics?? Please . . .

This last drew the response: "Please tell us what you wanna see. Schoolgirls that wear rosary?"[26]

Even in a world noted for the bizarre, the weird quality of these requests elicited some humorous responses and parodies:

* Jose > I'm looking for a 14 yr old doing a drawing of a tent using a red pen whilst whistling and there must be a green car in the background . . . :)
* Lurker #2 > Hold on, I think I got that one :))[27]

Other requests are felt to be simply too disgusting, beyond the pale even for a child pornography board:

Does anyone have some old pics from the camps in the Third Reich? I've heard that there is a whole series of SS men fucking small Jewish girls (b/w). I would like to see those pictures. Heil Hitler!

Almost certainly, this singularly disgusting request was not placed seriously but rather represented a provocation, a characteristic attempt by an "anti-pedo" critic of the board to sow dissension. Nevertheless, the question was taken seriously, and one reply ran as follows:

> Yes, I've also heard of this before, but why in your right mind would you want to see this in the first place? Its not even half [as] erotic as, say, the KG or even the Hel-lo series! You must be really sick to want to see that![28]

These exchanges demonstrate the extreme frankness that prevails on the boards, which is striking when we consider the extremely illegal nature of the behavior involved. People have no compunction about seeking such items, posting messages that might be read by thousands of others and that could be (and are) read by anti-pedophile groups and police. But it scarcely seems to matter. To that extent, moralist critics have some justification when they argue that the Internet has caused a near legalization of child pornography.

Though I draw no parallel between the behaviors involved, the legal situation is not unlike that of marijuana use in the late 1960s and early 1970s. In these years, police were still convinced that the drug was deeply dangerous, and courts inflicted severe prison terms on users; yet the sheer numbers of illegal users made controlling the substance all but impossible. At best, police could hope to arrest only a tiny minority of users or dealers. Moreover, the drug's illegal status helped cement the internal cohesion of a vigorous subculture, which saw itself as a courageous underground movement resisting social conformity. Within that world, people talked freely about drug matters and exchanged consumer reports, and these discussions were carried on in "underground" publications easily available to police. The situation is not dissimilar in the child porn world, in which enthusiasts participate enthusiastically in a deviant subculture of global proportions.

FOUR

A Society of Deviants

I think that everyone here, with the exception of trolls and LEA, are friends and family of a sort. I know that there aren't many people I personally know that I would let know of my tastes for the younger things in life. Here, I know it's safe (within reason, of course) for people to talk about lolis.

—P_Horse, Maestro board, February 26, 2000

Over the last half century, sociologists and criminologists have devoted much attention to studying forms of organized deviance, subcultures or gangs, in order to understand their values, ethics, and structures; but few of these studies present an example of deviant organization close to the world of Net child pornography. What should we even call this underworld, this milieu? I have been speaking of those who use Internet child porn as members of a *subculture*, and I believe that is the most appropriate word, but this particular subculture differs substantially from others that have been recorded through the years. Generally, the term implies a group who "build a body of shared knowledge through their contacts. This knowledge is called a subculture because it exists as specialized knowledge within the larger culture."[1] The network or community studied here certainly possesses a huge corpus of specialized knowledge, but this is built and transmitted entirely without direct, face-to-face contact. Individuals remain unknown to one another, to the extent of not knowing or caring whether a fellow deviant lives in the next street or on the other side of the globe. The whole phenomenon raises fascinating questions about that old sociological chestnut "What is community?" *Community* is, incidentally, the term favored by participants. We are reminded that most of the technical terms and concepts devised by sociologists to categorize human relations were devised before the massive changes wrought in social interactions by electronic technology and urgently need revision.

Organized Deviance?

The yawning gap between older categories and the present reality can be seen from the standard work of organized deviance by Joel Best and David Luckenbill. Their study divides deviants into classes, based on the nature and degree of their relationships:

> These organizational forms are defined in terms of four variables: whether the deviants associate with one another; whether they participate in deviance together; whether their deviance requires an elaborate division of labor; and whether their organization's activities extend over time and space.[2]

The spectrum ranges all the way from Loners through Colleagues, Peers, Teams, and ultimately to Formal Organizations, and the model works well for most types of deviance, from pickpockets and confidence men to robbery gangs and drug syndicates. But what is the relationship of participants in e-networks like the Maestro boards? Clearly they are highly deviant individuals, who in most cases operate strictly as loners, never having direct personal contact with another deviant. On the boards, people identify themselves solely through fictitious names or handles, and real names or locations are never known unless in the event of an arrest, which necessarily ends that person's participation in the child porn world.

Not only do participants never meet, but the mere suggestion that they ever could (outside a police cell) is greeted with derision. On one occasion, a naive poster asked, "How can I meet any one of you in person. I sure would like to hang out with you and talk about everything I seen and heard!!!" Responses were numerous and uniformly mocking:

> * **gremlyn** > thanx ocifer [officer], I'd love to go to the pedo picnic. FBI welcome!!
>
> * **Stupid** > what the hell . . . sure why not. We could start a club, maybe next door to the Girl Scouts? Nice neon sign in the window: 'Pedo Trade Meeting Every Friday at 5pm—bring the kids, we have on-site child care'??!! Why would you *want* to meet anyone? Enjoy the anonymous camaraderie . . . don't push your luck.
>
> * **Half man half Lager** > Nah . . . seriously guys, just think, we could *all* post our home addresses, phone numbers etc. . . . then Hey Presto!! Pretty soon we would *all* have the same address wouldn't we, no more expensive phone bills logging onto Boards like this, no more worrying about the Feds etc., three free meals a day . . . a new fucking "husband"!!! . . . Heaven!!
>
> * **Omega68** > What about a great pedo-convention on the south pole? I think this is the only place where the cops won't reach us.[3]

Yet the existence of such exchanges reminds us that these are not simple "Loners," cut off from either the deviant world or the social mainstream. Members do associate, quite intensely, through electronic means. This should classify them as "Colleagues," and this is the term that Best and Luckenbill apply to computer hackers; yet the fit is not particularly apt, since colleagues would normally be expected to meet and socialize when not engaged in their deviant activities. Some kind of personal interaction is also expected of "Peers," and the child porn networks really do not demonstrate the sort of hierarchy or division of labor required for teams and formal organizations. Are we dealing with a wholly new mode of social organization?

The Subculture

Despite these differences, the child porn world does have many of the features traditionally expected of a subculture. For one thing, the network maintains its unity and solidarity solely through shared interest: this is a society of deviants united by common passions, rather than any commercial nexus. There are instances in which money changes hands and videos are sold, but many Web sites that demand payment for access are bogus, and anyone gullible enough to pay will, if he is lucky, just lose the price of admission; if he is less fortunate, he will have earned a visit from the FBI. The vast majority of people who post or distribute pictures do so out of non-economic motives, and we can debate whether these should best be described as altruism or exhibitionism. Unlike most adult pornographic sites, child porn pages on the Web do not even derive income: who would advertise in such a context? Apparently, the Maestro ran his boards out of his own pocket, as what he saw as a public service to his "community." The non-commercial nature of the trade deserves emphasis, because so many writers on the topic still make highly inaccurate remarks about the supposedly profitable nature of the trade and its organized-crime ties: this image is reinforced by the misleading word *industry* for the child porn world.

Also characteristic of a subculture, the "loli" world is characterized by specialized knowledge and language that set it apart from the mainstream: this is par excellence a community demarcated by highly specialized expertise. The fact that a person finds his way to a "loli board" is no mean feat of skill and has ipso facto merited admission to the milieu, the community. Novices stress the extreme difficulty of finding this electronic Shangri-la:

* **Rupert** > I'd say it took me a good year to find this board.
* **Scientist** > I'm still a newbie. Found this bbs via *** via months of surfing.
* **Lamont Cranston** > I looked for a year before I found [board] 1, and then it was at least 6 months before I moved up to [board] 2.[4]

* **Love2See** > I searching 2 months for cp and the first pic sc I see it was *** from a banner of a loli site, and when I enter that site (my first porno site)—I was shocked. First hc pic it was a hel-lo, a sample from the site. After that I find ****—I was so happy . . . after that I find **** board, full of spam, and The Maestro board—end of story.[5]

Becoming an active board member demands serious computer literacy. As will be apparent from my description of posting porn on temporary Web pages, a good deal of technical background is required to participate. To gain attention or respect, one has to post pictures of some kind, and at a minimum, this requires knowledge of basic security techniques, such as finding a proxy. In some cases, many pictures and videos can be obtained just by visiting Web-friendly sites, but access to newer and more select material requires a knowledge of decoding Zip files and running the various programs needed for videos and movies. The boards feature lengthy lectures to novices ("newbies") on the skills and etiquette appropriate to this culture. Technical discussion on the boards is commonly at a sophisticated level, and the abstruse quality of some discussions can inspire mockery:

> * **Fred** > Help. My hyfendoufenator switch fell off the mother board and shorted out the rear area stabilator localiser junction. Now all my jpgs are upside down and inside out. SO? What's the pass?
>
> * **Crow** > I had the same problem, just switch the jumpers on the rear area stabilator localiser junction to the opposite of what it is now, and apply a nice sized wad of chewing gum to your hyfendoufenator switch and press firmly back in its place and your jpgs should be back to right side up, hope that helps you
>
> * **careful** > Of course, you checked to make sure the economizer input flow switch is set to "null" "lock" setting? Otherwise the hyfendoufenator may return a "bad file name" in which case you should remove the "nice size wad o' chewing gum" allocation bobber and restart the system. After restart, go out to the car (garage, etc.) and get "jumper cables," these should be attached to your motherboard and then plugged into a wall outlet, a couple of forks will work. When you get back from the hospital, restart and reformat your system . . . all should be fine now![6]

The question "What's the pass?" parodies novices' endless pleas for passwords to decode materials, when every experienced participant realizes that passwords are distributed only after a safe interval.

Apart from technical issues, individuals are soon inducted into a whole array of slang and argot that serve to separate participants from the common run of humanity. Many words are standard to the world of computer newsgroups and BBS's. Such would be *lurkers*, people who observe the proceedings in a group without participating, and *trolls*, wreckers who frequently post disruptive or hostile comments or who invent rumors in order to create dissent. Use of these terms is often framed by advice that has a proverbial quality: the phrase "Do not feed the trolls" means that participants are urged not to respond to provocative comments that might encourage wasteful controversy. Complaints about spam or deceptive sites are equally common to adult sex sites.

Other terms, however, are distinctive to the child porn world. The boards often discuss whether a particular site is on- or off-topic. This is a common concern on mainstream boards, which might reject a particular posting as inappropriate to the theme of a particular group, but in something like the Maestro board, *on-topic* has a much more specialized meaning, namely, whether a posting concerns underage subjects or not. *Off-topic* is a dismissive term for pornographic pictures of adult women: to quote one fan, stating his preferences: "where there's breasts and pubic hair / usually, I'm not there." Electronic child porn is sometimes described as The Topic, capitalized thus.

Other terms peculiar to this world include *LEA*, or law enforcement agencies, and the initially puzzling *bubba*. When a participant suggests a hazardous practice, such as trading pictures, he might be scornfully warned that "bubba is waiting," which means that he may end up sharing a prison cell with a large convict named Bubba, who will use him as a sex slave. ("Bubba" occasionally implied an added reference to President Clinton, who neatly symbolized both federal authority and sexual hypocrisy.) Another common phrase is "Surf safe!" which serves as the final line of many messages. In addition to being an exhortation to maintain proper security procedures, it has almost become a distinctive slogan of the whole culture, an unofficial membership code.

In addition to shared values and knowledge, the child porn world has its structures and hierarchies, though these are far looser than we might expect to find in any criminal gang or network. At first sight, the child porn community is utterly disorganized, decentralized, spontaneous, and *samizdat*, but that is somewhat misleading, to the extent that great respect is accorded to knowledgeable and experienced individuals. These are the figures who have become old-timers by dint of having operated and survived for several years, and who post the best and most novel pictures: they are the regulars, the "regs," who merit enormous respect as the repositories of both knowledge and illicit material. To quote Dark-star: "All the regs know each other even if they have changed their nicks. Members come and go. We get bible eaters, anti-pedo peeps, weirdo's, lea's flaming or setting up spam sites to fish for IPs or credit card numbers, they all go, but the regs stay." Above them exist the true demigods, the "wise ones." Novices are informed of the means by which they can enter and advance through this hierarchy. In a list of instructions for the Maestro board, Pirra8 writes, "Logical progression is: newbie, lurker, regular, chat member, poster, newsgroup poster, trader, wise one. Takes about a year to get to be a wise one. After that, you might get to be Admin, create your own paysite, or become an underworld guru."[7]

The wise ones possess almost mythical status, and names such as Pirra8, G-Man, Godfather Corleone, Loligagger, NewsRulez, and the Lord High Executioner are venerated. Elders are approached with phrases such as "I ask the Great Ones" and "I'm asking for guidance from the seniors," Though the language suggests parody, it is used with remarkable consistency, and much correspondence suggests that the leaders succeed in projecting images of power and authority. Names like Godfather Corleone indicate that the individuals involved deliberately try to cultivate this image of a leadership role, a difficult enterprise in such an anonymous universe. We have no idea if someone like the God-father is in fact the patriarch the name suggests, or a very young man, or a woman, or, indeed, a police provocateur.

The anonymity of the Internet allows people to assume whatever roles they choose, and others can accept or reject these personas at their choice. "Jayjay" initiated an extensive correspondence when he asked contributors to describe their visual impressions of the usual board participants:

Have you ever wondered what everybody looks like on this board? I form a picture of people when I read the posts. Here goes: admin I imagine as like NASA with a big screen in front of them deleting and tracing and making sure the ship stays on course. StillListener + Peter Pan + Darkstar and johnboy as scientists in white coats running around testing things. GFC [Godfather Corleone] as Bogart in *Casablanca* (I don't know where I got that one from). The Maestro as one of them ancient Tibetan monks. . . . Trolls as drunk wife beaters in scruffy mobile homes. Flatgirls as two students in a shared flat . . . cops as big fat slobs in white shirts smoking and eating around a little 14 inch VDU.[8]

Whatever the objective reality of the Godfather and other elite figures, the degree of authority they possess is indicated by the fierce reactions when some other individual posts a message appropriating one of these hallowed names. The ruse is immediately detected because the wording and content are unfaithful to what is expected of the great one in question. The impostor will be threatened by dozens of angry participants complaining of *lèse-majesté* and warning of virus attacks if the crime is repeated. Newbies are subject to stern lectures for violating the codes of the community and for failing to show proper respect. Answering complaints about the poor quality of recent postings, Count Dracula responded:

> Has it ever occurred to you that the regs might be getting pissed off with eternally dipping into their private loli collections to give out free and get remarks like yours flung back at them, it's time for all the newbies and lurkers to learn to get some new material, pics, vids, whatever, buy a digital camera or a camcorder do some home-mades and post to some site, that way we all benefit and the board becomes more harmonious instead of all this "where's the urls," "I need some loli" etc etc. . . . so don't be shy, get snapping and contributing.[9]

Considering the activities that form the everyday pursuits of this underworld, the passionate desire to preserve respect and appropriate standards is a little bewildering. At the same time, the prestige of the leaders is transient and fragile: how could it not be in a medium little more than a decade old, in which a few months' experience creates a regular? Any of the great ones can vanish from the scene at a moment's notice and be replaced by some new star. Equally, the culture is absolutely open to new arrivals, and a couple of strong postings will win a reputation and perhaps open the path to the status of wise one.

Normal People

How does one join this subculture? As we have seen, the reasons why adults become sexually interested in children are much debated, but given that this enthusiasm does exist, it is not difficult to see why it should find such a friendly environment on the Internet, with its anonymity and its ability to transcend jurisdictional borders. We can also appreciate how novices should find it so easy to be drawn into the subculture and, once involved, to absorb its values and practices. In many ways, the seemingly aberrant world of child porn on the Net represents not a total break with approved mainstream ways and mores but their extension into illegality.

Some degree of tolerance of illegality is common to Internet culture in general.[10] The whole world of electronic communication has developed so rapidly that rules and laws are poorly formulated, and it is common and approved practice for computer users to violate regulations. People who would never dream of committing larceny or burglary in the "real" material world think nothing of hacking an Internet site, using a purloined password, or copying software illegally, while a widespread opinion holds that copyright rules simply do not exist on the Net. If something works and produces benefit without harming an individual (as opposed to a faceless corporation), then it is acceptable and approved. Even if technically criminal, misdeeds on computers are likely to be viewed by many as pranks rather than heinous offenses, and this approach is largely shared by the media. When, as happens from time to time, a hacker succeeds in changing the Web site of a police agency so that it suddenly depicts hard-core pornographic material, the news media tend to report the story as quirky or humorous rather than as a dreadful crime. (Sabotaging or closing down a popular site is a different matter.) The idea of seeking forbidden material on the Internet is natural and even socially approved, so that the heroic deeds of hackers and outlaw computer wizards are the subject of a hundred Hollywood films. When an Israeli teenager hacked into important U.S. government sites, that nation's then–prime minister, Benjamin Netanyahu, offered the Americans a cursory apology but used the incident at home to boast of Israel's technological prowess and sense of adventure. Conversely, authorities who try to prevent these efforts are reactionaries, stuffed shirts, control freaks: the enemy.

Occasionally, the fervently libertarian ethos of the Internet can extend even to something as condemned as child porn. In a curious case in 1998, the manager of a small California ISP discovered a child porn Web site, which she duly reported to authorities, and then tried herself to gain more information about the site's operators. She encountered a fiercely critical reaction from other Internet users, including a hacking attack that shut down her site. The issue was less tolerance of child porn as such than her apparent vigilantism and her willingness to draw officialdom into what should ideally be the self-regulating world of the Net.[11]

On the Internet, rules are made to be broken. This attitude is facilitated by the user's psychological sense that whatever occurs in a computer transaction takes place within his or her own private space. Although one is visiting a site based in Singapore, the individual is viewing it on a screen at home in London or in an office in Los Angeles, and it is intuitively obvious that this is where the transaction is really occurring. One can, after all, interrupt the process at any time to get up and make coffee or wash the car. The attitude seems to be that it is my home, my desk, my computer, and my business what I do with it. This is one reason for the ferocious opposition to schemes to tax commercial transactions online: why should the State of California, say, be able to charge sales tax on business that is self-evidently done on my desktop in Connecticut? This sense of private space also promotes a sense of invulnerability: it is difficult to take seriously all the jeremiads about the lack of privacy on the Net when the user feels that he or she is pursuing a personal interest at home, with no one apparently watching. Even in the case of child pornography, the absolute legal prohibition on private use is not as widely understood as one may think. In a surprising recent survey, Kimberly McCabe questioned a sample of citizens who attended law enforcement–sponsored crime-watch meetings in two cities in the U.S. South, people who might be presumed to have some interest in criminal justice issues. Even so, a third of her sample agreed with the statement "Downloading child pornography from a newsgroup is legal." Just under 8 percent believed that "possession of sexual material involving a minor is legal," and the same proportion felt that "viewing computer-generated children in sexual situations is okay."[12]

Also making the child porn subculture more apparently acceptable is the lack of overtly deviant behaviors or markers associated with the activity. Participants do not assume an overtly deviant role in the way that they would if they joined a gang or cult: they need not shave their heads, wear special clothing, or attend a meeting every week or even every year, nor need they relocate to a compound or commune. Entering the child porn culture might mean assuming or affecting a deviant identity, but one that has no physical manifestations or that need continue after one has switched off the computer. This particular subculture is one that can be joined without physically moving into a strange or dangerous-seeming environment, a biker bar, sex club, or drug supermarket, though in practice, using the computer at home can lead to far more perilous consequences than any of these places.

It is useful to compare the process of accessing child porn on the Internet today with the semi-tolerated matter of purchasing a magazine of this sort in an urban bookstore in 1975. Although the bookstore patron was running little risk of official sanction, it was self-evident from the surroundings and the social context that the purchaser was in deviant territory, both physically and metaphorically. The store was likely in a "bad part of town," in a physical setting perhaps not far removed from active prostitution and drug use, and not somewhere one would wish to be seen. In contrast, the modern computer user is, in every sense, at home with child pornography. Today, there appears to be no entry fee to the subculture, no risk or commitment, and that is perhaps the most dangerous delusion in the whole process.

In many ways, too, child porn users are extrapolating from the socially commonplace. On the Internet, sexual material and adult pornography are extremely abundant and generally tolerated, despite the continuing protests of conservative moralists. Pornography sites are well frequented, and little social stigma attaches to seeking such material through improper means, for instance, by using computers in libraries or schools. Such misdeeds are often the subject of humor rather than serious condemnation, even when the users are young teenagers. A person accessing sex sites from a workplace computer might technically be violating corporate rules but, according to most views, is no more criminal than a colleague who takes home pens or paper clips. Many porn sites also "push the envelope" in terms of the strange and perverse practices they depict, including sadomasochism, bestiality, and toilet functions. Occasionally, too, amateur sites in which posters offer homemade pictures of wives and (adult) girlfriends will throw in a soft-core image of a pubescent girl, and the responses suggest that this action is seen only as mildly naughty, perhaps a form of tweaking authority. Seeking bizarre or shocking sexual images on the Internet does not of itself contradict deeply held social values, especially when—as it appears—the searching is done in private.

Collectors

Also "normal" to a degree is the motivation that drives participants. Though their immediate incentive is sexual gratification, much of the appeal of child porn is what we might call a collector fetish, the same kind of instinct that drives people to acquire collections of Meissen porcelain, baseball cards, militaria, or Star Trek memorabilia. As in these legitimate areas, child porn enthusiasts tend to be pack rats, with very large collections of images often intricately organized and cataloged. Allegedly, members of the Wonderland Club were required, as a condition of joining, to donate personal stockpiles of at least ten thousand child porn images, a figure quite in line with the hoards commonly reported in arrests and seizures. In one Wonderland case,

> when U.S. Customs agents raided his San Diego area home in 1998, they found a computer chockfull of 40,000 photos and 1,000 movies—nearly all kiddie porn, with some featuring infants and preteens. These images were meticulously organized by the children's names and stored in files with headings such as "li'l rape."

In 1999, Adrian Thompson from England was caught with the largest collection of images ever recorded in that country: he "had 100,000 hardcore pictures on his computer disks and had downloaded 22,000 images of young boys and girls aged between two and thirteen."[13] This individual was unusually well qualified for the electronic world, since he held a degree in computer science and cybernetics, but there is no reason why ordinary computer users should not have very substantial collections.

Recent developments in electronic transmission and storage make such vast collections feasible—and, incidentally, suggest still more reasons why the long-term eradication of child porn is going to be extraordinarily difficult. A single posting might include thumbnail images of hundreds of pictures, all of which could, in theory, be downloaded and stored in one afternoon. In May 2000, for instance, "Loko" announced the posting of a vast collection of the KG series: "Here are all the KGs I have (900+ pics—20 Mb)." Shortly afterward, "Dad" made his own contribution by declaring, "These are various pictures from a pay site that I found a way into. There is about 1,500 in all. . . . I searched all the pay sites I could find to get pics for you all, I tried 30 of them, it took me 8 hours, straight."[14] The fact that these images are in electronic form means that they can be stored in a very small space, without the substantial libraries that would have been required if they were in magazine form: the risks of detection thus diminish.

Once again, rapid advances in technology have had a vast impact. In the late 1980s, the common means of storing computer data was a floppy disk that might contain either 800K or 1.4 megabytes of memory. If we assume that each photograph took up about 30 or 40K, that means one of the larger disks would hold perhaps thirty-five images, so that a significant picture library might require a hundred floppy disks. Since then, floppy disks have largely been replaced by Zip disks, and in the crudest financial terms, the cost of storing a megabyte of memory fell from about nine dollars in 1984 to a mere nine cents in 2000. A normal 100 megabyte Zip disk can contain perhaps three thousand images, an entire visual library that can be slipped into a jacket pocket. A disk with 250 megabytes would contain a collection almost large enough to earn entry to something like the elite Wonderland Club. Incidental comments on the boards suggest that some regular enthusiasts hold their entire collections on two or three Zip disks. Zip disks are especially valuable for storing movies and mpgs, each of which might take up anywhere from two to ten megabytes and so would have been far beyond the capacity of the older floppies. CDs are also common:

> It has been stated a million times already, you should NEVER store anything illegal on your hd [hard drive], just too damn risky. . . . Better to save all your precious files on encrypted CD's. Investing in a CD recorder is well worth it in the long run and offers the best security you can get with this type of material. You can store up to 650MB on a single CD and they're easy to hide or destroy if the worst were to happen. Also, when you encrypt your CD's with PGPdisk or similar, you can rest assured that no one will ever know just what you have on them. And you can sleep a little better knowing just that![15]

CDs or disks would often be stored in a microwave oven, so that in the event of a raid, the entire collection would be vaporized in seconds simply by pressing the "sensor reheat" command.

Collecting and actually possessing images has some virtues for security purposes, since one has to access the photograph online only once and can view it when desired, without facing the additional risks involved in surfing perilous Web sites. This removes the danger that one's address will be repeatedly logged in these suspicious contexts. Even so, the practice has its own acute dangers, and the fact of making and keeping collections, even in electronic form, raises puzzling questions about the motivations of child porn enthusiasts. Owning a collection of child porn seems absolutely contrary to the strict security precautions and safe surfing so frequently recommended on the boards, since, if found, the images constitute irrefutable evidence of criminal behavior. Since pictures are posted so frequently, enthusiasts might be better advised simply to download them temporarily as needed and then discard them to avoid the accumulation of damning evidence.

The fact that people violate these basic rules suggests that collectors are operating from motives apart from the purely sexual, and which are perhaps as difficult to comprehend as those of legitimate hobbyists, whom outsiders often see as fanatical. Child porn fans must be looking for something rather more complex than simple masturbation aids. In both cases, licit and illicit, there is a desire for the satisfaction that comes from possessing rare or distinctive objects, such as a Mickey Mantle rookie card or a first edition of Tolkien's *The Hobbit*. And though such objects can be immensely valuable, most collectors seek and own these things chiefly for the pride of possession. As we have seen, money is rarely involved in the child porn underworld, which is the preserve of the truly motivated collectors. Perhaps, too, there is a sense of one-upmanship, a satisfaction in owning and knowing things forbidden to other people.

The collector phenomenon has attracted some scholarly attention, and it is useful to compare porn enthusiasts with their legitimate counterparts. Studying the latter, Brenda Danet and Tamar Katriel argue that collectors are "striving for a sense of closure, completion and perfection." The authors "identified five strategies used by their subjects: completing a series, filling a space, creating a visually pleasing display, manipulating the scale of objects, and aspiring to perfect objects, as in restoring a vintage car to mint condition."[16] The mere fact of acquiring a collection is thus only a first stage in the process. Once the treasured objects have been obtained, the collector might spend many hours in cataloging, rearranging, and reorganizing them, as much for the purpose of displaying them in the most powerful way as for effective retrieval. In undertaking these meticulous chores, collectors are seeking a sense of dominance and control over the material. In the case of child pornography, there may also be a sense that the collector is gaining total possession, albeit symbolic, over the child subjects themselves.

The sense for completion or perfection is particularly marked in child porn collecting. Hobbyists seek unbroken series of the various photo shoots such as KG or Tiny Americans, and they pride themselves on their achievement in seeking out and amassing items. Collections posted on Web sites are avidly combed for fills, that is, missing items in a series, and until the practice became too dangerous, these images were often obtained through private trading. A characteristic exchange might run as follows:

> * **lum** > A question, if I might, for other collectors! Looking through my collection of MCLT ****.jpgs, I notice several large gaps in the numbering. Have the following series ever been put up? I am looking for 0800 series, 0900 series, 1020-1100, 1206-1285, 1400-1525, 1560-2420, 2540-3050, 3100-3395, 3600-4400, 6000 series, 8000 series. I would appreciate a little feedback. Thanks.
>
> * **Kid** > Most of the series have been posted before except for 2000, 4000, 5000 and 6000 series. These series are most difficult to find. I only see a few pix posted in newsgroups and I still looking for more of these series. I have never seen the 6000 series and I think no one has it.[17]

This correspondence again reminds us of the sheer extent of many of the series in circulation: a complete collection just of MCLT ("my collection of lolitas and teens") would include eight or nine thousand images, and that is only one series out of many. The idea of reciprocity emerges from another exchange:

> I posted the Merick Euro series, I have the Vera Merick series. I need the third series. Or any other Merick series. If you don't have that, I

need these. Kitty Island fills needed: 1, 7, 10, 14, 16, 18, 20, 21, 23, 26, 27, 28, 31, 36, 37, 38, 41, 47, 48, 61, a2. Anna Fills needed: The whole series. Please give me the fills, we can make this board really cool again. I post, you fill, you post, I fill.[18]

Some new fills are greeted ecstatically. One famous and much-reproduced shoot from a 1970s European magazine depicted a lesbian interaction between a pre-pubescent girl and an adult woman, allegedly her sister. Most presentations of this set involved perhaps a dozen items, but one poster presented a much fuller collection of photos, to the excitement and enthusiasm of numerous "fans," who could now fill in their collections. In addition to familiar older series, great value attaches to new items, especially any with out-of-the-ordinary content.

The fanatical nature of the collector instinct is suggested by the intense conversation on the boards during 1999 and 2000 concerning the KG and KX series, then the hottest items available. The videos, in particular, were

> some of the most highly sought after material ever produced. The only way you, or anybody else for that matter, would ever get those vids is by having connections with the producers or traders.[19]

The kindergarten images circulated widely, but with marginally different contents, so that a fan had to visit several sites to collect a full set of, say, Inga pictures. The process of collection led to intense discussion and speculation about what else might be available; Darkstar wrote:

> All kg and kx contributions very welcome, if you have any substantial new pics maybe some hc Inga or more girls doing vibrators etc you can post to *abpep-t* and ask nearly whatever you want posted in return, even prior to you posting yours up full, many regs have fills they need in the kg especially sets kg54 and above. All posts welcome. Surf Safe.[20]

The activity described here represents the new and safe form of trading: I post something publicly, and you reciprocate; the more I post, the more you post, and we both get what we want. At no point is there the kind of direct private interaction that might lead to an encounter with police provocateurs.

The volume of material available for trade is stunning:

> There is in excess of 100 sets of the kindergarten sets some with 30 pics in a set, others with over 100, these are mainly sc [soft core]. The kx series is the hc [hard-core] version and there is similar amounts. Also there is rumored to be a videotape too but this is unconfirmed. If you want any of these items you are going to need top class trades, probably original material, so you might see some of these items occasionally, all at once is unlikely.[21]

By some accounts, the total number of images in the whole KG/KX set runs into the thousands. Anyone wishing to collect the complete set had better supply "original material," which in this context almost certainly means actual records of interactions with young female family members or neighbors. The price might seem appalling in terms of the consequences for the children involved, as well as for the risk suffered by the culprit; but this is clearly thought a worthwhile risk, given the extremely high premium placed on these items.

Ultimately, the subculture is driven by the quest for new material, the urge to complete collections. To quote Pirra8 again:

> I'd like for all to try an experiment—go to ****, ****, etc.—sign up for a web site—and try posting 1 picture—on-topic. See how much fun it is. After the first four hours it takes you to get one 500K picture up—imagine the work getting dropped in half an hour. Then—imagine your life, reputation, and stability being in jeopardy when you post. Hmm—why do posters do it? Because we love torture? The answer is—we want you to return posts to get new stuff. Your goal is to become a poster. Otherwise, don't say anything. Just sit there and eat the scraps that come your way.[22]

Socialization

Though it seems difficult to understand how an average person might be socialized into such an aberrant underworld, the majority of users who discover a child porn board already have a predilection for this type of material and probably share many of the attitudes of the subculture (though some posts do suggest that individuals were "converted" after discovering the material). It is unlikely that people could just stumble across a pedo board by unfocused surfing, though they might encounter an individual photograph or two. One either receives information about a board from an existing contact or finds a site after long surfing through sites devoted to child-sex themes, located mainly in relatively tolerant countries like Japan. What changes is not that the Web explorer suddenly discovers child pornography but rather that he finds he is not alone in his deviant interests:

> * **Chris** > Does anyone know how many pedophiles there are in this world? Sometimes I feel like I'm the only one. . . . I don't think noone know me interest but I am just 24 and I feel very lonely in my age, do you think there are more in my age who is pedo?
> * **Oasis** > No, you are not alone. We all share your emotions. We are into kids, that's why we are here, you know. There are no stupid questions, just answers. But allow me to say, that you made me smile tonight. How many of us exist? Well most of us are lonesome surfers and collectors, because you can't trust noone but yourself. Better tell noone about your hobby or obsession, that could get you in trouble. Have a nice time on this board.[23]

Joining the subculture marks less an entry into new activities and interests than an escalation of pre-existing behaviors, supported by a new sense of community.

New participants in the Maestro board often announced their relief, and even awe, at having found this site: for "Milky Way," "this place has been a haven for me for the past 18 months."[24] Another contribution:

* I am a 3 weeks newbie lurking and trying to learn as per advice from a regular. . . . When I arrived to this board, sick in my heart to find only commerce in the rest of the Net, I thought: This is what the new world should be, sharing without expecting reward, free help to whoever needs it, and no judgment of other people's tastes and inclinations, race, colour, or political beliefs. This board is teaching how to become better.[25]

The sense of having found a congenial home is not limited to novices:

* **Owl** > By the way, why do these people who have been around so long still stay? From what they've all said they pay for the newsgroups and believe me (I started at the first of the year) they don't need to come here for new pics! There are thousands of fantastic pics they get from the NG's. They came and stayed for the discussions and social aspect of having others to talk to who have a very specific interest frowned on by the rest of society. Well with all the bitching that was going on, why would they want to stick around?[26]

In these exchanges, we often read of the board as a "home" or "haven," in other words, a place one can visit. The sense of the electronic world as a real place originates as a metaphor but acquires a remarkably concrete reality through linguistic usage: someone may *hang out* or *drop in* at a particular board, *enter a room, bump into* a friend there, *cross paths* with someone, and so on. To illustrate this, one board participant was wondering about the absence of Goddess, a regular from the Maestro board: "Any news from her??? Did somebody piss her off here?" DukeofEarl replied, "I saw Goddess and Greasy over at the ****board the other night, and yes, she is as pissed as hell. People around here calling everyone LEA."[27] Clearly, DukeofEarl had not "seen" Goddess, nor had he been physically at the location mentioned; rather, his computer allowed him to enter a particular electronic network. The phrase "around here" is equally metaphorical in suggesting that the writer is in a real, material room. Nevertheless, he expressed the common fiction that the boards represent distinct places where social interaction can occur in much the same way as at a bar or a party. This helps support the notion that the boards are safe space that one can visit at will, where like-minded friends can reliably be found.

Once one discovers the pedo boards and groups that are central to the Net subculture, it is all too easy to be drawn in, to become socialized. One factor is the sheer volume of information on these sites, which can initially scare off novices but ultimately promotes socialization. As with the Usenet, the first reaction to a board can be one of shock and discouragement, if not at the child porn subject matter then at the overwhelming level of the technical discussion, the shrill and abusive tone of many messages, and the ostentatious scorn poured on anyone who dares to ask a naive question. The content is also dense: at any given point, the Web page of the main Maestro board contained some five hundred lines of text, five thousand words or so, and perhaps twice that, and this content would change rapidly during the day. Nor is it possible to search the page for specific topics, for example, to see if any new sites have been posted simply by searching for the letters "http": as remarked earlier, posters will present sites in a form such as "h++p" in order to avoid search engines. To find the URLs which are his main goal, a user must read, or at least skim, rather than dip at random. For anyone who chooses to persevere in consulting the boards, though, it also soon becomes clear that these are nothing like the hyped sex sites that promise far more than they produce. For those interested in this kind of sexuality, this is the Real Thing.

Reading the messages in pursuit of sites or software, one is likely to acquire gradually the peculiar language, mores, and thought patterns of this world and thus be inducted subtly into the subculture. One learns the meaning of terms such as *LEA* and *bubba*, scorns those who fail to surf safe, realizes the prestige attached to the wise ones, groans at the obstreperous behavior of trolls. How could anyone not know what *abpept* stands for, or fail to understand the running joke about participants as faculty or alumni of Pedo University, good old "PU"? Recently, psychologists have argued (controversially) for the existence of a kind of Internet addiction, in which users spend ever more time on the screen and sever ties with the non-electronic world.[28] In the case of electronic porn, this tendency may be reinforced by a kind of desensitization, a hunger for ever more illegal material. While a novice might be amazed and stimulated by the first few soft-core pornographic images, these are all too likely to become routine, and one turns avidly to the harder-core sites. As board participants themselves acknowledge, involvement thus becomes a cumulative process:

> * **Lookangle** > With this hobby we get bored after a while with the usual and we risk a bit to get new stuff or get actual experience. It's a natural progression. Like stealing. You start small. Get bored. Go for bigger stuff. Get caught. The lesson for all of us is: Constant restraint and vigilance.[29]

> *__Rakjing__—hello, loli-lovers! about 6 weeks before I came to this board first time and I love it. Surely you know it by yourself, that you want every day more and more and more.[30]

One difficulty is that the activity of collecting has no natural conclusion. There is no obvious stage at which an aficionado might declare that his collection is now complete, so that he can now move on to some other pastime. Even when the collection reaches ten thousand images, and he has assembled all the KX series, say, there will always be more.

The process of involvement is accelerated by the speed and intensity of the activity on some boards. The highly transient nature of the content means that anyone looking at a board at different points of any given day will effectively see a quite different phenomenon. At 8 A.M., for instance, a poster might be drawing attention to a new site, which will be gone by noon, by which time yet another site may be posted, and members will be commenting on the passing of the earlier page. This does not necessarily mean that activity is always so intense, and days can pass without the posting of significant new sites; but the level of chat and information exchange proceeds apace. The rapidity of change means that participants had to visit the Maestro site on a very regular basis if they hoped to benefit from it. Visiting a site like this just once a day, or even every few days, is to invite a sense of exclusion, to see the bygone records of what has been but is there no longer. A strong premium is thus placed on frequent visiting and careful study. The more often one visits and reads, the more one becomes involved, and perhaps sees oneself as part of the broader community of participants.

Danger

Also promoting a kind of group identification is the pervasive sense of danger. Participants acquire a sense of sharing in a dangerous, clandestine world where one possesses information utterly unknown to most of the world. Few international spies operate with so many pursuing enemies worldwide, and if caught, these individuals usually face far less severe penalties than the pornographers. As Darkstar warns:

> Downloading pics onto your pc constitutes possession of cp in most jurisdictions. Found and you will be fried and sizzled in the local press and dead meat for the rest of your life . . . wow, it's just like those witchcraft days now! . . . Review your security else you will be washing floors and keeping bubba warm at nights. . . . Surf Safe.[31]

The constant emphasis on safety and self-defense is evident from the abundance of technical information, which constitutes a majority of postings on the boards. Users learn how and where to download encryption or anti-virus software, how to obtain proxies and passwords. Novices are warned about the crucial necessity of using proxies and taking other precautions to avoid tracking. Posters may suggest sites where one can go to check a proxy; if the site shows one's real IP, the proxy has failed and must be replaced forthwith. This is an issue of prime concern when visiting illegal sites: without such safeguards, "you might as well as leave a calling card and put your computer in the front yard so everyone can view."[32] Novices are also told to refuse the "cookies" that are the most common means of building up a record of which sites are visited by a given computer. Another concern frequently expressed involves clearing tracks, since computers preserve records of the sites they have visited.

Participants will instruct novices in the essential importance of cleaning the computer's cache regularly to erase images, which might otherwise constitute legal evidence of possession of child pornography. In addition, there are lessons in seeking and destroying any vestiges that might lurk in unsuspected corners of a machine:

> * **Scooby** > I believe that the most secure way to beat the LEA is to have nothing on your hard drive. Delete cookies, BC-wipe all files once downloaded and stored to another medium such as a floppy, clear history and cache etc. If you have nothing on your comp, the LEA won't have any thing that will hold up in court.[33]

More recently, the danger of hacker attacks from anti-pedophile groups has caused an upsurge of interest in maintaining "firewalls" around the computer, to resist unwanted intrusions while on the Net. The depth of paranoia evident in such discussions is so intense as to lend itself to humor: following one singularly abstruse exchange, "Mr. Bungle" offered this hint:

> My suggestion is every week or so, take your hard drive out of the comp. Set it on a giant electromagnet for an hour or so. Then take it into your back yard and place it into the center of a 4 square meter bonfire. Only real way to be 'SAFE.'[34]

The level of paranoia on the boards is intense. Sooner or later, some contributor will accuse every regular and even every great one of being a covert agent of law enforcement and raise doubts about some particular site as a potential "trap site," where visits are monitored by police. Or perhaps the whole Maestro network was itself a massive ploy by Interpol or the National Security Agency? Charges of being a police agent or provocateur greet any invitation to trade, to exchange e-mails, or to meet in person. Invitations to participate in confidential academic research projects are met with particular derision, reasonably so given that no promise of anonymity in such circumstances could be upheld in the face of police demands for the identity of child pornographers. When one student announced his wish to undertake "a project for my school about Internet-criminals," a few of the numerous responses ran as follows:

> * **David** > thanx Mr. officer, but we do know, your squad is monitoring this board.
> * **Officer Bob Speed** > Is that you, Thumper??? Christ, we'd all thought we'd seen the last of you and that worthless partner of yours when you went crosstown to work porno . . . told you to stay in traffic if you wanted to get promoted, but oh no, you knew best.
> * **fearless** > do you have underage girls in your school? please post some pics of them as a present ;))[35]

Suspicions reach Himalayan heights when anything changes significantly, for instance, when a board changes its address or suspends operations even for a few days. After one such technical reshuffle on the Maestro boards in 2000, conspiracy theories ran rampant: "The Detective" wrote:

> Imagine the following situation (speculative!): Police have caught *** and ***. In order to prosecute loli fans all over the world they set up a new board (because they were not able to crack the old one), and now they redirect all of us to the new board . . . I had this idea because I can NOT imagine any reasons why the old board should be given up.[36]

"Bummer" agreed:

> If anyone tells you not to be paranoid, especially during these strange last few days, get away from them. Paranoia is what makes animals survive in the jungle, paranoia is what makes you lock your door at night, paranoia is why we use proxies and firewalls. It keeps us safe. As for the recent allegations about a former *** admin being a LEA, double-agent, or religious zealot, I have seen no solid evidence. But anyone who was at *** in the last couple of months must have noticed that 90% of the regulars all suddenly vanished at once. What happened? They all at once all decided to start a new hobby like stamp collecting?

;) Obviously, *** was not 100% what it claimed to be (or once was). I think the recent break-up was probably the safest thing.[37]

The level of hysteria around this time reached heights sufficient to provoke several of the greatest names in the subculture to announce their resignations from the board, including such legends as Godfather Corleone and Pirra8.

The volume of mutual accusations and suspicions is so persistent that it inevitably invites parody, and posters adopt names like "LEA Mole." In response to one query about what participants were doing at that particular moment, "Joel the Troll" wrote, "I'm eating a donut, the watch officer bought a dozen, surfing with my laptop on my desk, in the corner, near a window, in the Vice unit. I'm stroking my member, it's getting hard, as I think of the dumbass pedo I'm gonna bust in a couple hours."[38] In another exchange, "Puzzled" asked a question that often appears on the boards:

> * Is it true that FBI has this site?
> * **jayjay** > I dare say they visit very often—but remember this site is not illegal—but if there is any easy pickings they will be easily picked
> * **FBI** > yes we do. but don't tell anyone, is top secret!!
> * **INTERPOL** > We are here, too. But you don't worry, go on.
> * **anonymous** > I don't know about the FBI, but I'm sure LEA does keep tabs on this board. They are here, waiting and watching all that goes on. And I'm sure some of the regs here are really them posting and trying to fit in with all of us! So always be careful with any info, links or anything else you find at this board! You just can't trust anybody here, no matter what they may say![39]

A sense of constant danger and likely surveillance entirely prevents the formation of the kind of personal solidarity that occurs so naturally in other subcultures, but it unquestionably encourages a mood of drama and even excitement. The child porn world resembles other deviant subcultures in the sense of steadily generating solidarity against the hostile outside world. People know that they and their fellow deviants are carrying on an activity utterly condemned by mainstream society, and curiously, perhaps, they seem to accept in their own minds that their behaviors are utterly wrong. The inner contradictions that we so often encounter in Internet conversations form the major theme of the next chapter. For present purposes, though, we may be surprised how much the sense of danger and persecution strengthens the subculture, by providing a sense of common purpose and identity. The more pedophiles and pornographers are attacked by law enforcement agencies, mass media, and anti-pedos, the greater the sense of community against common enemies. It is difficult otherwise to see why participants should remain in so genuinely threatening an environment, which seems nevertheless to attract many new surfers each day.

FIVE

Moralities

It's fashionable on this board to proselytize about how good it would be for children to have sexual contact with a ped. and have the pictures posted for our pleasure . . . stand on that soapbox and soon you'll be standing in the dock . . . just enjoy your sin . . . keep quiet . . . and pray to God you don't hear the knock.
—Farfhad, Maestro board, September 25, 1999

Subcultures are often characterized by distinctive systems of values that, to a greater or lesser extent, set them apart from mainstream society. Deviant groups like criminal gangs and sexual subcultures appear to operate on value systems utterly alien to those of "normal" people, and this is certainly true of the pedo boards. Even in the most innocent postings regarding technical, computer-related issues, participants are seeking only to improve their access to images that the vast majority of people, in virtually all societies, would regard as unpardonably vile.

At first sight, there seems to be a contradiction here. Earlier, I argued that much of what the boards did was basically an extension or extrapolation of "normal" values, particularly within the electronic world, and yet a glimpse at the conversations on the boards suggests that participants are evil incarnate, utterly rejecting all social norms about children and sexuality. But this appearance of a radically deviant value system would be misleading, since the boards are also the setting for intense and passionate debate about the morality of the traffic and for abundant self-questioning. Some participants state quite openly that they believe what they are doing is wrong; some recognize that they are fulfilling a deviant role, others do not; some proclaim that they are interested only in "innocent" fantasies, while others admit to actual molestation. We thus find an extraordinarily broad spectrum of attitudes and opinions, and even in this bizarre setting, much of the discourse expresses relatively normal, mainstream morality and concern. I have no illusions that the available materials represent any kind of statistically valid survey of the subculture, but this really is all we have to work from.

In understanding these exchanges, it is useful to recall the long sociological debate over deviant subcultures, and particularly the concept of neutralization. In the mid–twentieth century, academic studies emphasized the belief systems of deviant groups such as criminal gangs, which were seen as diametrically opposite to those of the mainstream.[1] Studies of delinquent gangs discussed how these subcultures might have formulated such thoroughly aberrant beliefs and suggested how these mores could have been formed. Perhaps they grew out of the knowledge that a person could not succeed in the approved regular world, and so delinquents gravitated to groups where they could acquire status by following the warped standards of that little anti-society. The problem was that, on closer examination, delinquents did not in fact demonstrate values and beliefs too different from those of the mainstream. On most social and political issues, gangsters and organized criminals tend to be extremely conservative, while their attitudes toward gender and family are exactly appropriate for their particular class and ethnic background. In their personal goals, too, deviants are often quite conventional. Organized criminals want just the same possessions and status symbols that their honest conventional neighbors might dream about, but they use different means to get where they want to go.

Struck by the conventionality of many deviants, criminologists noticed how their subjects rationalized or justified actions that, in essence, they knew to be wrong. The common term used for this practice is *neutralization*, a term associated with the scholars David Matza and Gresham Sykes. Neutralization takes many forms. A prostitute may speak of an encounter as a *date*, a term that minimizes the deviant or criminal aspect of the transaction. In its original usage, a *john* was a generic term for a man, specifically a boyfriend, rather than, as later, a paying client. A criminal act such as a robbery can be justified by a number of excuses or denial techniques, such as the denial of responsibility ("It's not my fault"); the denial of injury ("They can afford it"); denial of the victim ("They had it coming"); condemnation of the condemners ("The police are bigger crooks than I am"); and the appeal to higher loyalties ("The gang is my life"). Use of these techniques suggests that the deviants in question internally accepted the standards of the wider society and needed to justify their deeds in a way that made them acceptable, at least to the individual voicing these excuses.

As we will see, some of the participants on the pedo boards seem to speak in exactly the language described by theorists of neutralization. Classic neutralization techniques emerge most obviously in the debates initiated by those individuals who overtly raise doubts about the morality of what they are doing. In response to these caveats, other contributors justify their behavior in terms that seem, to outsiders, to represent forms of self-deception. One such rhetorical tactic is a denial of the victim, or rather a denial of victimization: children are commonly assumed to have consented to the actions or directly to have sought sex, so the experience is consensual. Even if the child is three or five, she was still asking for it. Linked to this is the denial of injury, since the sexual activity is seen as rewarding and even educational for the child, rather than selfish or exploitative. There is also abundant evidence of the "condemnation of the condemners," as enemies of child porn are repeatedly attacked as hypocrites and cynical.

The massive deployment of every available neutralization technique may indicate yet again the relative normality of the board participants and their attitudes: we need not imagine the boards as a gathering place for monsters. This interpretation has significant policy consequences. "Monsters" or fanatics may be willing to ignore all risks to achieve their goals, reminiscent of the worst stereotypes of desperate heroin addicts, but normal people have a much greater capacity to assess risk and thus to be deterred. The great majority of people who bought child porn in the

1970s were happy to look at it when it was easily available but simply gave up seeking it in the following decade, when law enforcement pressures became too heavy.[2] If users share fairly normal, mainstream attitudes and fears, then this at least raises the hope that effective enforcement might discourage a significant share of them from joining or remaining in the child porn subculture.

All Men Are Pedos

Though subculture members accept and often use the description "pedo" for pedophile, this does not imply any or all of the negative associations customarily applied by mainstream society. At most, the word is used in its etymological sense, a "lover of youth," parallel to the jokey-sounding "loli-lover." Though many admit to being pedophiles, many fans of child pornography claim to be no more than that, fans, for whom the material is only an element of a distinctive lifestyle. The diversity of attitudes emerged in response to the question "At what age did you figure out that you were an loli lover? And how did you realize the truth?"[3] Several rejected the idea of a pathological condition:

> * **JanesAddiction** > I'm not a "Loli Lover" . . . I have a 19 year old girlfriend and I'd prefer taking her (or any knowledgeable adult) to bed any day over a Loli (tho a 60 y/o mite consider a 19 y/o a loli!). I like them all . . . short or tall. My fascination isn't for the short-eyes, it's more the temptation of the forbidden: 'Waddaya mean I can't look at something?! Let me see!!'. It's the rebellious side that drives me to the hunt for pics and movies . . . I just don't like being told 'You can't.' I have seen some *very* pretty girls in my searches, but it's a fantasy! As long as it's not confused with reality (or attempted to be made reality), then it's okay. I don't look-down on true loli lovers tho . . . my place is not to judge. As long as there's no *overt* harm/force involved, hey, different strokes for different folks.

In a different thread, "Humbert Humbert" wrote, "Am not a pedo, just like the beauty of pre-pubescent/adolescent girls. Therefore, I don't think I am a perv. Just rational minded." (Humbert, of course, takes his nickname from the pedophilic hero of Vladimir Nabokov's *Lolita*.)[4] The idea that a taste for child pornography is neither abnormal nor pathological naturally makes it easier to be drawn into the subculture.

Some participants reject pedophile status altogether, while many more challenge the image of child-lovers as a pathological category. One common argument is that "everybody does it," that sexual attraction to children is far more widespread than mainstream society dares accept, and that persecuting child pornography is an extreme form of hypocrisy. This seems a predictable form of neutralization, but writers seek to justify it with various types of evidence. The recurrent question "How many pedos are there in the world?" inspired many replies:

* **Absolutely Correct** > Somehow, some way, society will soon realize that there are too many of 'us' for them to keep trying to suppress. Doctors, Lawyers, Politicians, Scientists . . . *We are everywhere*. I could be your best friend, your teacher, the police chief . . . anybody . . . you just don't know. And now it's time for women to accept this reality.[5]

* **baldpubes** > I disagree that we are one of the worlds largest minorities. I say we are the largest majorities. I say there only two kinds of people in this world, the ones who tell the truth and admit they are pedos, and the ones who lie about it, at the same time they are stealing glances up their ten year old neighbor girl's dress.[6]

* **Stiffbizkit** > All men are pedos, only we admit it. How many men are there in the world? You have your answer.[7]

* **dad** > Actually I don't differentiate between "pedos" and "non pedos" . . . I think that all men are sexually attracted to children, some men dismiss this attraction and think no more of it. Some of us don't dismiss this attraction and dwell more on it. I for one don't think of myself as a pedo, I think of myself as a man that is attracted to women of all ages, from 7 to 77, I am not broken or wrong, I am attracted to child and I can't help that.[8]

* __we > And just think about the pedos that have never seen this place, And all that have no access to the net, and all that don't even have computers, there's *fucking millions* of us.[9]

* Love2See > Dad, you are right, I think 90% of the males are attracted to little girls, but a part don't admit that for themselves. The society educate them to believe this it's wrong . . . but if you go deep in culture and history you will find these things are very normal. In the past cp did not exist . . . to be attracted to lolita it was very normal . . . Romeo and Juliet have only 13 yrs, long time ago girls start to have sexual relationship from 12 yr etc.[10]

The idea that historical study justifies "child love" is often heard:

* J.L.Byrd > We're not so much the fringe group you may think. Our interest has always been apparent in civilization. Witness the literature, the popularity of on-topic brothels in Europe and Asia, and the *volumes* of old material from 100 years ago to the 70s. Throughout US history, our kind has been free to pursue our interest, until very recently.[11]

Some contributors attempt to substantiate their claims from official and social scientific sources:

*A pedophile > According to the USDH [U.S. Department of Health], and the American Psychiatric Association there are approximately 100,000–400,000 active pedophiles (as opposed to molesters) in the United States. So about 0.3% of the US population fits that category.[12]

* Comiskey > In the Kinsey book *Human Sexual Response*, from about 1955, there was a mother's description of watching her 4-year-old rubbing herself off against a pillow.[13]

Hedonism and Ideology

Many contributors to the boards have a quite sophisticated attitude to the traffic of which they form part—inevitably, given the educated

nature of most participants. People with this degree of computer expertise often hold some kind of professional or technical position and
are sufficiently educated to apply some degree of self-analysis and
conscious rationalization. Though some contributors appear to be
barely literate, at the other extreme we find learned messages such as
this reading list, posted by "Sikk" to help novices understand the
subculture:

> You might also try *Lo's Diary* by Pia Pera, *Collusion* by Evan Zimroth,
> *Pussycat Fever* by Kathy Acker, *120 Days of Sodom* by Marquis de Sade,
> *The Blue Lagoon* by Henry D. Stacpoole, *Pretty Baby* by William Har-
> rison, *Nude Men* by Amanda Filipachi, *Dream Children* by A. N. Wil-
> son, *The Photographer's Sweethearts* by Diana Hartog, *First Love* by
> Joyce Carol Oates, *Marble Skin* by Slavenka Drakulic and *Firefly* by
> Piers Anthony.[14]

I doubt that many academics in university English departments could
produce such an erudite list. Subtle hints of cultivation are also found in
many passing phrases in postings, as well as in chosen nicknames such as
"Origo-Mali," Latin for "source of evil."

The boards regularly feature lengthy discussions about the ethics of
the traffic, in which participants generally assert a libertarian value system. It is open to debate whether the ideologies are sincerely held or
whether they should more properly be viewed as forms of neutralization.
A question such as "This board is for . . ." evokes a particularly large response, with comments like these:

> **J.L.Byrd >** Persons with natural but politically incorrect tastes in erot-
> ica come to share, in secret, beautiful, natural and stimulating but for-
> bidden material, the likes of which has been enjoyed and celebrated by
> healthy adults from the beginnings of time . . . until the current one-
> worlder liberal takeover of western culture.

> *** a quiet fan >** this board is for people who like and appreciate the
> human body. We also like thrills we get at looking at little boys and
> girls in their birthday suits. We have a freedom of choice and speech

on this board which is rare in this day and age. We also don't impose
or force our views on others on this board.[15]

Sometimes, the value system described is explicitly and aggressively
counter-cultural, a kind of Sadeian hedonism, asserting that sexual pleasure is something that the strong can take at will. More commonly, views
expressed are an extrapolation of views that have a wider currency, or
which at least gained popularity during the 1970s: again, they are not too
far removed from the normal spectrum of beliefs. Some advocates of an
alternative ethic contend that sexuality is good and beneficial, and a re-
pressed and repressive society denies this to its children. By promoting
the idea that children are sexually active creatures, the subculture sees itself as promoting and extending sexual liberation, much as teenagers and
young adults were liberated during the 1950s and 1960s.

The politicization of the subculture should not be exaggerated,
since the long discussions are often interrupted by protests from those
simply demanding more URLs, more dirty pictures, and rejecting the
philosophizing as irrelevant to the real nature of the board. Yet ethical
and political themes do surface very frequently and usually remain
within a broadly libertarian context. Feminism is particularly casti-
gated for its role in demanding anti-pornography laws and creating a
climate of puritanism:

> * **J.L.Byrd** > We like this erotic material . . . so do outsiders, who
> react violently because they're terrified to admit they might be 'de-
> viant' as described by the emasculating females who seem to run
> things today. What's needed is a top-to-bottom change, starting
> with Bubba [Clinton] and his government-as-father-figure that
> "empowers" the New Woman, right down to the libber in a short
> skirt who turns on you and snarls: 'What're YOU looking at?!'
> When western culture is overhauled, there will not be the need for
> secret places such as this.
> * **LoliLuvr** > UK is in the grip of a coordinated pedo witchhunt being
> organized by women's groups . . . when will guys learn to organize
> yourself and fight back instead of whining, enforce your right to look

and touch the womens groups are enforcing the opposite, do something don't just whine, if you want loli get organized.[16]

Occasionally, board contributors speculate about the possibility of forming a movement to gain respectability, on the analogy of other once-despised sexual minorities such as homosexuals, though most commentators realize that such a scheme is hopelessly unrealistic. Nevertheless, a strong consensus holds that pedophiles possess moral superiority, in the sense of being able to exercise complete sexual freedom. Participants scoff at suggestions that the condition causes harm either to the individual or to the children in whom he is interested:

* **guilt-less** > hi, guys. listen, I've been thinking. My life of being a pedo has led me to drinking, drugz, murder, bribery and jay-walking. Last week my wife left me and my dog bit me. Somebody blew up my car at work and I am ready to throw myself in a vat of lard and drown myself. So I will be going away for a while. Farewell all you other evil doers . . . praise God and learn the wickedness of your ways.
* **billy do-right** > yes, guilt-less. I agree. Many a year have I suffered through this dead-end road of worthlessness. I dump innocent little girls' bodies in ditches regularly, and feel it is time for a change. I thank you for your inspiration.
* **Lugnut** > Man, I know what you mean. Things are so bad around here that my little kitty hanged himself. He left a note with his little paw print on it—but mate, you must be low to jaywalk.[17]

Sometimes, political ideologies expressed go much further than mere libertarianism to a kind of right-wing anarchism, which rejects both police authoritarianism and the various manifestations of political correctness:

* **G-MAN** > Innocent people are falling victim to the uncivilized methods of U.S. authorities. Every time I think that there may be hope for freedom and democracy in the U.S. they go and prove they don't give a . . . Anyway: stay away from this oppressive country as much as possible!!!

* **Nikostealth** > You folks from other countries may not know this, and far too many here don't realize it either, but these "officials" are running an (under our constitution) illegal gov., with illegal laws. Our constitution gives us the right, at anytime, to overthrow our government, by force if necessary. We have an election coming up soon, and are hoping to see better days through it. . . . However, we are *far* closer to a civil war in this country than many think. If things don't begin to change, I believe we will see a surge of support for the many militias already in place, and the formation of many more. Our leaders are under the arrogant (and delusional) belief that they could handle a uprising of citizens determined to restore freedom. . . . They can not. And they will not.

* **Phleb** > One must always remember, there are three million (very quiet) NRA members. Should the fit ever hit the shan, they will be on the side of the Constitution, not the pro-tem government.

* **J.L.Byrd** > I believe Nikostealth is right—we are on the brink of a major revolt against the politically-correct social engineering leadership. . . . The reason it hasn't happened yet is that our freedoms are being taken while the populace is being distracted by bread and circuses. When this loss of freedom sinks in and hits close to home, there will be either a civil uprising or a partitioning of North America . . . that's assuming we manage to keep our firearms.[18]

Befitting the ethical and political sentiments so commonly affected, board contributors are keen to differentiate themselves from mere criminals: even in a universe devoted to child pornography, some activities are beyond the pale. This curious distinction was illustrated when "Spider Man" boasted that his job gave him access to many people's credit card numbers, and he sought advice about how this purloined information could be used to gain access to pay Web sites.[19] The response was frosty in the extreme:

* **Origo-Mali** > As much as I could help, I will not be akin to criminal activity such as this. It may be considered wrong to look at young girls, but most here do not feel that way, but robbing money from someone else is considered wrong by everyone.

* **fun** > Sorry Spider Man, We are someone who are fun-loving without causing harm. Money theft is crime. Hope every one on this board are of similar line as Origo.

Children's Rights

Another conventional idea regularly espoused on the boards is that of children's rights. However odd this may sound to outsiders, many of the "hobbyists" writing on the boards sincerely view themselves as part of a children's rights movement. Meanwhile, outsiders who oppose child porn are attacked as hypocrites who cynically exploit this issue to distract attention from real dangers to children, such as poverty, family breakdown, violence, and abusive families:

* **Gingerbread Man** > The government does not have the right to censor what I look at or how I think or feel. That's what Hitler did, and everyone believes he was wrong. The overwhelming amount of violence on TV is hurting our youth tremendously, but there is no censorship in sight for that. Kids are beautiful and must be protected. . . . From the *right* people. Not from those who love them most (us).[20]

* **adolph** > This forum is *all* about children!! . . . from a grown-up's point of view. How to love and nurture their hearts and minds as well as their bodies, . . . and a celebration of their beauty and innocence, . . . and a classroom to share and learn how to properly appreciate, and learn what truly helps them grow, . . . and what impedes that growth, . . . (and ours!!) without physically subjecting them to our own urges, fantasies, or personal histories . . . be they benign or traumatic . . . it's my true hope and belief, that this board reduces the crimes and abuses of the precious children in our world!!![21]

* I just hope society gets the message where the real abuse problem lies and it isn't guys or girls looking at pics on the net! And the parents up in arms should look closely around them in their families that's where the real abuser lurks. There is a difference for those unenlightened

ones amongst you who come on here between looking at girls pictures and actually committing abuse. I myself could never do that. I'm not saying what I do is right but it's harmless compared to the adult, often a relative, who actually abuses.[22]

> * **Dr. Who** > This little hobby is all that's kept me sane through the years. As most of us do, I love children. The thought of hurting one is abhorrent to me![23]

Board participants often assert that their goals go beyond mere hedonism and affect an overarching love and veneration for children. The reader never knows exactly how to take such affirmations, but some of the exchanges are suggestive. In one incident, an anti-porn group posted a picture of a child with a caption identifying her as a victim of Marc Dutroux, the notorious Belgian serial killer who abducted children in order to exploit them for the purposes of pornography and pedophile rings. This posting ignited a lively correspondence on the boards. Several postings expressed extreme rage on hearing of Dutroux's crime, suggesting that they would like ten minutes alone with this monster to express their moral outrage in person. "OMG [Oh my God] . . . That's fucking horrible!!! Who is this sick, filthy piece of shit??? Is he dead? He fucking well should be."[24] This is a strikingly "normal" response, the sort of outburst commonly heard in any working-class bar when the television news reports some brutal crime against the innocent. "Loli-lovers" thus make every effort to distinguish themselves from those who harm or exploit children:

> * **baldpubes** > Heard the latest on the Jon-Benet murder? Her parents are now saying it was a pedophile who killed her and to that I say, bullshit. No true pedophile could do that. The person that did that to Jon-Benet was nothing but a sick ass slimeball lower than any animal and I myself would have no trouble at all pushing the button or pulling the lever and sending that animal straight to hell.
> * **Megatron** > baldpubes, you are totally correct saying that no true lolilover would ever harm a child.[25]

In the Dutroux correspondence, others professed bafflement that such individuals could exist: how could anyone harm a child, much less kill her? I quote one response: "I feel sick . . . if it is truth . . . my god . . . poor child." Also suggestive here is the correspondence that developed in November 1999, when news broke of a South American serial child killer nicknamed "El Loco." A participant named "notme-officer" began the string by writing: "With the love of children in mind may I ask this board for a moment or two to give thought and prayer for the 140 child victims of El Loco. Not forgetting their parents. God Rest." Some replies:

* **Fatty** > I agree with you also.
* **LTN** > Agreed, notme. I also have a child and could not imagine what the world would like be without him.[26]

Given the privacy of the setting, it is hard to believe that these emotions are intended to deceive or to promote a good public image for the pedophile subculture. I tend to take these affirmations at face value rather than as neutralization.

View Evil, Do No Evil

Adrian Thompson, the British child porn enthusiast convicted in 2000, adopted as a motto the acronym VEDNE, which stands for "View Evil, Do No Evil," and that phrase neatly encapsulates the attitudes of many board participants, or at least their public personas.[27] Throughout the correspondence on the boards, numerous contributors emphasize the innocence of their interest, their hobby. They are "just looking"; they would not enact their fantasies in a real-world context; and they express vigorous hostility toward anyone who genuinely has sex with a child—though Thompson's motto concedes that the material he was collecting was "evil."

The actual relationship between child porn and child abuse is open to debate, no matter how firmly such a linkage has come to be viewed as a social orthodoxy. The difficulty is that solid data on the question are all but unobtainable, and official figures are highly suspect. To illustrate the problems with available evidence, let us assume that 90 percent of child porn consumers never become involved in abuse or molestation and confine their illegal activities to merely viewing and collecting images. I have no idea what the actual figure is, but as I will suggest, nor does anybody else. These individuals are extremely unlikely to find their way into the criminal justice system unless they attempt to trade images, and barring accidental finds on their hard drives. Conversely, the minority of users who are also molesters are far more likely to be arrested and prosecuted. They might try to seduce youngsters online or abduct or molest the children of friends or neighbors. For whatever reason, the police will probably apprehend them and will discover child porn collections upon searching their belongings. In consequence, the 10 percent of CP consumers who are also abusers will make up a sizable (and wholly disproportionate) majority of child porn arrests. This allows anti-porn activists to state, quite accurately, that "in the vast majority of child porn arrests, the individual involved is also found to be a molester": listeners are encouraged to draw the (unwarranted) conclusion that child pornographers are necessarily abusers, and perhaps vice versa. In fact, the statistics establish no causal link between child porn materials and actual behavior, any more than the similar observation that most sex criminals also enjoy adult porn. The statement "Most rapists watch porn videos" cannot be translated as "Most people who watch porn videos become rapists." Conceivably, perhaps 90 or 95 percent of child porn fans commit abuse, or perhaps the figure is closer to 5 or 10 percent; the reality is just unknowable.

Whatever the objective truth, participants on the child porn boards naturally favor the view that abusers are a small, unrepresentative minority within the community, and that most "loli fans" are just looking, not acting—viewing evil but not doing it. Comments of this type are plentiful on the boards:

* **Norman** > There is nothing better than seeing young girls enjoying themselves, whether non-nude, s/c or h/c, as long as they are happy.[28]

* **Dr. Who** > Pedo-sexuality *is* a genetic "flaw", it can be controlled but not eliminated. I have controlled it all my life and it ain't easy, but it can be done. However that doesn't stop the brain. Luckily my fantasizing while sitting on a park bench, hurts no one![29]

* **lomalee** > As long as you keep it in your head, no one will be hurt but you. . . . Keep it in your head (and your pants).[30]

* **newbee** > You may say I'm crazy, but have you ever think of these girls (the one whose pics and clips we look for) like saviours? Thanks for these girls, we can let our libidos play with the kleenex or with our imagination while we're with our women, instead of go to the streets or to a girl we know and maybe hurt her or force her to do something that can be dangerous for us. C'mon, guys: we know we don't have many chances: or we live a chaste life just looking and chatting with those girls or we look for pics and clips. Of course, there's the other way—going to action—but it's an exception.[31]

Posters explicitly challenge the link between a taste for pornography and actual molestation; indeed, the *abpep-t* FAQ asserts:

Pedophiles are not molesters!!! The vast majority of posters in *abpep-t* abhor the notion of child abuse and molestation. Some won't even condone consensual sex between children and adults. Do not post requests for help like 'how can I get into a young girl's panties' or 'where should I go to find kids to fuck.' If you do, you will be flamed out of existence.

These views are often echoed on the boards:

* **Froid+** > Think about this . . . Looking at a bottle of whiskey doesn't make you an alcoholic . . . does looking at this make you a child molester . . . (you figure it out)!
* **Smile** > does that mean if I read *Mayfair* I'm going to rape a woman? Or if I buy car magazines I'm going to steal a car?[32]

Participants who discuss real-life sex with children are denounced forthrightly:

> *** Searcher**—How can I get a little girl to suck my cock (and tell nothing to anyone)?[33]

> *** DR.LURK >** It's slime like you that give the true good people of the pedo reality a bad name. You are not a true loli lover but a violent sexual deviant who should not have the privilege of being with the good people of this board, or even on this earth around the beautiful loli. You and yours are a major reason we are hated by the general society. Now do us all a favor and *Go stand in front of a speeding train.*
> *** notmeofficer >** I'm not one to give lecture, but if you need 'relief' go find some pics that way no one gets hurt, well, only you if you're caught . . . I wonder how many little girls have been 'saved' by the posters on this board . . . in other words 'stick it in your floppy drive not in little ones' . . . we dream, we fantasize, we sometimes wish . . . but I think most here love little ones, so keep your thoughts in your head . . . they can't harm no one there.[34]
> *** Teddybear >** Personally I would never do anything to harm a child in any way. That includes paying for any material and in that way support any people making money out of hurting children.[35]

Exponents of the "look, don't touch" school scorn molesters who believe they cause no harm to their victims, and many of these critical comments could easily have come from a mainstream attack on child abusers:

> *** BlindCrippledCrazy >** and then there was the little girl who really didn't enjoy the 'fun times with daddy', but being a typical child and wanting badly to make her daddy happy and love her (because he seemed to get mad when she didn't want to play... maybe he didn't love her anymore?) She spent many days and nights trying to avoid playtime, but daddy would always find her. When mommy left to go to work she would try to go out and play. He would always call her in. All she really liked was the snuggling close part afterwards . . . she wished they could just do that. But, daddy always took what daddy wanted and rationalized it in the end. No cops. No telling.

They all grew up with the secret quiet. But that father missed out on the *true* love of a child and the child forever harbored resentment towards her dad . . . who's the real loser? (Dad of course) GET REAL! they're children.[36]

The irony in all this, of course, is that what the "lookers" are seeking is pictures of children actually being abused, a point not lost on some critics:

> * **Nikostealth** > I know this is an unpopular thought with some . . . But we're going to *have* to move away from the "Look don't touch" concept (Ducking the beer bottles thrown at me). For the simple fact that one of the oldest and most effective anti-pedo arguments is that for us to look, *someone* not only touched but took pix of it. . . . There's too much H/C [hard core] out there for us to deny it, so we need to find newer and better arguments. I, personally, take the stand that sex is sex and rape is rape at *any* age. And that kids are people, not livestock, and they have the right to say what they want or don't want for there own bodies.[37]

Molesters

Some deny they have sex with children; others not only admit to such behavior but claim it is proper and justified. Contradicting the image of "just a hobby," a great many passing references and jokes suggest that "hobbyists" are assumed to be active in the seduction or molestation of children. When board traffic is particularly light in the summer months, someone will joke that this reflects the advent of the school holidays, when most regulars will be out hanging around playgrounds.

We can scarcely determine how many contributors to "pedo boards" become involved in actual molestation, since most experienced contributors would presumably not be foolish enough to confess behavior in writing, even in this fairly private setting. Still, some postings actually do claim to record authentic experiences of molestation, and in harrowing terms. Dracula claims:

My girlfriend is 13 and I'm 37 and we been going out since she was 11. Just last year I did her friend and her at the same time. I know a lot of girls between the ages of 9–17 and I had a few of them but I know they would never tell any one for the cops already asked my girlfriend if we had sex and she told them no!

Another account, from "Soul-less," reads as follows:

Three days ago I found out my daughter had to tell her mum (ex-wife) I abused her, my daughter and I have always had strong love and a special bond. My daughter [loved] her boyfriend enough to tell him about us. He bashed her one night and said if she left him he would ring the police and tell them everything. He did ring them, and the poor innocent girl lied for me . . . and went back to him, he bashed her again last week and she cracked. I am waiting for the cops to come any minute, my two sons know and I don't think I'll ever see the kids again . . . I am a living dead man. Learn from my mess. . . . If it means prison I'll try suicide cos that is not as big a fear as not seeing the kids.[38]

In answer to a question about the age at which girls begin to orgasm, one contributor wrote:

I can tell something, I licked my four year old daughter's pussy, in two minutes she taste very good, then her face comes red and hot, really she have a orgasm, believe me.[39]

These accounts vary in plausibility: some ring painfully true, others may be pornographic fantasies. Nevertheless, a common assumption in the subculture holds that posters might also be molesters. Witness the following:

Latest LEA Sting Results: Yesterday, 11/23/99, LEA arrested a Mr. **** from Carolina Beach, North Carolina USA. For producing and distributing video tapes and photographs of him and his 11 yr. old daughter having sex. Confiscated were 12 videos and over 2000 photos, video camcorder, cameras, and a computer. . . . *If any of the regulars here disappeared as of yesterday, we will know who that regu-*

lar was. And if so, he probably shared some of that material here with an undercover agent. Be very careful, who you share material with. [my emphasis]

Furious discussion follows such exposés of the linkage between child porn and real-life abuse. One of the hottest debates followed the conviction of a German man who had abused a nine-year-old girl called Marion, who was the child of a neighboring family. In the process, he created a series of dozens of images that circulated globally. Through the ensuing controversy on the boards, the prevailing assumption was that the actual sex was a loving and responsible act between adult and child, and that any harm which could be expected from the situation would result from the interference of law enforcement and therapists:

> * **DukeDolphinX** > I hope the little Marion will not receive a trauma . . . I'm afraid of what the psychologists are capable to do. . . . But as always the people and the authorities don't care about the happiness of the children, they want do only their affairs.
> * **Darkstar** > Marion will become a darling of the "victim" culture and will denounce her loli luver as sexual predator and pedo. She will be destroyed just like Helena was in England, farmed out to families to "care" for her whilst she received therapy etc etc.[40]

A German writer used the incident to upbraid that nation's Bundeskriminalamt, or BKA (the federal police), equivalent to the American FBI:

> * **Can'tBelieve** > dear BKA . . . I know you'll read this . . . think about what *you* have done to this child . . . you did at least the same as this guy did . . . and maybe caused much more hurts than he did . . . thank you.
> * **Darkstar** > Marion obviously enjoyed her time with the poster, look at what she did for him, all that posing, and for a beautiful girl like that to miss out on *it*, how long you think till she wants another guy, no amount of abuse counseling is gonna convince her that the pleasure she received was really abusive and painful, oh what a fucking mad world![41]

Yet after all these outraged moralistic comments, some writers took particular note of what they found to be an intriguing aspect of the story as reported, which aroused purely selfish desires: "The complete photo shoot consisted of 290 pictures; but only 45 of the set had been posted to well-known newsgroups. . . . Where are the remaining 245 pics of this series?"[42]

The Illusion of Consent

Interactions on the pedo boards leave no doubt that some subculture members, at least, are personally involved in sexual activity with children, but they report or discuss this in radically different ways: there are degrees of deviance. At one extreme, people write in ways that suggest a total neglect of conventional values and attitudes, and the supportive environment of the boards permits them to speak with stunning frankness. In a discussion of a "Vicky" movie, in which a ten-year-old girl sexually services an adult man, one posting responds, "It's definitely one of the best available! that guy is one lucky s.o.b.! She's been trained very well, she knows exactly what to do! I just wish we could see everything he does to her! Thanks again, . . . for providing a little paradise for all of us!!!"[43] This is a voice that conventional thought associates with the grimmest stereotype of the child molester, the heartless exploiter of children who tramples all assumptions about the innocence and vulnerability of children, and who sees children as objects, victims, potential sex slaves. A similar callousness emerges from "Nanny's" rave review of the KX series: "I posted some more kx—Inga gets a mouth full of sperm, oh, its a dream series." At the time of filming, Inga was six.

The same abhorrent approach emerges from many of the fantasy stories that appear on the boards. While most imagine children giving some sort of voluntary consent to sex, a great many are unabashedly dreams of rape and abduction. In one British contribution by "UK Snowy" called "Off the Bone," the author fantasizes how he picks up a young French hitchhiker with her three-year-old daughter. He abuses and rapes the mother, intimidating her with warnings: "'Listen you French whore,' I shouted at her forlorn face. 'Quit the fucking kicking or I'll hurt the kid.'" He then rapes the child:

> She passed out I think, because she suddenly went limp, like a rag doll, but I wanted to ravage this foreign party and make her pay, like her mother, for my misery. Easily lifting her and more or less dropping her onto me, I enjoyed the most taboo sex I could ever imagine. It was cruel, heartless, despicable I know, but it was also the most intense feeling of power, of release, that I couldn't imagine being experienced in any other way. . . . Her three years of life experience, would not be the same anymore.

Despite the conventional reference to how cruelly wrong the rape was, there is no sense here that the author feels any remorse about his fantasies. Such examples, inconceivably dreadful, suggest that the pedo boards represent a society not just of deviants but of monsters, whose values are irredeemably alien, pure evil.

Other participants present the sexual activity in a radically different context and claim it is perfectly consonant with the libertarian children's rights rhetoric so often found on the boards. In this setting, compulsion and consent are obviously hot-button issues. The age of subjects is hotly debated in this regard: just when are children too young to be depicted? Participants have very strong feelings on these issues, and fans of nine- and ten-year-old subjects are ardent critics of the despised perverts who favor toddlers. The implication is that "loli-fans" are not merely pleasure seekers who exploit children as sex objects: rather, they are sufficiently enlightened to recognize that older children can share sexual pleasure. The more heartily they denounce the aficionados of babies and toddlers, the more such "fans" seek to portray themselves as upholding an alternative libertarian value system.

Throughout the postings and the story fantasies, the common assumption, or illusion, is that children consent to sexual behavior, however grotesquely this idea violates common sense. Far more characteristic of the sex stories than the rape fantasy quoted above is an item such as "Girlfriend's Surprise," in which the narrator describes a sexual encounter with a steady girlfriend in her mid-twenties. Suddenly, the bedroom door opens and in rush her two daughters, "Cathy, a real cute 8 year old with pretty blonde hair, large expressful eyes. Then there's Darlene. A very active 3 year old brunette." They fondle him sexually, and his girlfriend announces that this is a surprise she has in store for him: "It's OK! Both my kids know all about sex. They've been doing it with their daddy since they were two! They've been after me for weeks to have sex with you. I've told them what a great lover you are." The story then recounts an orgy featuring the girlfriend and the two very enthusiastic little girls ("'Yeah, and I *like* it too!' Darlene chimes in. 'I *like* to suck daddy's cock for him!'"). Often in such tales, the male narrator is seduced by a child and, indeed, is shocked by her enthusiastic passion.

A few writers describe children taking the lead in making pornographic materials. "Tomcat" writes:

> I got the impression that more and more younger people are surfing on topic and making stuff for themselves for fun not for commercial. For example there are pics named *** and so on, it seems the little girl (11 years old?) made them herself, you can see her holding the camera on herself while photographing her own pussy. Probably she posted them herself, too. Funny, or? Guess this will increase, too as youth of today has another approach to sexuality than we older people.[44]

Another correspondent quickly repudiated the suggestion about the series in question, proving that other individuals must have taken the pictures, but the fact that the suggestion was made shows how desperately child porn fans wish to believe they are dealing with consenting partners.

The illusion of consent is so strong that a fierce reaction greets any contradictory evidence. After one series was posted, "Someone" asked:

> Are any of you aware that this child is being abused against her will? If you look at these photo you will notice that the person holding the camera is also pinning the child's feet with theirs, while the man performing the act has his knees on her chest like cops do when making an arrest. If this is what the regs call child love, I wonder what you all would do if you hated that child.

Responses were numerous and uniformly skeptical:

> * **bud** > get your eyes examined . . . where do you see any pinning?
> * **Methusla** > These are vid-caps from a video that was made in Germany around the late 80's, or at least that was when I first saw the VHS. She and her brother and an adult male (probably their father) feature in several other vids. No force is used, nor is the girl restrained in any way, she is a full participant. 'Someone' needs to go get some new glasses and a life.

Other instances of compulsion are less equivocal. One notorious series of pictures that appears regularly on the Web sites involves a man having intercourse with "Natasha," a girl of six or seven, whose face betrays obvious fear and distress, and in one particular photo it is reputedly clear that the penetration is causing her intense pain. Whenever this photo set appears, as it does regularly, some commentators will invariably denounce it as sick and contrary to the whole libertarian purpose of the boards. "AlSmithee," typically, wrote that "I love this site and many of its posts, but the images of very small girls being obviously hurt are not for me . . . in the Natasha pics the younger girl is obviously deeply distressed." Because of such attacks, the penetration photo is often omitted when the series is posted.[45]

You Cannot Justify What We Do

Items like the Natasha series foment real debate on the boards, in which quite acute questions are raised. In a parallel exchange, "Hoho" asked why the young girl "Hea" cried during sex, in the series bearing her name. Several contributors made the dazzlingly obvious response:

> * **OnTheRoad** > perhaps it hurts . . . ?
> * **Phil** > Isn't that rather obvious? She doesn't like what he's doing to her. And neither do I.
> * **Dogmeat** > Time for a wakeup call. This is part of pedophilia. Your browser has a stop button. The net has something for everyone. Press that stop button and look after your head.[46]

In another correspondence, "Knightshade" began by asking:

> Why should children be robbed of their early sexual development? It's just a matter of politics. If a kid wants to, why shouldn't he/she? This is my ideal, and I believe most everyone will agree.[47]

"LEA Mole" replied:

> You are dead wrong!! If kids want to drink or hitchhike to New York, should they be allowed to? Of course not! Number two, 99.9% of these kids don't want to be doing this. Look at their eyes, their faces. I see fear and loathing, what do you see? Most of these kids are forced into this position by an authority figure in their lives. Their trust and innocence are shattered. They may become used to it, but like it . . . no.

Darkstar countered:

> Have you swallowed the abuse agenda hook line and sinker? Some bad pedos don't make all child luvers bad an some kids who don't like it don't mean all kids won't like it. There are many other ways to exploit child's too, wanna complain about these too. Like being dumped in social welfare hostels or indoctrinated about sexism, racism, and feminism from an early age, what do they grow up to be like?? Remember Maoism, student revolution, remember socialism, communism, well, feminism and sexism will go the same way.
> * **lea mole** > Darkstar, I haven't swallowed ANY agenda, I'm just putting things in perspective from a child's point of view. You cannot justify what we do by comparing it to anything else. We do it . . . it is wrong. It is not justified by anything but our own pathetic rationalization. Hell, a heroin junky can rationalize to you the need for another shoot-up, but we both know the reality. Face it, we are deviates . . . perverts if you will. We do it because we don't have the guts to stop. Deep down inside, we are disgusted with ourselves, because we know we are wrong and that makes us ashamed.
> * **Loligagger** > lomalee or lea mole or whatever, that was spoken like a true Quantico Graduate!!

A "Quantico graduate" would be an alumnus of the FBI training academy in Virginia.

This exchange illustrates a surprising feature of the boards, namely, that many contributors overtly state that the whole child porn traffic in which they are engaged, directly or indirectly, is wrong and harmful, and that they have profoundly divided feelings about having access to the materials. In one exchange, "Farfhad" commented that

> to do what we do requires that that some four year old ends up sucking her dad's dick and gets the pics sent to newsgroups for our pleasure . . . society's reluctance to allow freedom for that to happen does not surprise or upset me one bit . . . learn to live with what you do . . . or give it up . . . don't waste time deluding yourself with how your rights might have been invaded . . . you are the invader of others rights.[48]

Another perennially emotive theme is that of the long-term effects of adult-child sex. Here are extracts from another exchange, in which at least some of the views heard are staunchly conventional:

> * **CuriousGeorge** > Do you ever wonder what girls like Hela and all the other chickadees you find in here are doing these days? I mean you gotta kinda wonder, are they walking the streets for money, are they strippin' in some seedy club, are they dead and buried because they committed suicide after dealing with the pain and ridicule after they grew up and found out that their girlfriends weren't getting boffed by their dad? Do they know that their sweet innocent childhood pictures are being floated around the net for millions to see only to come across friends or an acquaintance who says, "Hay Hela, I saw your 'family' pictures on the net the other day. You know, the ones of your dad doin' ya up the butt. Gosh, what a guy."
> * **zx** > Having friends or acquaintances would require some kind of social skill, which, as you said, was probably banged out of these victims by dad's 'love'.
> * **Outlander** > Sometimes I wonder if anybody around here thinks about those thoughts. You make good points. I wonder if the people

that post this stuff came across HC [hard-core] pics of their niece, would they post it? Or if they happen to find old photos of their cousin with a mouth full of bologna when she was eight, would they post it? And why shouldn't they? I mean these girls are somebody's niece. They are somebody's cousin. When you think about it too much, it kinda makes ya ill. Doesn't it?

* ??? > here we go again, people trying to make us feel guilty about our hobby.

* neo-petronius > this is not exactly the place for moral concerns, is it? . . . All I'm saying is, if one visits this site one has already made certain decisions that make moral concerns somewhat, that is, completely irrelevant. You've already made your decision. Any further discussion just sounds like self-pity.

* J.L.Byrd > I've said it before: Anyone who is troubled by what's offered here—*leave*. If no one—and that includes you guys—came here, places like this board would close down! How does it feel to sponsor KP [kiddie porn]?[49]

Such charges of hypocrisy surface in most such exchanges, after some contributor has denounced a particular series. The obvious, unanswerable, question is, so why are you here in the first place? One such critic, "Goob," was denounced as

a whining troll, and of the worst kind too! Talking smack about 'Hea' but all the while jacking-off to it! He claims that it's wrong but fails to mention that he is here, at this board, d/l and collecting! Come on, give me a break![50]

Vigorous debates also erupt over the core question of what exactly causes individuals to pursue child porn: is it a sickness, an obsession, or (as commonly asserted) "just a hobby." Though participants know all too well of the ample evidence of a linkage between child porn and molestation, they persist in speaking of a *hobby*, a term that implies this is a harmless private pursuit. Some people collect stamps, some baseball cards, and some pictures of naked children. One contributor remarks that particular photos were taken when our hobby wasn't forced into seedy backrooms. These were taken when it was all out in the open and perfectly normal. Probably by a reputable photographer somewhere in Europe, and her (or her parents) paid, and treated, well.[51]

In response, other, more senior participants scoff at the term *hobby*, asking in effect what other mere hobby or pastime requires an individual to risk the total loss of liberty and reputation:

A 'hobby' is sort of a laugh, isn't it fellas? Why, it seems lately on this board we have seen so many come out and say it's an addiction. Someone called it a loliholic. I think we should always pull ourselves into question, to re-evaluate ourselves, consider where we are at, and who we use to be at one time in our lives.[52]

The term *hobby* might be considered the ultimate form of neutralization, a denial of behavior: part of what a participant himself describes as "our own pathetic rationalization."

Ultimately, we can never say with any certainty whether the value systems debated in this subculture are anything more than masks or charades that participants use to deceive both themselves and others. Nevertheless, the substantial space these issues receive indicates how fervently many "loli enthusiasts" try to construct appropriate identities for themselves, quite different from the nightmarish stereotypes of pedophile and molester or even the demeaning image of the compulsive porn user. In their own minds they are dissidents and rebels, persecuted victims in the struggle for universal sexual liberation. Other contributors have no such illusions and essentially agree with media and law enforcement that child porn is completely beyond the pale.

| SIX |

Policing the Net

You already have zero privacy—get over it.
—Scott McNealy, CEO, Sun Microsystems

The extent of the pedophile presence on the Web may seem startling to those who regard computer networks as an ultimate Orwellian nightmare. Over the last decade, the privacy issue has attracted ever more concern and increasingly demands the attention of legislators. The fear is that the combined efforts of governments, police, and corporations are all but eliminating personal privacy. We might not be too far removed from the terrifying scenes in adventure films such as *Enemy of the State*, in which incomprehensibly vast government data banks unerringly and almost instantaneously track down anyone using a telephone or sending an e-mail. While admitting that privacy issues potentially pose an enormous threat to rights and liberties, we must ask why, in such an environment, the authorities cannot succeed in thwarting a electronic traffic that permits individuals to build up libraries of five or ten thousand wholly illegal images. Assuredly, it is not because law enforcement agencies in the United States or elsewhere are timid about proactive policing or launching stings; nor do they fear a backlash of public sympathy in favor of the pedophiles. Yet, obviously, the trade survives, with its network of boards and newsgroups. Why? Can traditional law enforcement techniques and approaches hope to deal with such a technologically sophisticated enemy?

Easy Prey

Since 1977, there has been a technological race between child pornographers and the police forces who wish to combat them, and at least until the coming of the Web, law enforcement held the advantage. As long as pornographic images existed in material form, their transmission and storage posed major problems, the worst of which lay in any kind of trafficking. The possessor of a child porn picture or video was safe only as long as he owned and viewed it in private and never did anything that might attract the attention of the authorities. Once a magazine or a film was handed from one individual to a trusted friend, there was an immediate danger of police intervention, for who could tell who might be reliable? The longest-standing contact and conspirator might turn out to be a turncoat to the authorities, perhaps cooperating with them to bargain for a lighter sentence in his own case. Successively, each new measure of communication or transmission was closed down, from the stores through mail order and importation.

At first sight, the Internet seemed to continue this pattern, in that we frequently read of arrests of online pornographers who face severe penalties; to that extent, charges that child porn has been decriminalized are exaggerated. Also, police agencies have invested a great deal of effort in combating this type of crime. Nevertheless, the vast bulk of arrests still involve low-level or plainly careless perpetrators, and this is likely to remain the case for the foreseeable future.

As we have seen, the most common type of easy arrest still occurs when an individual stores child porn on a hard drive, which can come to light in various ways, such as when the computer is used by another person. As the Gary Glitter case indicated, computer repair is another perilous area, though the experienced regulars on the boards were astonished at so blatant a blunder:

* **Norman** > GG's crime was stupidity. Handing a laptop crammed with CP to a comp shop. DOH!
* **LoliLuvr** > For everyone's info, it was his cache that got him caught, it was full of pics he had looked at weeks earlier or pages where he only

looked at one pic, this along with net payments made allowed them to track all his connections, so get tooled up for some safety.[1]

The Glitter case reinforced the danger of possessing any suspicious material on a hard drive, not because of the police but as a result of prying repair staff:

> * **me** > the thing that gets me is that one does not need to look at the pictures on the hard drive to fix a computer. So if they are found than that means that the repair shop was snooping on your computer.
> * **Homer** > I work with computers for a living, I will admit that when we fix a computer up we always snoop around, and so does other people I know in this biz.[2]

In other instances, police have been more proactive, going online to investigate pornographers and pedophiles. Police have been particularly successful in catching molesters who seek to entice victims encountered through computers. In these so-called traveler cases, police agencies have achieved a success rate comparable to that obtained earlier against child porn mail order and imports. Contributors to the pedo boards speak in contemptuous terms of anyone caught through a bungled attempt at on-line seduction. The common assumption is that anyone in an AOL chat room claiming to be a lonely young girl seeking companionship is likely to be an agent of the FBI or of a vigilante group such as the Guardian Angels. The case will then proceed like this one described by an FBI agent in an affidavit submitted in a recent prosecution:

> On March 8th, 1999, I was logged onto IRC [Internet relay chat]. I joined a chat channel called *****. I was utilizing a female screen name. I knew from my training and experience that this was a channel regularly used by adult males who were seeking minor girls for sexual purposes. At 3:39 PM I received a private message from an individual using the screen name hotseattle. I identified myself as a 13 year-old girl from Los Angeles. Hotseattle said that he was a 33 year-old male from Seattle who traveled to Los Angeles frequently on business. During the conversation, hotseattle said that he was interested in meeting

in Los Angeles "sometime" to "kiss, make out, and play and stuff." He also said that he would "lick and suck you all over." . . . I provided hot-seattle with my e-mail address and he provided his to me . . . Hotseattle said that he had a digital camera that he could use to make "any" type of pictures I liked . . . Hotseattle told me that he wanted to get me alone in his hotel room and have me strip naked for him.

Electronic interaction became increasingly torrid over the following months, until in September, the agent arranged a rendezvous with "hot-seattle" in Santa Monica, where a young-looking female deputy was waiting, wearing an outfit prearranged online. The suspect was arrested when he approached her, and he faced federal charges, since hotseattle had crossed state lines for the encounter. The alleged "hotseattle" was Patrick Naughton, a former official of the Disney corporation, presumably a sophisticated and well-informed individual. Nevertheless, Naughton had apparently been carrying on dialogues with two separate agents who were posing as pubescent girls. (While admitting the Internet contacts, Naughton denied that any actual molestation was intended).[3]

Such seduction cases often result in charges of child porn possession in addition to attempted molestation, since individuals who are both sexually interested in children and computer literate probably have private porn collections, which emerge when police search their premises. "Patrolling" chat-rooms and IRC can be a productive way of catching child pornographers. In addition to placing ostensible lolitas online, another common form of bait involves offering to trade images. Instead of claiming to be a thirteen-year-old girl, another FBI agent might claim to have a video of his niece taking a shower and offer that in exchange to a like-minded pervert. Federal and state law enforcement agencies have organized substantial programs to coordinate these efforts. In 1994, the FBI set up a special program called Innocent Images to catch would-be on-line seducers and traders, and the program has enjoyed many successes: investigations rose from 698 in 1998 to 1,497 in 1999, and convictions run at around two hundred a year. Since "traveler" suspects usually leave such a substantial trail of evidence, it is scarcely surprising that such cases boast a conviction rate variously estimated at 95 to 99 percent: this is easy hunting.[4]

The federal government has also offered support for training personnel in this potentially difficult area. In 1998, Congress authorized the Office of Juvenile Justice and Delinquency Prevention to fund the creation of "State and local law enforcement cyber units to investigate child sexual exploitation. . . . Designed to encourage communities to adopt a multidisciplinary, multijurisdictional response to online enticement and child pornography cases, the Internet Crimes Against Children Task Force (ICAC Task Force) Program ensures that participating State and local law enforcement agencies can acquire the necessary knowledge, equipment, and personnel resources to prevent, interdict, or investigate ICAC offenses." The most significant aspect of this approach is in recognizing the need to overcome interjurisdictional jealousies and disputes. These efforts are reinforced at the local level, most successfully in the Northwest, where federal, state, and local endeavors are coordinated through a CLEW (Computer Law Enforcement of Washington) agreement:

> In addition to providing computers and technicians who can tease data out of computer systems and hard drives, the program will train law enforcement personnel to seize computers and components using methods that preserve their data. The group also hopes to establish uniform rules for getting search warrants for Internet-based and computer data that would be respected by all the states, so that a search warrant from Washington state could be used to seize a server in Arizona.

This all sounds impressive, but it remains to be seen whether such schemes will bear fruit, except in catching more starry-eyed would-be seducers.[5]

The ISPs

Another fruitful field for police operations has been the major Internet service providers, the ISPs, which serve as the essential gateways to the

Internet and where activity can most closely be observed and supervised. The legal status of ISPs is open to some debate, with implications far beyond child pornography, extending as they do to issues like libel and copyright violation. Should an ISP be seen in terms of a television station, which is liable for material it broadcasts, or is it more like the U.S. mail, which just provides a medium for material over which it has no legal responsibility? Federal law clearly indicates that the provider is seen solely as a carrier on the lines of the U.S. mail, yet some recent investigations and court decisions suggest that ISPs can be held liable under the model of the television station (and some foreign nations have also adopted such an expansive view of ISP liability). In 1998, New York State's attorney general closed down two ISPs and seized their equipment as part of an international child pornography investigation, which focused on images drawn from the newsgroups *abpep-t* and *abpee-t*.[6] Though the legality of such an action is controversial, ISPs are well aware of possible legal consequences in an area as unpopular as child pornography and have a powerful vested interest in complying with authorities to the maximum possible extent.

Much of the most visible action against child pornography in the 1990s concerned AOL, which had achieved a hegemonic position in the market. Given its enormous scale, it also became, unknowingly, a major vehicle for child pornography. Though AOL management was genuinely concerned about the use of the network for sinister purposes, the company also needed to be seen to be aiding suppression. At least from 1993, the news media were frequently reporting cases of online abuse and pornography, under headlines that regularly featured the name AOL. In 1995, typically, the *Boston Globe* headlined "Police Probe America Online–Pornography Link." This was desperately bad publicity and clearly invited official regulation. In 1995 also, anti-porn activist Barry Crimmins was urging Congress that "this crackdown must also include serious punitive measures against companies like AOL." As an anonymous contributor remarked to a pedo board discussion, "AOL has a policy of avoiding government legislation by showing they can police the Internet without new laws." Moreover, if the ISP showed any lack of enthusiasm in the anti-porn crusade, this would certainly cause trouble if and when AOL issues came before Congress, for instance, during corporate mergers.[7]

For whatever reason, the company responded by assisting authorities in tracing individuals who frequented illegal sites or who traded porn through its chat rooms, and a series of major investigations and arrests followed. In 1993, forty people in fourteen states were arrested for circulating child pornography online in a federal investigation named "Operation Longarm." U.S. Customs agents raided the alleged headquarters of what was called a "worldwide computerized child porn ring," and the federal government declared that computers represented the key front in the war on child pornography. In 1995, a hundred individuals were arrested in the Cincinnati area for downloading child pornography via AOL. The same year, AOL users were the target of a major sting operation that culminated in fifteen arrests and 120 searches of homes and offices around the nation, the charges involving both child pornography and the sexual solicitation of children online. This operation, "Innocent Images," was the first to bring to public attention the FBI program of that name.[8]

It is far from clear exactly how AOL was assisting law enforcement, except in helping agents examine and supervise chat rooms in which trading might be occurring. Substantial difficulties stand in the way of using the providers to monitor or suppress child porn. The volume of traffic on any ISP is far too large for any serious surveillance to be applied, to find, say, who is accessing illegal sites. Nor would there be any incentive to do so unless in response to a direct demand or threat from law enforcement or following specific public complaints. Though the impression in the media was that the company was observing Web surfing or porn trafficking, the sheer scale of such an endeavor makes this implausible. Individuals arrested in the various sweeps were probably caught through their activity in chat rooms but AOL and law enforcement agencies let it be thought they had been detected through their surfing activities, in order to deter other AOL users. Porn enthusiasts recognized this and wrote accordingly:

* Curious George > The only way that one could conceive of doing this would be use a program searching for keywords in the extensive user log records of millions and millions of users. This would be expensive, time-consuming, resource-consuming, and produce little results. The results of this expensive project would have to be further narrowed down, creating more expense. For example, a keyword search yielded 100,000 AOL users who visited a site with loli in the url within the last 2 months. This search would have to be further narrowed down. Who d/l [downloaded] stuff off the site, who was on the site the longest, how many times did they visit the site, were they on the site to condemn it or because they enjoyed it? Eventually a computer wouldn't be able to do the job, a human would have to search these many log records and decide what should be done about it, further wasting AOL's time, money, and human resources, and for what? Nothing.[9]

* Methusla > Re ISP's logging activities, it's not in their interests to make waves, as regardless of whether they rat on you, or LEA walk in with a warrant, they lose credibility & business. If all ISP's in the world, logged every piece of traffic, how many millions. of gigabytes of HD space would this take? Not to mention time and staff hours.[10]

* aol refugee > AOL is not allowed to track your surfing habits to outside sites any more than they are allowed to read you e-mail . . . unless they've received complaints. In other words, don't be dumb enough to trade pre[teen] pics in their chat rooms, or to surf without using a proxy (outside your country, of course). AOL does *suck*, but so long as you know this stuff you should be OK. Safety before pleasure.[11]

Despite doubts about exactly what AOL was doing, the message was successfully projected that AOL was a very bad medium for child pornographers to operate in. After 1995, the serious porn traffickers left this provider entirely, and on the boards, novices are repeatedly warned to have no truck with the network:

* fnord > if you are using AOL and on this bbs don't expect not to get caught, AOL is pretty much anti-p*rn through and through.

* **HangMan** > cops have it easier grabbing AOL users as it's harder for them to anonymously surf. Seeing that the head of AOL has announced a war with pedos using its services is also a deterrent.
* **Darkstar** > Just stay away from AOL they are a security nightmare. . . . They tend to be the first port of call for most cop shops looking for an on-topic arrest.
* **Lolig@gger** > Darkstar is correct! AOL is bad news for on-topic material viewers.[12]

Such comments are wonderful news for the AOL corporation, which, as "a security nightmare," "anti-porn through and through," is effectively vindicated from any association with the child porn trade.

The Hard Core

Many who use child porn online are exposed and arrested with little difficulty, but in the vast majority of cases, those who are arrested have almost gone out of their way to attract attention by committing one of the cardinal sins of this world—online seduction, using AOL, and so on. There are many ways in which online pedophiles can get caught. The irony in all this, though, is that all the information about arrest and suppression presented so far in this chapter is freely available on pedo boards such as the Maestro sites, which flourished for years despite all the law enforcement campaigns. While law enforcement can generate headlines by means of an almost endless number of low-quality arrests of minor users, the largely reactive nature of policing means that next to no effort is devoted to apprehending hard-core dealers and traffickers, as opposed to naive amateurs. We might even suggest that the authorities made a grave mistake in driving the pornographers off AOL, since traffickers were then forced to construct the complex international networks now in use and thus are far more difficult to observe and trace. The pedoboard subculture generally avoids the obvious mistakes that cause the downfall of a Gary Glitter or a Patrick Naughton. Instead, they post pictures at *abpep-t,* find and swap material on "floating" temporary sites, and make extensive use of anonymous proxies, as well as advanced encryption techniques.[13]

Reading the boards, we must be struck by the relative lack of serious concern about law enforcement activity—as distinct from the constant nagging paranoia that X or Y is a police provocateur, activity that seems to represent almost a pastime. Board participants are well aware of the various traps and investigations and regularly post news clippings and summaries of criminal cases as they arise, so other enthusiasts can learn about law enforcement techniques and be sure not to make the same mistakes themselves. The FBI affidavit in the Naughton case, quoted above, was taken from a Web site to which I was alerted by a posting on the Maestro board and on which the elaborate legal document is reproduced in full. In addition, the boards report news of investigations from many other countries and in many languages, offering a global coverage that would scarcely be possible if one relied on the media databases generally available in the United States. It is only through the boards that I have been able to track down relevant news stories in the German, Spanish, Italian, British, and Czech media.

Pornographers also scrutinize reports of any current investigations. The Lord High Executioner began, "I recall reading out at the INTERPOL website that there was going to be this conference to tighten down on lolitas being uploaded onto the Net," and he commented on this event in light of recent changes in Web sites. Putting the trends together, he concluded that there might be truth in rumors of "a Super Secret Investigation/Operation being conducted by the FBI in cooperation with International authorities through INTERPOL to try and catch people just looking and/or uploading/downloading Lolitas."[14] Given the very open character of the Web, we might think that the pornographers should be under constant police surveillance, but sometimes we must ask just who is keeping an eye on whom.

The apparent immunity of the hard core is not absolute, since police agencies have caught some very serious traffickers, but such instances stand out because they are so exceptional. The best example to date of just how the hard-core subculture can be disrupted by a proactive investigation is the Wonderland network. In this instance at least, the culprits identified were serious professionals using the full panoply of security measures, yet they were discovered. Significantly, the breakthrough in this affair came not through *Enemy of the State* electronic gadgetry but through old-fashioned police techniques of the sort that are very familiar from conventional operations against professional or organized crime or against other international crimes, such as terrorism. In summary, police found some illegal activity largely through chance and put pressure on accused individuals to act as informants until a wider and much more serious network was identified and wound up. The Wonderland investigation began in 1996 with a prosecution of sixteen people in San Jose who were charged with taking part in an online child porn network. (It is not clear how this particular operation was uncovered in the first place.) One or more of those of those charged cooperated with law enforcement, presumably in hopes of improving their own legal situation, and that led to the identification of a British participant. U.S. and British authorities together discovered the existence of Wonderland and began an international investigation coordinated through Interpol.

Just how the group was penetrated remains mysterious. As *Time* magazine reported vaguely enough, "U.S. agents tried surfing into Wondernet but failed to gain entry." Patiently, police reportedly lurked "in the cybershadows outside the Wondernet, watching transactions until they penetrated the veil of screen names and obtained the real names and addresses of 34 U.S.-based club members." Police forces in a dozen nations carried out more than a hundred more or less simultaneous dawn raids, the tight coordination being essential if participants were not to be alerted through e-mail and thus given the opportunity to flee or destroy evidence. Obviously, customs and other agencies were reluctant to spell out their tactics in too great detail for fear of alerting other pornographers to improve their security measures in future. They may also have been chary about describing any tactics that involved police actually trading in child porn themselves, which one would think would be an indispensable means of establishing their bona fides. As in operations involving drugs or terrorism, law enforcement must deal in illegal commodities in order to be effective, but authorities must avoid admitting that they ever dealt with anything as sensitive as child porn, even to offer bait.[15]

The Wonderland case shows both the potential and the constraints of proactive policing in this area, and even this triumph for law enforcement indicates the limitations of what policing can really do. Apprehending child pornographers of this sophistication is a highly expensive and time-consuming affair, requiring immense technical expertise and diplomatic skill. Powerful bureaucratic pressures give agencies an incentive to keep producing statistics as a measure of effective performance, and it is just much easier to produce a hundred low-level arrests than to pursue one high-level investigation. Following through on major investigations thus requires a clear and sustained commitment of resources and political will. Official avoidance of difficult high-tech targets is closely paralleled in the response to other forms of high-profile crime involving computers. A 1999 study of computer-related fraud cases indicated that a strikingly low number of case referrals resulted in prosecution, and only a tiny minority led to conviction. The reasons for this pattern are all too familiar from the child porn cases discussed above; evidence is difficult to gain, and cases are technically complex:

> It can be very difficult to detect and investigate a computer fraud crime . . . intruders can cover their tracks by erasing various logs on the targeted computer system. Even when a complaint is lodged with law enforcement, it can be difficult to trace the crime back to a specific, identifiable criminal. . . . The chain of intervening computers leading to the targeted machine "can run through Sweden, Norway, anywhere in the world."[16]

Jurisdictional boundaries are very uncertain: "There is no U.S. Attorney for Cyberspace." In consequence, agencies avoid proactive investigations of such crimes.

Even when pursued to completion, the long-term impact of something like the Wonderland sweep is uncertain. It affected only a tiny proportion of the whole subculture, and many self-described veterans of Wonderland remain at large and contribute regularly to the pedo boards, though they were forced to abandon their long-cherished nicknames. Crucially, too, countless images originally shared among this narrow circle have now moved into the public domain via the boards. Customs originally boasted that authorities "turned up a data base of more than 100,000 sexual photographs of naked boys and girls, some younger than two, some engaged in sexual acts with adults." Yet *discovering* this hoard did not mean that all or any of it was removed from circulation, in the way that confiscating a ton of cocaine eradicates it from the illicit drug market. For the vast majority of participants and "loli-lovers," even so massive an international purge was a minor hiccup in business as usual, the main effect of which was to stimulate new thinking about superior security.[17]

Nor is it clear that Wonderland had a serious or lasting deterrent effect. Certainly, there was a short-term impact: to quote Darkstar, "peeps are wary and still remember Wonderland, that frightened off lots of people who had some very kewl [cool] collections."[18] But the rapidly changing nature of the Internet-using population means that long-term consequences are strictly limited. For every one veteran scared off in 1998, perhaps ten more novices who had never heard of Wonderland discovered the boards afresh in the next year or so. Like so much else in the Internet world, the pedo subculture has a very short collective memory, in which a year or two is ancient history. Police agencies must be aware that even mounting a dozen "Operation Wonderlands" does no more than scratch the surface of the trade; and at some point, other priorities are going to come along for law enforcement, with competing demands for resources. Even if they arrest hundreds or thousands of child porn users each year, the staggering mathematics of Internet usage imply that the traffic will continue.

Law enforcement agencies can continue to undertake massive "search and destroy" investigations and are guaranteed to reap good headlines in the process, but the nature of this type of commerce means that police cannot achieve the same kind of permanently crippling effect that they would expect in winding up a terrorist group like the Red Brigades or the Weather Underground. In the case of child porn, police cannot take out leaders or agitators, because there are none. Nor can they destroy infrastructures, on the analogy of raiding drug labs, because the institutions of the porn trade are neither fixed nor localized.

Stopping the Trade?

Given all that, what opportunities are available to law enforcement to combat the trade, either to strike at the kind of experienced dealers we encounter on the boards or to diminish their audience significantly? Various possibilities come to mind, in the form of surveillance techniques that, theoretically, might identify visitors to child porn sites. Though a single law enforcement sweep might exercise only a short-term deterrent effect, a continuing sense that Web traffic is being watched could be much more potent. For the moment, let us postpone discussion of whether such a policy might be legal, ethical, or, ultimately, desirable.

In recent months, the possibility of some kind of blanket surveillance system has been warmly debated on the boards in the context of technological advances by intelligence agencies worldwide. There have for years been rumors of the workings of Project Echelon, a super-secret surveillance facility with the ability to intercept and examine virtually any form of international communication: the system is based in the United States, in cooperation with Great Britain, Canada, Australia, and New Zealand. In 1999, Echelon moved outside the realm of the traditional conspiracy theorists when respectable European media reported not only that Echelon was operational but that it had for years been conducting economic espionage against American trade competitors, including "friendly" countries in the European Community. The implications for intercepting and monitoring illegal Web traffic are enormous. According to the ACLU:

> Several credible reports that suggest that this global electronic communications surveillance system presents an extreme threat to the privacy

of people all over the world. According to these reports, ECHELON attempts to capture staggering volumes of satellite, microwave, cellular and fiber-optic traffic, including communications to and from North America. This vast quantity of voice and data communications are then processed through sophisticated filtering technologies.[19]

Something like Echelon has now become documented fact, as Great Britain has constructed a well-funded new surveillance system, which became operational in 2000. This is under the control of MI5, the nation's old-established political police force, which had lost its raison d'être with the collapse of Communism but now has claimed a new lease on life as the chief enemy of cybercrime. The facility is known as GTAC, the Government Technical Assistance Centre. Like earlier British surveillance systems, GTAC would work closely with other networks in allied countries with the goal of detecting and defeating international criminal activity in areas such as terrorism, narcotics trafficking, and, of course, child pornography. In the debates surrounding the new facility, advocates repeatedly used the fight against child porn as its principal justification.

The fight against child porn was also cited to justify a draconian Regulation of Investigative Powers (RIP) Act proposed by the British government in 2000. Under this law, all ISPs would be required to connect their servers to the MI5 monitoring center:

> The government is to require Internet service providers, such as Freeserve and AOL, to have hardware links to the new computer facility so that messages can be traced across the Internet. The security service [MI5] and the police will still need Home Office permission to search for e-mails and Internet traffic, but they can apply for general warrants that would enable them to intercept communications for a company or an organization.

These connections would "allow anyone to watch the websites you are browsing in real time," and authorities could monitor one in five hundred telephone connections to the Internet. The new network would essentially have the power to monitor all e-mail and Internet communication sent in Britain. The RIP law would make it easier for police to force providers to supply a list of the Web sites visited by customers. And there were other worrying innovations. If unable to deliver encryption keys demanded by police, accused individuals would be forced to prove that they were innocent of criminal intent, a dramatic reversal of the presumption of innocence long guaranteed under English law.

Not surprisingly, these proposals were deeply controversial, and the British government was forced to settle for a less sweeping measure; but it remains to be seen whether something like the RIP will be implemented in practice, if not with full legal warrant. In another manifestation of overbroad powers, British and other European customs authorities now use "profiling" tactics to decide when to search the laptop computers of people seeking to enter the United Kingdom, on the grounds that the machines might contain child porn. Such profiling methods, long used in anti-drug efforts, are notoriously intrusive and unreliable, but once again, the severity of the menace is felt to justify the practice.[20]

In theory, the combined efforts of the FBI, NSA, GTAC, and allied units should be able to detect most illicit child porn traffic on the Web, in a stunning example of global law enforcement cooperation. In addition to alarming civil libertarians, these developments sparked panic on the pedo boards: pornographers are well aware of the new ice age in which they operate and of the dangers of intensified international police cooperation. When one optimistic contributor suggested that international efforts might be limited by legal considerations, "Smile" answered scornfully:

> * nothing's illegal for the LEA. Government agencies work hand in hand nowadays. Someone of your intelligence knows that. The law exists for those on the outside. If the US LEA wants to look at logs in another country, they ask the LEA in the relevant country and get the answers they need. They have better communication lines than we do.[21]

Knowledgeable members of the subculture are under no illusions about their operations being invulnerable to serious official surveillance:

qwert345 > it does not matter what type of security system or walls or proxy you have, everything can be traceable and tracked within time, corresponding on here will be placed on file on an embedded tape/file to be monitored to see what I d/l, view, or follow. I have seen from this board and others . . . if you contribute . . . you will be caught and mostly if you distribute the items. Surf safe and plan safe.[22]

But the defeat of child porn is simply not just around the corner. For one thing, it is far from clear how successfully agencies such as the National Security Agency (NSA) and MI5 could employ their dazzling new technologies (even if they can be implemented without legal and political objections). As illustrated by the ISPs, a computer system can find many thousands of messages with suspicious content, but at some stage, slow and fallible humans have to make the decision as to which need detailed investigation and prosecution. All intelligence services know that being swamped by data is the one of the surest ways to doom an investigation. Tracking the electronic career of an individual or group would be easy, but searching randomly for child porn activity is unrealistic. Responding to scare stories about GTAC, board regular "NickNack" wrote:

A few years ago, they were talking about this subject. And the answer from the Internet society was very simple, if you are going to do that, we are going to send every email including words like ETA, RAF, KKK etc. And then it's simply not working.[23]

Imagine if GTAC did find that, in a given year, fifty thousand British people sent e-mails featuring the words *child porn*, and that all these individuals could be reliably identified. Are police then supposed to abandon all other work to begin building criminal cases against these new suspects? Skeptics might also ask why, if MI5 is as omniscient as some accounts suggest, the Irish Republican Army continues to thrive more than three decades into its guerrilla war against Great Britain, a struggle in which it has repeatedly launched devastatingly successful attacks on the British mainland. Have IRA supporters or arms smugglers never used phones, faxes, or e-mails?

The problems listed for GTAC and its like also apply at the level of ordinary policing. It is no easy matter to determine exactly when an individual is visiting a suspect Web site, and blanket surveillance in search of child porn would turn up a huge number of false positives. Searching for obvious key words or phrases in URLs (*sex, porn, nude, erotic*, and so on) would discover people using everything *except* child pornography, as would any attempt to isolate words such as *child, kiddie, underage*, or *lolita*. As users of filtering software have discovered, these searches can produce ludicrous results. One barred access to photographs from a Mars probe, since the URL of the relevant NASA site included the phrase "marsexplorer" and thus contained the taboo letters "sex." Another possibility might be to create a cleared list of sites that users were authorized to visit and exclude all others, but this would largely defeat the usefulness of the Internet. A more targeted approach would be to search for users visiting well-known bulletin boards with fixed URLs: this would work only as long as the boards remained at that precise address, which they do not do for more than a few months.

Trap Sites

Another sweeping solution would be for some agency such as the FBI or Interpol to establish a trap site, a Web site or bulletin board that either presented quite genuine child porn material or allowed contributors to supply information about authentic sites and URLs. All users of a site would have their IP addresses logged, which at least would provide prima facie evidence for search warrants. In many cases, these searches would likely turn up abundant quantities of child porn, and only a single image would be sufficient to justify conviction.

The question of whether trap sites presently exist is hotly debated on the boards, and many contributors raise the question of whether something like the Maestro board itself might be such a snare. Most, however, reject the trap site notion as a kind of urban legend. The reasons for skepticism are simple. In the first place, it is frankly incredible that any police agency could get away with placing in the public domain the cornucopia of illegal smut required to mount a sting on a long-term basis. To attract traffic, the honey trap would have to include hundreds or thousands of genuine images, which once made available would continue to circulate ad infinitum. It would be deeply embarrassing for a law enforcement bureaucrat to admit to a Congressional investigation that his or her agency had regrettably become one of the world's largest distributors of child pornography, no matter in how good a cause. As Pirra8 declared in one of the incessant controversies about provocateurs on the boards, "I know Goddess is *not* LEA—because LEA would not post the quality stuff that she has. And, the quantity."[24] Another of the main activists on the boards offered a humorous slant on the notion that a federal agency might be circulating child porn in order to entrap users:

> * **Godfather Corleone** > Yes it's correct! As a matter of fact, we are working on this project now, I can't really say much about it but the goal is to upload 10,000,000 images and clips in three years to make as many people interested in lolita as possible—then we strike! ;) I've heard ***, *** and Pirra8 are top chiefs within the FBI and personally I'm hoping for a position there as well! ;)[25]

Only somewhat less embarrassing would be the statement that the U.S. Customs Service or some other agency knew that a given site was distributing such material, but that the agency had tolerated its existence for six months or a year.

Furthermore, collecting IP addresses is rarely of much use since virtually all board participants use proxies, so the only individuals identified would be the inexperienced who were "surfing naked." The widespread use of proxies is rarely noted in law enforcement sources, and when it is, it is almost with a sense of astonishment. In 2000, for instance, FBI director Louis Freeh testified to a Senate panel on recent hacker attacks against federal Web sites, and he noted that perpetrators in many cases falsified the Internet addresses of the computers involved in launching attacks, "meaning that the address that appeared on the target's log was not the true address of the system that sent the messages."[26] Though using proxies is second nature to many computer users, the practice needed spelling out for the bemused legislators.

To be valuable, any information collected about IPs would require as an additional step finding the real identities lying behind the proxies:

> Your safety lies in the amount of work it is for LEA to get info from proxyserver logs. They would have to go right away to the server itself. (If they wrote, the logs would have been overwritten by the time they got a reply). It's a lot of work to go through all those logs. And the server will most likely demand a warrant or a court order. Otherwise the anonymity function of their proxy wouldn't be worth anything.[27]

To quote another poster, "MI5 can monitor my proxys for as long as they want."[28] A serious and effective sting might involve not only establishing a porn site under law enforcement control but also bogus proxy sites—but the complications here become ever more elaborate. Even without a proxy, a person remote-accessing the Internet by means of a modem is assigned a random IP on each visit, so tracking would do little good in such cases. Also, the fact of merely visiting a given site violates no law, so establishing that a computer with a given IP address was used to access a porn site proves nothing for certain about the identity of a perpetrator. The computer might have been used by someone other than the owner, or the owner might not have been downloading images.

The other problem with trap sites involves, as the name implies, entrapment, which is likely to be the principal defense of anyone charged in such a case. The line between entrapment and a legitimate sting operation is often hard to draw clearly, but the key difference is whether an accused person would have performed the illegal behavior anyway, or whether he or she was led into it by law enforcement. Are police generating crimes that would not have occurred without their incitement and the invitation of law enforcement authorities? Child pornography provides the context for one of the major recent legal decisions in this area, in which unacceptable police behavior was delineated. The case involved a Nebraska farmer who had ordered adult homosexual-oriented materials through the mail. Guessing that he would be likely to purchase child pornography, undercover U.S. Postal Service agents bombarded him with invitations to buy such articles until finally he succumbed and was charged with illegal possession. In this case, not only did the U.S. Supreme Court determine that law enforcement had engaged in entrapment, but the defendant was even the subject of friendly coverage in national media outlets such as the *New York Times* and *60 Minutes*, which normally feel that no measures are severe enough to be used against child pornographers.[29]

Entrapment is a particular concern in chat room sting operations like that which captured Patrick Naughton. The courts are usually sensitive to these issues, and in a recent case, a federal appeals court struck down a conviction with a damning warning to police: "There is surely enough real crime in our society that it is unnecessary for our law enforcement officals to spend months luring an obviously lonely and confused individual to cross the line between fantasy and criminality." Doubts about entrapment go far toward explaining the surprisingly light sentences handed down in such cyberstalking cases, when the common defense is that no actual child was in danger, leaving this technically a victimless offense. (Matters are different when child pornography is present.) The FBI affidavit in the Naughton case went to great pains to list the times on which the supposed young girl reminded Naughton of the legal situation and gave him numerous opportunities to rethink and back out.[30]

With all these caveats, some recent cases seem, at first sight, to suggest that trap sites are in use. In one, an elementary school teacher in southern California was arrested after he "allegedly downloaded 60 images from a Web site based in the Netherlands, according to court documents. At least nine of the images depicted children." The man "was arrested after a six-month federal investigation that traced the electronic fingerprints left when Internet users visit Web sites." This story caused consternation when it was posted on the pedo boards, because it raised the specter that someone identified "just looking" at pictures on a given site could be picked up at any time, and some novices seemed on the verge of abandoning the boards. More experienced users, though, raised doubts about the official reporting. Some claimed that the individual had been engaged in other suspicious activities, including possible molestation, and a student reported him to a relative in law enforcement: "they only picked on him because he was a teacher, and that makes people nervous when a teacher had on-topic stuff." One contributor implied that the suspect's interests were already public knowledge, suggesting that he was indiscreet and throwing a completely different light on the "trap site" story: "I know this because this guy teaches at a local school here in Calif. We have known him for years." If that is correct—and it cannot be verified—then the suspect was already sharing material with friends, albeit in a tight-knit group, and was rash about security precautions.

Also raising questions about the news reporting, it is hard to credit that a prosecutor would go to court solely on the evidence of such "electronic tracks" without the existence of actual images in the possession of an accused person, and the story as reported leaves unclear whether actual possession was involved, which is quite different from "just looking." Some participants on the pedo boards made the plausible comment that the story was reported as it was in order to deter future casual visitors to CP sites:

* **G-MAN** > It really just looks like a showcase story to me.
* **BigMan** > This story is lot of *bull*. . . . Just be cool guys!!
* **Morgoth** > What a joke . . . nothing to worry about for us, but that teach is a real moron, and unlucky, too. Even so, the particular case does confirm both that IP addresses are recorded in some instances, and that agencies cooperate across international boundaries.[31]

As a final solution to the child porn problem, the trap-site notion leaves much to be desired, but it is a recurrent nightmare for pornographers. The idea has given rise to a number of pseudo–trap sites, practical jokes to which obnoxious novices are commonly exposed. An individual persistently clamoring for good URLs may be directed to a particular site, where he will find his screen filling with something like the following text, possibly accompanied by dramatic sound effects:

You are entering an Official United States Government System, which may be used only for authorized purposes. Unauthorized attempts to access the information stored on this system will result in criminal prosecution. The Government monitors and audits the usage of this system, and all persons are hereby notified that use of this system constitutes consent to such monitoring and auditing.

The terrified user will then be told that his IP address has been logged, and an icon of his computer hard drive appears on screen, as the "official system" tells him that the contents are now being stored in an official database for further examination. Many controversial groups, including political extremists, use tricks like this to scare the unwary, though it is nothing more than a prank that can be performed by anyone with a solid knowledge of programming.

Police can accomplish much in a concerted war on child pornography and can make access that much more difficult, especially if they work closely with ISPs and vigilante organizations: together, they might offer sufficient deterrence to shrink the child porn traffic massively. Even so, the problems identified with blanket surveillance techniques raise doubts that total elimination would ever be a serious possibility. Apart from the other qualifications and caveats mentioned earlier, any long-term analysis of the war between police and pornographers must take account of the astonishing technological changes over the last few years: recall that the Web in its modern shape dates only from 1993. When pornographers themselves speculate about the future, they recognize the countless dangers they face, but many are sanguine, placing their hopes in new technologies such as Freenet, coupled with the difficulty of pinning down servers located in countries beyond the reach of Western police agencies. To quote Darkstar again, "LEA will never get rid of us."[32] The experience of the last two decades suggests that his optimism may be justified.

| SEVEN |

Vigilantes and Militias

Am I in real danger or are these people just trolls with no
LEA connection? Please guys, I need to sleep but I can't.
For the first time in my life I'm scared. I'm paranoiac,
thinking somebody will knock my door at any moment.
—R-board, June 25, 2000

Though trap sites as such might be mythical, some Web sites have acquired the reputation of being dangerous for porn enthusiasts, for reasons that might be instructive for future prevention efforts. Significantly,
the most feared and effective such sites have nothing to do with government or any official agency but have rather been created by private companies or grassroots groups, which for a variety of reasons wish to remove
pedophile material from the Web. Activism by private enterprise reflects
frustration at the general failure of law enforcement to deal with the core
of the child porn subculture. The consequence is that here, finally, we
find anti-porn activists who genuinely scare the subculture. This development raises intriguing questions about the whole issue of law enforcement and criminal sanctions. If existing tactics have not achieved suppression, might we hope for more from new methods, perhaps drawing
on the expertise of private companies and entrepreneurs? Mass arrests
and roundups may be neither feasible nor desirable: the prisons are full
enough already. But some of the innovative strategies now directed
against child porn might be starting to have the deterrent effect that we
have not hitherto witnessed in this elusive area. In the context of the Internet, some forms of deterrence will work far better than others, and an

ongoing threat posed by technologically sophisticated activists is far more effective than the sporadic danger posed by traditionally conceived police purges.

The deployment of private resources against the child porn underworld is a relatively recent development, which only really took off during 2000, yet it rapidly scored quite striking successes. In just a few months, private activism had achieved far more than police and official law enforcement had done in a decade. The achievement was especially impressive in terms of the potential deterrent effect. Yet in many ways, this private activism is even more troubling than the prospects of some kind of Echelon or GTAC system, in that private enterprise warfare constitutes vigilantism, lies wholly beyond any official or legal regulation, and sets frightening precedents for the future of the Internet. Once again, we face the dilemma of deciding just when the cost of fighting child porn becomes too high.

Self-Defense

In its initial phases, the private attack on child porn institutions represented a clear form of self-defense, to which companies were forced to resort given the lack of official assistance. One early case study involved *angelfire.com*, which, as we have seen, was for several months in 1999 a favored venue for temporary child porn sites, to the fury of the site's administration. Individuals would acquire a temporary home page and post pornographic images, which were accessed worldwide until *angelfire*'s employees found and closed the page. In late 1999, an exasperated company announced that it was taking action and would cooperate closely henceforth with law enforcement. Anyone attempting to visit a site touted as CP found the following message:

> The files you have attempted to access have been removed from our servers for facilitating the distribution of illegal content via the Internet. Our abuse staff will be working closely with the federal and/or international authorities to aid in the prosecution of the responsible individual(s). Our procedures will include the provision of all pertinent

member information, copies of the site, IP addresses, activity logs, and—if necessary—access logs for all parties accessing this URL. This is part of a new and strengthened partnership dedicated to bringing purveyors of illegal material—especially that content involving children—to justice.[1]

This message had a blockbuster effect on the boards, remarkably so given what we have noted about the problems of identifying genuine IP addresses as opposed to proxies. Nor, initially, was it even clear that the message was authentic, as opposed to a trick by pranksters or anti-pedophile pressure groups. What made it so intimidating was the phrase "access logs," suggesting that people would be attracting police attention solely for visiting a site rather than posting or trading. After all the rumors, this genuinely was an authentic trap site. The Lord High Executioner was skeptical, as he reminded readers that the proposed reaction was legally perilous:

> Are we to honestly believe that the access logs will be used? Well, they do need special permission from the FCC to do such a thing, but I doubt if they are going to do so *unless* they specifically say they need them. To be honest, I believe like the others out here, that they really can't nail us for just 'accessing' a site to only look. That's insane. However, as some of you have pointed out to me a good few times, every time you download a flick to watch you are necessarily breaking the law and in possession of lolitas along with copying pics down to your HD.

The effect of the crackdown was to pass the word among the cognoscenti that "*angelfire* seems to be a trap for people in US," and all contributors were urged to find a different outlet for material.[2] Thereafter, any news of a posting on a new *angelfire* page was greeted by stern warnings not to go there, citing the authoritative judgment of the Executioner and other wise ones that "something might be up" in this particular case:

> * **Sleeper** > *Angelfire* made it *very clear* that they *will* log you and send *all* of the information to the proper authorities for prosecution. . . . Or

they also made a *very* strong hint that it would not be out of the realm of possibility of infecting your computer with a virus . . . well, that's what they said here about two months ago. . . . We already had three people crash from downloading from *Angelfire* a few weeks ago. It's your call though. . . . Take care.[3]

This is, in short, one instance where deterrence actually seems to have worked well, and other providers under siege from pornographers took note. The *sexhound.net* site acted similarly in 2000, in response to a major wave of kiddie porn postings. Though, as its name suggests, *sexhound* is no stranger to explicit material, it adopted a very stern line against child porn, and administrators posted a warning on the Maestro board:

Sites posted on this board are deleted from *Sexhound* ASAP. Move the board, we will find it again. Post pics on *Sexhound* and you will spend time in prison. We are launching an all out war on your kind. You will not win. You will pay with your freedom. You cannot hide on the Internet. Post on *Sexhound* and you will suffer the legal consequences. If you think this a troll [i.e., a fake posting], just post a *Sexhound* link that contains CP and you will see how fast it disappears. But once it's gone we will put all of our knowledge into tracking down the person who uploaded the files. Stay away from *Sexhound* if you value your freedom.

The Maestro's administration responded obligingly, announcing: "To all posters: Don't upload any sites at *sexhound.net*. It is not worth the time. The sites will be deleted too soon to be viewed by our members."[4] Today, both *angelfire* and *sexhound* are considered taboo on the pedo boards, a modest triumph for the principle of deterrence.

Before treating this as a model for the elimination of Net porn, we should remember some special circumstances of the case. Above all, *angelfire* and *sexhound* could be abandoned as outlets because it was easy to find hundreds of other comparable providers with fewer scruples, and it simply was not worthwhile taking the risk. As "Licker" observed, "Who cares about what *Sexhound* Admin thinks of *us*? . . . C'mon posters.

There are plenty of other free hosts on the WWW."[5] If there ever was a general crackdown on such open sites—and to be effective, it would have to be genuinely global in nature—loli-lovers would probably be more willing to proceed despite the threats, secure in their use of anonymous proxies. Child porn can easily be driven from *some* sites precisely because it is so easy to go elsewhere.

Nuking Pedos

Still, these battles raise the interesting point that the subculture is much more immediately concerned about detection or sabotage from private commercial firms like AOL and *angelfire* than about official government agencies. Other private groups also inspire immediate concern, especially amateur or vigilante groups devoted to combating child pornography, which are believed to be much more familiar with technology than are police forces. We should draw a sharp distinction here between highly expert professional groups and the well-publicized amateurs who surf the Net in order to entrap stalkers and seducers: what so terrified pornographers about *Sexhound*'s threat was the line "all of our knowledge!"[6]

Some information has surfaced about organized hacking groups dedicated to fighting child pornography online. One such is Ethical Hackers Against Pedophilia, "a group that works with law enforcement to track down online child pornographers." Another is *Condemned.org*, founded in 1999 as a network of "some thirty seasoned information security professionals, white hat hackers and technologists." Reportedly, the group was founded by an Australian woman named "Blueberry," who reported her horror on discovering child porn on the Net:

> "It's really stomach-churning, horrific stuff and you see a child in a nappy [diaper] being raped and screaming," she said. She started *Condemned.org* in 1999 as a labor of love, pooling five computers on her living room floor and scouting out sites while her kids were in school. Now, they have volunteers around the world and backing from security and software companies.[7]

We might be skeptical about this origin story, with its potent image of a housewife being stirred to mount an amateur crusade in response to stumbling into a den of horrors. It is inconceivable that an average computer user would suddenly or accidentally discover the sort of material described here, if she had not already been searching for it or if she had not received addresses from other activists. This makes it more likely that *Condemned.org* grew out of a pre-existing vigilante effort, perhaps in cooperation with law enforcement. Whatever its origins, the group invites the reporting of illegal sites and then seeks to remove them through legal means, often by simply approaching the provider in question:

"In the first four months running, we've removed over 500 [child porn] URLs," reported Blueberry. "When that method fails, however, some members resort to direct action":

> Although no one at the organization would admit to hacking servers in the U.S., [he] acknowledged that a few *Condemned.org* volunteers have taken out thirteen overseas sites this way. "We have hacked some of these sites in areas of the world where there are no laws," he said. "In those countries, we've taken servers completely offline with buffer overflows or straight exploits written by a couple of guys on our staff. Once we get in, we erase their file directories and everything on their hard drives."[8]

Condemned joined several other anti-porn organizations, including "EHAP, founded in 1997 by two hackers with the handles RSnake and Chalk, and *antichildporn.org*, founded in 1999 by a Minneapolis woman who calls herself Natasha Grigori":[9]

> When antichildporn.org gets a tip about a pedophile bulletin board, they let loose a "spider" on the board that ferrets out URLs, filenames, passwords and e-mail addresses from hundreds of pages of text, saving hours of work. . . . The next release of their tool will comb through the URLs and e-mail addresses, using public records to match them with owners, locations, phone numbers and Internet service providers.

The relationship between such vigilantism and official law enforcement is uncertain, and the matter is very delicate. Agencies sympathize with private campaigns against child porn sites, but their public stance must be cautious, since hackers are often violating the law themselves. This is especially dangerous when anti-porn activists visit sites to verify that they are offering illegal material, since even downloading a single image, for whatever motive, is a significant violation of federal law. To quote a recent journalistic study, "off the record, law enforcement officials said they do work with the groups—quietly. They're afraid of getting caught in the backlash in case the groups do anything wrong."[10]

Trojan Wars

Just how effective are the vigilantes? We would be unwise to take anti-pedo claims at face value. Groups inevitably want to make themselves appear as effective as possible, and anti-pedophile groups may well see an advantage in keeping pornographers in a constant state of nervousness. Nevertheless, some boards were hit very hard, and some destroyed. Whatever the truth, by 2000 every glitch or temporary shutdown on a pedo board was boasted as a triumph by hacker groups. When one participant asked why a favorite site seemed to have ceased operations, another contributor crowed: "The fucker's dead and gone! *** BBS gone, *** gone, *** locked down until I say so. My next project is *** clubs, and after that we start on this board. Enjoy it while it lasts, pedos."[11]

Skilled hackers and vigilantes are widely rumored to deploy electronic sabotage against participants in the form of viruses and even more devastating sleeper programs, "trojans," or trojan horses, designed to "nuke" their targets. The capacities of these trojans are considerable. To quote a victim, a hacking tool such as the "Cult of the Dead Cow's Back Orifice 2000"

allows a hacker to take control of machines that run Windows—executing applications, reading and transferring files, even restarting or locking up a computer. It gives its user more control of a remote Windows machine than the person at the keyboard has. I also discovered that trojan horses are nasty beasts—malicious, security-breaking programs disguised as something benign like a screensaver or a game. They run in the background so you don't know they're there—until some hacker exploits them to take control of your computer. . . . I make a more appetizing meal for hackers since I have a solely Windows environment.[12]

Worse still, these trojans are deployed not just against major posters or Web masters but against the low-level "peeps" who just visit and observe sites:

* **Darkstar** > The board is presently being monitored by hackerz groups their intentions is to nuke as many peeps as possible, they are also trying to accumulate personal info, so be vigilant. Install *Atguard* and keep an eye open for those inbounds, there is active trojan testing going on, if it's successful they intend to post onto the infected IRC channel and claim pedo wipeout status.[13]

Such booby-trapped sites have appeared with increasing frequency, reducing board participants to a state of furious frustration and calling forth expressions of warped chivalry:

* **Lord High Executioner** > Sounds like the anti-pedos are launching another offensive. . . . Luring people into these sites and then making sure something happens to their comp is completely dishonorable. Why don't they just meet us in battle? One who attacks by not showing his face is completely dishonorable. But, then again, these anti-pedos will try anything.[14]

One message, from "Argono," purported to come from the standpoint of a saboteur, describing some of the tactics that might be used to disrupt and destroy "pedos":

What's the best pedo nuker? Well, many of them have a proxy, and . . . many not. That's the game. Build a porn-site, load the url in a pedo-bbs and view the logfiles. Fifty percent are on the road without proxy. And then start the nuke with the IP's from the logfiles, yes, I see many, many open ports. You can become an admin-status in his/her computer. And the game goes on :-))[15]

Warnings and threats accumulated in early 2000:

Take note again and again: Up until now we have been just testing the waters and making the right contacts. We are joining forces to rid the web of boards such as this one. We will no longer act as troll or RF's. What you have seen in the last three weeks is nothing compared to what is coming your way. Joining forces will be Pedo Patrol, RAP, LEA, Pedo Watch, PACA, Lycos, Insite, CTIN, Fof4, HACP and over 3000 volunteers. Please enjoy the time you have, for it is short.[16]

The Blitz

After some weeks of such warnings and feints, "the game" reached a sudden peak of ferocity in June 2000, which in the child porn world rapidly gained the status of "a day that will live in infamy." All the major hacker groups launched a concerted attack directed specifically at the Maestro's boards, and within the space of a few days, all disappeared under concerted troll attack; so did many less-prestigious sites. Some just vanished, temporarily or permanently, and others merely repeated anti-child porn messages in endless loops. Then attack caused general confusion:

Nearly all the top on-topic board have been spammed and destroyed. Have they moved or what? Do you know of any other good boards? The following boards are up shit creek—***board, BBS2, EnglishBBS, Panty Raiders, LoliBoard, etc. What the hell's happening?[17]

This was bad enough for the pornographers, but worse was to come. For several months, one new board had become the main center of activity in the Maestro network, and now, an anti-pedo site suddenly listed not just the proxies but the *authentic* IPs of everyone who had posted material on that site for several weeks past, together with the associated pseudonyms. "Nicks and matching IP numbers or DNS names were posted onto the board by some troll claiming to be an anti-pedo, who had been monitoring the board for a while. This naturally compromised some peeps' security."[18] In theory, such posting made it possible for police to find each and every one of these computers with its owners and to trace back every illicit image posted on that machine over several months. By tracking pseudonyms, it would perhaps be possible to accumulate posting records over several years. Moreover, the IPs were posted at an anti-porn site based in Denmark, which any board participant could visit to see if he had been exposed. All visitors to the site received a complicated trojan that would trace their future Web activity.

Exactly how the remarkable feat of tracking real IPs was achieved remains uncertain, and ignorance naturally contributed to ferocious paranoia and mutual suspicion. Reconstructing the events, it seemed even to knowledgeable participants that there must have been some kind of inside job, that one of the administrators at the apex of the child porn world must have handed over the private logs to an anti-pedo group. The suspect most frequently cited was Godfather Corleone, whom we have often met as a revered mentor of this subculture. This charge was widely rejected, not least on the obvious grounds that he had posted such spectacularly illegal material over the years. Also, a malicious traitor within the walls could have done far more harm by turning information over to law enforcement directly, rather than proceeding via a private group:

> * **whisker** > This is the second time today someone has alluded to GFC tipping off ****. What evidence does anyone have? And if it were true (which I think is unlikely) why would he waste his time with a one-man non-LEA boob like ****? Why not turn everyone in directly to LEA?
> * **Articule** > If GFC had to "cut" a deal, wouldn't it be with LEA? Big secret sweeps followed by many press conferences (not to belittle the real problems that some posters *might* be having). I believe it was us and our lack of computer savvy, out on the board, or possibly a rogue regular (that collected IP's seen in IRC chat).[19]

On balance, the private hacker groups probably found their own way directly into the Maestro network, bypassing all the legendary security procedures.

Whatever the means of access, the June attack had devastating effects, far greater than those of Wonderland and all its recent counterparts combined. One typical response follows, from "Anon":

> I'm scared to death . . . I've just returned from a trip and last night while I was trying to find out what was going on with Maestro's boards I followed a link posted by johnboy that took me to an antipedo group site. I was surprised and scared as hell when I saw my nick, the dates, my proxy IP on a list alongside to my own postings but that's not what really troubles me. There is a line, only one (enough) that tells my real IP, oh God! . . . Now I've moved all CP into CDs, deleted files, wiped free space, reformatted HD, etc. and I'm praying. Guys, how could this happen? Was the board under LEA control? Was there a treacherous admin between the board staff? Or was the site hacked in some way that allowed this people to get the data?[20]

Another letter in the same vein, by "Concerned":

> I saw several nicks of myself on the list and they showed the same address. I think this is dangerous and if the LEA have the information right now this is trouble. Can anyone calm me down a bit, I don't want the cops ringing on my door in the morning. I only d/l pics and wrote links. I never posted pics myself, but will that make a difference in the end? I hope this board is safe. Who knows? No paranoia but this time we have reasons to be concerned.[21]

Most of the established nicknames on the boards perished within hours of the attack, probably never to be reused. The administrator of another long-active board was one of many who declared his retirement about this time:

> After taking advice from several respected persons, I regret to announce that I will no longer be using my admin password at any of the Maestro's boards . . . I have not taken this decision lightly, after over twelve months of involvement there. But I have serious concerns, and would urge others to be very cautious at this time at those sites. . . . And remember—a wrong decision in this hobby could affect the rest of your life![22]

Others echoed his sentiments:

> * **Reposter** > I as well am done in the business of the boards. News is
> safe and that is my new playground.
> * **Gandalf** > Probably a good idea. I am taking a break myself, from
> the whole thing.
> * **Freebird** > I too have decided to lay low since seeing my nic and IP
> posted. During the time period in question, I don't think I reposted
> any links and I'm not that overly paranoid.[23]

Observers of the boards noticed the passing of an era:

> * **2sly4u2** > where are all posters? GFC, Pirra8, ILEY, Smiling Jack,
> Ramses, Darkstar and so on??? Sure, a lot of familiar names are still here
> but where are the posters . . . the real regulars????!!! All I can see now
> are fresh ones posting here for a few months only??
> * **An old reg** > Darkstar has been in and out . . . Ramses has retired,
> along with GFC, and I believe P8 has done the same. Haven't heard
> from SmilingJack . . . keep your eyes peeled though, and be very care-
> ful round here![24]

As to the long-term effects, the Maestro boards were an obvious ca-
sualty, for subculture members a painfully felt loss. As one obituary
noted, the chat board "always offered a dynamic give-and-take within
The Topic I had never experienced before . . . and I miss it now."[25]
Though these boards revived after the June attack, all knowledgeable
participants believed that they were hopelessly compromised, and that
henceforth, they should be presumed to be trap sites, which at least monitored one's IP and probably delivered trojans as well. "Danube" wrote
that the old main Maestro board "is really scary. Find another on-topic
board." Admin noted, "In my view, it is risky to visit, and dangerous to
post at." Morgoth agreed with these evaluations:

> Abandon Ship! The boards may or may not have been compromised,
> but don't bet your ass you are safe. Learn to use News. Get a good pay-
> server, and you'll be all set. *Do not risk your ass on the Maestro Boards!*
> . . . Time to move on.[26]

Shortly after the Maestro wars, vigilantes began a subtler but equally devastating attack on the more public clubs such as *egroups*, which generally ran soft-core pictures that were at least semi-legal in some countries. Now, hitherto unknown posters suddenly posted extreme hardcore pictures on some relatively mild groups, leading to furious controversy within the board and complaints to corporate management. Though moderators rush to delete such offensive materials, it is generally too late once they have appeared, and the groups were indelibly labeled as venues for hard-core child porn. The consequence was the almost immediate forced closure of many of the most popular groups, all within a few weeks. It is commonly alleged that the posters in question are anti-porn activists who are deliberately poisoning a site in order to destroy it, and this idea is made plausible by the consistent and repeated nature of attacks. Again and again, we find the same modus operandi and even the same pseudonyms. If this view is correct, then the vigilantes are running a major risk, since they are themselves handling extremely illegal materials and, in theory, could be facing long prison terms. Still, their kamikaze tactic has proved highly effective, in closing specific boards and perhaps in driving firms like *egroups* to take the logical step of banning all sexual material on their networks.

Defiance

Looking at the reactions of subculture members during the June meltdown is instructive for the possibility of controlling or eliminating the child porn trade by technological counter-measures. A good number of participants seem to have been genuinely scared, and many announced that they were quitting, at least temporarily. Presumably many others defected without bothering to notify the boards of the fact. Yet even at this terrifying moment, a resolute hard core remained. In the note quoted above, "Anon" declared quite convincingly that he was terrified, scared, paranoid, and taking all manner of desperate security measures, yet it is significant that he did not take the obvious precaution, namely, destroying all the child porn materials, which alone would constitute a case against him in court. Interestingly, too, it was at just this point that child porn activity surged on public sites such as *egroups* and MSN: far from driving people deeper underground, suppressing the Maestro boards just turned some users to still more overt activity.

For many on the boards, the reaction to the purge was unconcern or active defiance, which was all the easier when participants were based outside the United States or Western Europe:

> * **Wizard II** > OK, OK, You got me!! I give up!! Here is my address and Email address and phone number. Come take me away!! Address is: Under your daughters bed, Email Address is: mydick@yourdaughtersmouth.com, Phone is: 1-800-YNG-CLIT . . . *Come get me! I am waiting!!*
>
> * **The Uncle Willy** > Sirs: Before try to act against this site I recommend you to ask your lawyer, do you think we stay sited while you are using your stupid tricks? As you see, I used my real name and email, I have nothing to hide since in Japan and my own country, this kind of material is not illegal, and you can't scare us with your menaces, if you wish to act seriously, do it or shut up.
>
> * **Once again . . .** > The almighty, rich white American comes and tells *the world* what they can and cannot do, with the illusion that they control the net, and all peoples. Give it a rest, *We* are everywhere, in great numbers. We are your Dads, uncles, cousins, nephews . . . your best friend . . . the judge . . . lawyers . . . politicians . . . priests . . . and on and on and on . . . perhaps you are the ones who need to be "cured."[27]

Once the initial panic had subsided, members realized that even the fact of having their IPs announced did not necessarily mean the end of the world, because police still faced the basic problem of coordinating a response. How could agencies cope with such a mass of information?

> * I may be wrong, but upon reflection I think that there is little to worry about re these fucks logging IP's. No LEA worth their salt has the time nor the resources to bother with these shits. I would not worry about them at all.

* I can't see how a machine address would be used in a criminal trial situation. It would be too vague. No ability to identify the actual perpetrator of a crime. However as a data-base for future cross-matching with a combination of other details a perpetrators known location might be achieved. But will LEA utilize all this detail?
* The tricks employed by our hacker friends to glean proxy IP's does not bother me, I don't see LEA wasting any more time on tracking the kind of posting that is done here at present.[28]

Tentatively, we can say the optimists were probably right. At the time of writing, several months after the crisis, there is no evidence that police agencies used any of these leads to undertake the kind of sweep that the subculture dreaded, or indeed that a single arrest could be directly attributed to the gigantic security lapse. Within days, the pornographers were launching a counter-attack against the hackers. The simplest form of counter-attack was to report hackers to their ISPs for participating in such "denial of service" attacks, which constitute a serious offense in the electronic world and which are quite sufficient to have one's account terminated by, say, America Online. As one pedo board administrator wrote to an enemy hacker, "If you continue to harass these folks, I will be forced to file a lawsuit through AOL and yes, AOL is *very* interested in you and are tracking you as I speak. I personally have called them and reported you for breach of TOS [terms of service]." In such a setting, it is no defense to claim that the hacking activity is intended to achieve what most would regard as a higher goal, namely, the suppression of child porn traffic.

Soon, too, surviving pedo boards were filled with personal information of the anti-pedo activists. The volume and detail of information provided is startling. IPs and e-mail addresses were posted, with notes urging, "Hackers are needed to put him out of business. This is a static DSL address. Go get him boys!" In one instance, the IP address of a U.S.-based anti-pedo activist was posted together with his real name, date of birth, career record, address, and the names and ages of his wife and children. The posting also contained the family's unlisted phone number, his social security number, and his driver's license number: "still checking medical and financial records. Enjoy, will update tomorrow." This material, ample to support a powerful attack on the man's life, was presented by Hackmaster as "my way of giving back!" As another would-be revenge poster warned, "It's not nice to fool with Mother Nature."[29]

By now, it will be apparent that even destroying the main pedo boards left others afloat, and these active sites were still capable of a good deal of mischief. These remaining sites remained active throughout the attacks and continued posting new child porn sites. Some postings were attracting an impressive nine or ten thousand hits on any given day, and announcements about the revival or relocation of one of the hacked boards received twenty thousand or more. Some subculture members revived their own long-dormant boards in order to help meet the demand from patrons now cut loose from the world of the Maestro, and several new boards were now launched, mainly based in Japan. As we have seen with the police campaigns, crackdowns could succeed in scaring away the less committed, but the subculture remained intact. Some members even argued that it had gained from the nightmare, in reinforcing the need for better security, more appropriate to current dangers:

Johnboy > I know that some here have very strong and negative feelings toward the owner of ***'s site. I did have similar feelings when I first went there and saw my nic and proxy IP posted. But now, as time goes by, I realize that this posting was a 'blessing in disguise' more than anything else. It is sites (and events) like ***'s that keep us on our toes and keeps us from having a false sense of security. And that will keep us from our real danger—LEA. I might even go as far as to say ***'s site has done us more *good* than harm . . . we are trying out new ways to make certain that we are as safe as possible (e.g. Spider, looping proxies, modifying Date/Time settings) and we are passing this information along to others . . . I always felt that I had taken the necessary precautions needed in our hobby but I am definitely more secure now than I was just one month ago. I believe that events like ***'s have to happen every 6 months or so to keep us from lulling ourselves into a false sense of security. So, in a weird way, the owner of *** has done more to help our community than he could ever imagine.[30]

Ultimately, surviving participants could afford to be blasé, even seeing this disaster as a transient non-event, an irritant but no more. "Kid-flash" wrote:

> There are quite a few posts from peeps asking many questions about what is going on . . . we are in the midst of a huge anti-pedo assault . . . these people are very much hating us even though they do not understand us . . . they are also very good at what they are doing . . . understand that we are the majority . . . they will never beat us . . . this is a harsh time for collectors and especially for newbies . . . if you look around enough and visit news and take all recommended security you should be ok . . . eventually we will gain control and enjoy the wonders of our hobby . . . in the mean time . . . Relax! . . . it is not the end of pedo-land . . . we will always be here because we are the majority . . . and when you meet a cute little loli tell her how pretty she is . . . you may see her on the Net someday.[31]

Gains and Losses

As in the case of policing, the work of the private anti-porn groups indicates both the potential and the limitations of any future campaigns of suppression. On the positive side, such covert electronic warfare inspires child pornographers with a degree of fear not associated with any criminal justice agency, except during the very best publicized international sweeps. The experience neatly illustrates a familiar part of the theory of deterrence, which is that the likelihood of being detected is far more important than the notional penalty one might face. Though viewing child porn sites might, theoretically, attract massive punishment from the federal government, the odds of detection are felt to be slim, say, one chance in many thousands. In contrast, the odds of encountering a virus or trojan planted by a vigilante are very strong indeed, perhaps 10 or 25 percent, and this high likelihood of damage is clearly enough to make one stop and think. Perhaps a host of trap sites duly mined with devious electronic snares would provide the kind of general deterrence that the Wonderland investigations did not.

Private vigilantes have many advantages over law enforcement, not least in being freer to operate outside the law. How could a targeted pornographer respond to an annihilating cyberattack? Even in the unlikely eventuality that he could identify his electronic assailant, he could scarcely go to the police. We may also see an economic lesson in this story. Well-funded private enterprise can afford to pay for the best technical expertise, which is generally not available to police agencies, at least outside the intelligence community. During the boom in electronic commerce that began in the mid-1990s, it was a frequent complaint that no public agency could afford the best information technology assistance because the most competent people were immediately snapped up by burgeoning, better-funded private companies, and the police are no exception to this rule. Lacking cutting-edge expertise, police efforts against electronic pornography are inevitably concentrated on the relatively easy business of tracking chat-room stalkers. If federal intervention cannot be relied on, then tracking the child porn subculture may well demand the kind of expertise found among private industry specialists and freelance hackers. Such private forces might be the necessary vanguard in any war against child porn.

Having said this, we should note that even such intense cyberwarfare did not win a total victory, and even if the main boards were put out of action, participants were relieved to recall that at least the newsgroups remained intact. Moreover, we have to ask at what cost the private groups achieved their gains. Clandestine measures against pedophile sites are multiply controversial. They clearly violate cybercrime laws in many nations, and it is scant relief to hear that private groups take care to violate no U.S. criminal laws. Other countries, too, have laws that deserve respect, even those with which the United States may not sympathize. Nor is it clear that the use of spiders and trojans might not, in fact, violate U.S. law, since recent legal decisions have tended to view electronic data in terms of physical property, intrusions on which constitute clear trespass. And private wars against pedo boards may make police investigations impossible by destroying evidence.

These campaigns also create worrying precedents. Many observers would accept that child porn is so uniquely horrible that no restraints are necessary in fighting it. But there is no shortage of other movements with their own ideas of absolute right and wrong; so if child porn sites can be destroyed by extra-legal means, what other unpopular targets might new vigilantes set for themselves? Some moralists see adult pornography as an unqualified evil, on a par with child-sex images. Might we see pro-choice and pro-life activists, gay and anti-gay advocates, uprooting each other's Web sites on the grounds that their respective rivals represented an absolute evil equivalent to child porn? Imagine a religious-oriented site campaigning against social tolerance of homosexuality and carrying the testimony of individuals who report being cured of this condition. Some would see such a site as a legitimate expression of religious opinion, while others might describe it as a manifestation of anti-gay hate speech, which deserves to be rooted out by whatever vigilante action is necessary. One person's free speech is another's hate crime. If carried to its predictable conclusion, this kind of private electronic warfare could virtually kill the Net as a medium for discussion and controversy. The age of cybermilitias may be dawning.

The survival of the subculture in the face of such withering assaults is powerful testimony to its resilience and the difficulty of destroying it, even by venturing outside the constraints of law. By far the greatest strength of the child porn underworld is its global character, its ability to escape suppression by any one legal system or nation-state. In coming years, this international dimension may prove the greatest single obstacle to any successful move against the subculture.

EIGHT

A Global Community

Q: If most of the postings are illegal, why is this group still up?
A: The Internet is not subject to any national jurisdiction. Participating (i.e. posting and downloading) is.

—*abpep-t* FAQ

New communication technologies have often been extolled for promoting the unification of humanity and the reduction of international tensions; when radio first developed in the 1920s, the BBC adopted the idealistic motto "And nation shall speak peace unto nation." The Internet has accelerated the process of globalization at a breathtaking pace, but a side effect of this has been to pose wholly novel problems for the enforcement of laws. Effective policing presupposes the existence of some clear jurisdiction. In cyberspace, issues of law and jurisdiction are often very cloudy indeed, and in large measure, the child pornography subculture exists because it is beyond the boundaries of any particular state or legal jurisdiction. Certainly, police agencies have cooperated across borders in order to share information and make arrests: the Wonderland affair demonstrates that. Having said this, the gaps in international policing remain obvious.[1]

Understandably, legislators believe firmly in notions of jurisdiction and national sovereignty, ideas that presuppose the existence of the nation-state in the form in which it has existed since the Renaissance. Now nation-states have never possessed the total imperial authority within their own boundaries that governments and political thinkers have affected to believe. No country could control its domestic affairs in total isolation as long as it engaged in international trade or other transactions, signed treaties, and entered alliances. National independence was massively eroded during the nineteenth century by the rapid growth of technology, media, and, above all, financial structures. Except for the most remote fastnesses utterly cut off from the global community, complete domestic autonomy was as much of a dream as economic autarchy. Perhaps the last truly autonomous nations on the planet ceased to exist when the British invaded Tibet in 1904 and the Italians seized Ethiopia in the 1930s. Still, the coming of the Internet has made the reduction of national sovereignty glaringly obvious by demonstrating the irrelevance of national boundaries and the extreme difficulty of national efforts at regulation, commercial or moral. Attempts to regulate the child porn trade have thus forced a new degree of international cooperation and an unprecedented harmonization of morality legislation and police procedures. The problem in coming years will be in attempting to project any such consensus to the whole globe, for only in this way can the electronic child porn culture be denied a home base.[2]

Global Community

A glimpse at any of the boards will demonstrate the thoroughly globalized nature of the child pornography trade. The whole child porn underworld survives and flourishes by exploiting differences between the legal systems of different countries, between countries that have radically different attitudes toward childhood sexuality. Also crucial are seemingly marginal distinctions over the age of consent and the definition of obscenity. Through the early 1980s, child pornography magazines were still legally and publicly accessible in the Netherlands, posing severe difficulties for police in other European nations, who fought hard against importation. Though hard-core child porn had largely moved underground by the 1990s, several countries retained relatively relaxed attitudes about child sexuality, which affected their views of what could legitimately be portrayed on the Web. While U.S. law strictly prohibits all depictions of nude or suggestively clad children, European countries tend to be more liberal about showing simple nudity in a non-sexual context, as in a nudist camp. Naturist magazines such as the German *Jung und Frei* and the French *Jeune et Naturel* circulated freely in Europe through the late 1990s. At least until recently, there was no reason why a Swedish server could not present a picture of a group of naked ten-year-old girls on a beach playing volleyball, though this picture would be strictly contraband when it was received on American soil. Nor did most European countries share the American horror of the art photographs of naked children by David Hamilton and others.[3]

In addition, many of the hard-core images circulated on the Net are the incidental products of "sex tourism." These portray white men having sex with young Asian or Latina girls and are presumably souvenirs taken by tourists visiting third world countries during the 1980s and 1990s: Thailand, Sri Lanka, and Indonesia are the main Asian venues, while the Latin American pictures could be from any of a dozen countries. These pictures are distinguished from others of the genre by the fact that the men in question rarely attempt to conceal their faces, presumably secure in the knowledge that they were committing no crime under local laws. As we will see, the legal environment has since changed to make such neglect of security precautions very risky indeed.[4]

The boards are enviably cosmopolitan. While the major sites are based in Japan, most users are from North America and Europe, and the main working languages are English and German. Specific debates may proceed in a variety of other languages, including Spanish, Swedish, Dutch, Portuguese, and, indeed, most of the European languages. There are exchanges in tongues such as Turkish, Tagalog, and Guarani, as well as other languages that I cannot identify, though I can at least recognize all the European languages. In a typical board exchange, two participants may be based in the United States, two in Europe, one in Malaysia, and one in Japan; there is no way for the casual observer to discover this. Indications might be provided by linguistic peculiarities, for example, the use of English or Australian spelling or slang such as "I'm off to the pub for a pint," "colour" for "color," or "knickers" for girls' underwear, while complainers are "whingers." Equally likely, participants in a quite different nation might be affecting these habits in order to divert attention from their real location, just as the often dreadful spelling and grammar found in messages may be a ruse to feign ignorance of English.

Deception of this kind is rampant on the boards. When listing survival tips for subculture members, one board participant included the advice "Write in English in this board and never in your own mother language, if you have one. Don't speak about very personal things, which could help to identify you after collecting some more informations."[5] The phrasing of the second sentence ("more informations") implies that the poster, "Thor," is not a native speaker, but he might well be an American or Canadian pretending to employ foreign usage. In another instance, "Rocky" quoted a story from a Detroit newspaper and concluded, "Is any one heard of this news and which country this *Detroit* belong to?" I have no idea if this is genuine ignorance or ingenious camouflage. "Darkstar" remarks, "Don't forget the wise ones who have been here for years know all this, and be telling you they live in the UK or Belize, Canada, whilst they really in Cali[fornia]."[6]

Similar caution is advised for those making pornographic images, since actual locations might well be revealed by incidental objects in the background. In one celebrated case, the maker of the Marion series was detected because the setting was recognized as being in Germany, leading federal police in that nation to circulate Marion's photograph. Responding to this arrest, one board member wrote, "This case is a good example what not to do when posting. Many people look alike on a world wide basis, however when you show locations and identifiable clothing to verify identity you are asking for trouble."[7] It would not be beyond the capacity of a pornographer to litter a room with magazines in some foreign language in order to conceal the fact that the shoot was actually occurring in, say, Illinois. The need for such cosmopolitanism is constantly emphasized. When asked for the best means of securing a truly anonymous e-mail account, "Helper" wrote, "*Do not* use sites like Hotmail. . . . Best to go to some boolah-boolah country in Africa or Asia, or sites in the '.nu' neighborhood [Nauru]. Never your own country, as this only makes legal issues easier for LEA's."[8] Darkstar advised, "Just use good proxies, make sure they have nym status, and operate out of territories like Tibet, China, Taiwan, Russia, Singapore, Mongolia etc. And alter the time domain in your computer, this is an ID parameter in conjunction with your isp IP that ties you down."[9]

In addition, the description I gave earlier of the typical posting of a porn Web site indicates a total neglect of frontiers. The site is posted by an American on a European server, announced on a Japanese server, with passwords posted at a site notionally based in Nauru or Tonga, while those downloading the pictures might be from fifty countries. One would need a thorough education in international law to understand the problems in legal jurisdiction this poses: what crimes have been committed, where, and what agencies might conceivably be involved? And where exactly has this occurred, except in the emerging nation of Cyberia? Though the whole transaction originates on one computer in California, the complete story has literally unfolded across the globe.

Global Policing

There is evidence of growing harmonization of policing efforts worldwide, mainly in response to public outcry about crimes against children. During the 1960s and 1970s, most Western nations did not regard sexual crimes against the young as a high priority for law enforcement, partly because the general atmosphere of sexual liberalism promoted a much greater tolerance of most forms of sexual deviance. Moreover, expert opinion commonly held that sexual abuse or molestation was not a very widespread crime, and that offenders were inadequate individuals in need of psychiatric help, rather than violent predators. This relaxed image was also reflected in popular culture treatments such as the 1971 film *Straw Dogs*, in which a likable, mentally defective molester named Henry is morally superior to the mob of thugs who denounce and persecute him. Any suggestions of organized conspiratorial activity by someone like Henry would have seemed ludicrous, and images of "sex fiends" or "pedophile rings" would have been condemned as sensationalistic nonsense. In such an environment, it would have been absurd to develop sophisticated international policing techniques to hunt down mere molesters.[10]

Matters changed with the rapid growth of concern about child sexual abuse, and from 1985 onward, a generalized American panic over sexual threats to children disseminated throughout Western Europe. There developed a growing international consensus about the need to protect children, a movement that was intensified during the 1990s by repeated scandals involving sex rings and serial child murders in several West European nations. One of the most damaging was the British case of the "London pedophile ring," a group of several men reputedly involved in multiple child murders. The case made major headlines in the early 1990s and again at the end of the decade, when offenders were persecuted and, in some cases, attacked or killed upon release from prison. Another notorious British case involved Robert Black, arrested in 1990, who was implicated in the murder of three small girls and proved to be a violent pedophile with a predilection for child pornography. Cases such as these radically changed the image of the pedophile from a pathetic inadequate to a violent rapist and even a killer, who demanded stringent policy responses.[11]

This pernicious image was strongly reinforced during 1996 and 1997 by the case of Marc Dutroux of Charleroi, Belgium, who kidnapped a series of young girls. Victims were sexually abused, murdered, and secretly buried. Some of the victims were held for weeks or months in a cell built into the basement of his house, and the sexual crimes were videotaped. He may also have been selling children internationally as sexual slaves. Dutroux had a number of accomplices, some of whom were reputedly highly placed, making this a "pedophile ring" reminiscent of the recent British charges. Several hundred thousand citizens demonstrated in the streets of Brussels, demanding action against pedophiles and justice for their victims, in what became a traumatic national crisis.

Not only did sex murders of children seem alarmingly commonplace, but there were suggestions of linkages across borders, again indicating the thorough inadequacy of existing police responses to the crisis. The

Dutroux case indeed involved an international ring, with participants in Germany and the Netherlands. Other such rings have continued to surface in subsequent years. In 2000, for instance, a pedophile ring in the Baltic nation of Latvia was alleged to include the prime minister, the minister of justice, and other leading politicians: the group was reportedly active in child pornography and selling children as sex slaves overseas. Such affairs gave credence to conspiracy theories like those expounded on the board by Darkstar, who proclaimed that "there is a vast underworld of pedo rings and secret societies in Europe."[12] Police in various countries also explored the idea that itinerant criminals might have killed child victims in multiple countries. Robert Black had traveled widely across Europe in pursuit of child pornography, and there was speculation that violent offenses might have occurred on these trips.

As a result, various nations adopted quite draconian laws against "pedophiles" and ventured boldly into innovative forms of international law. One primary area of concern was that of sex tourism, which, as we have already seen, is a productive source of child porn images. The matter was legally complex because the men in question were not generally committing crimes against local laws, and it is difficult to prosecute individuals for crimes committed on foreign soil. During the crisis atmosphere of the mid-1990s, however, several nations took steps to suppress sex tourism. Norway, Sweden, and Finland were the first to use the principle of extra-territoriality for these purposes, permitting criminal charges to be brought for acts not committed on the soil of the nation in question. Between 1993 and 1996, these policies were imitated by Germany, France, Australia, and Belgium. Britain established an innovative system to punish its citizens who engaged in this activity, allowing courts to prosecute those who organize trips abroad for child abusers. Given the immense difficulty of detecting or prosecuting the crimes, the measure was largely symbolic, but it again suggests the urgent political need to be seen to be striking at pedophiles. The British proposal was announced at what was titled the "First World Congress Against the Commercial Sexual Exploitation of Children" meeting in Sweden.[13] The proliferation of such gatherings, no less than the intense legislative activity, could not fail to give the impression that sex offenders were an authentic international peril of immense scope and seriousness, deserving dramatic revisions of existing legal principles. Holding the conference in Sweden sent a powerful symbolic message that standards had changed in tolerant Scandinavia, no less than in other nations.

An international desire to curb child exploitation overseas led to new legal devices in Europe itself, including countries that had once been regarded as libertarian havens. In Sweden today, the minimum age for appearing in sex videos is eighteen, as in the United States, and it is no longer possible to possess nudist photos or old nudist magazines dealing with girls or boys under that age. The Netherlands has established a telephone hotline and a Web site permitting people to complain about Internet child porn sites. Complaints are relayed to the provider, which is required to withdraw the sites in order to forestall police intervention. At the same time, the German government attempted to make ISPs liable for content they knew to be illegal. Working on this principle, the government tried to force the Compuserve corporation to bar its four million users from accessing two hundred newsgroups with sexual content: crucially, this meant many of the *alt.binaries.pictures.erotica* group. A senior Compuserve official was then charged criminally, not for any personal involvement in child pornography but for failing to ensure that his company suppressed such traffic. (The conviction was subsequently overturned.) All in all, attitudes toward child porn have been transformed across Europe. When a naive inquirer posted a message asking, "Where can I buy those materials without any penalty, tell me a country in Europe where I can get it?" the answer was straightforward: "Without any penalty? Try Atlantis."[14]

Major police offensives ensued against users and producers of child porn. In 1997, French police arrested several hundred individuals for purchasing or possessing child pornography, actions that led to a number of suicides. The event was a direct response to the recent publicity over a series of sex murders and suggests the power of the perceived linkage between child pornography and actual violence against children.[15] The international panic over sex offenders and child pornography provided the justification for remarkable, and alarming, new types of law enforcement technology, such as the GTAC surveillance system introduced by Britain's MI5. Meanwhile, the European Union funded an ambitious police coordination project known by the acronym COPINE ("Combating Paedophile Information Networks in Europe"; the word is also French for "girlfriend").[16]

There were several cases of international cooperation in addition to the Wonderland affair, which so impressively illustrated the ability of police in a dozen nations to coordinate simultaneous raids. As early as 1993, U.S. federal agents investigated Americans using Danish BBS's to traffic in child porn. In Great Britain, a 1995 police operation codenamed "Starburst" led to fifteen arrests for child pornography trafficking in Britain and produced over thirty other suspects abroad. Arrests followed in Hong Kong, Germany, Singapore, South Africa, Canada, and the United States, and one German suspect provided information on another forty suspects across the globe. One of those arrested was a British Catholic priest, who owned what has been described as "the largest known collection of illegal matter yet gathered electronically," at least in the United Kingdom.

Direct U.S. intervention led to the exposure of another British "ring." U.S. Customs contacted the West Midlands police:

> Vice Squad officers then swooped on the Department of Metallurgy at Birmingham University and discovered thousands of pictures stored in the computer system of youngsters engaged in obscene acts. The material could be accessed through the Internet across the world. **** had built up an extensive library of explicit pornography called The Archive, featuring children as young as three, on a computer at Birmingham University where he worked.[17]

The scale of international cooperation is suggested by the multinational nature of some recent prosecutions. In a recent U.S. prosecution of Web masters for distributing child porn, the accused included two American residents, two Indonesians, and a Russian.[18]

One of the most far-reaching international investigations occurred in

1998, after a German national was found murdered in the Dutch city of Haarlem. Police searching his apartment found computer materials and disks featuring extensive images of children. This led to the exposure of a widespread international pornography ring operating from the town of Zandvoort; the group used small children and toddlers as subjects. I quote from a newspaper report: "The police said they had also found voluminous records of what appear to be clients and suppliers from countries including Israel, Ukraine, Britain, Russia and the United States. They said they believed that some of the photographed children were from Eastern Europe, while some of the short films were made on the Portuguese island of Madeira." The affair was critical in raising public awareness of child pornography and pedophile rings in Europe. If even the Netherlands was cracking down in this area, then international attitudes were changing rapidly.[19]

Limits of Repression

Yet, in Europe as in the United States, it is far too early to declare any kind of victory. Despite recent examples of international cooperation, the vast majority of child porn investigations globally are reactive and arise from chance discoveries, just as in the United States. The Zandvoort case just mentioned began with a highly fortuitous event, namely, a murder. The case was also wildly atypical in featuring a centralized network with address books for private circulation. The vast majority of Net porn is just made freely available for anyone who wishes to take it, with the poster knowing nothing of the identity of his recipients.

Some added complications also prevail in the international environment, since different countries place a very different weight on various types of crime, and moral offenses evoke the least solidarity. Even after the crackdowns of the mid-1990s, it is far from certain that child porn materials were thoroughly cleaned up in the more liberal European countries. It is an open secret that much distribution and trading continues on the Internet, with users employing the English language to disguise their real locations. In 2000, "Holland" asked, in Dutch, "I've been active on the Maestro's board for a while now and wonder if there are any Dutch people here." G-Man replied that, "There are a number of Dutch people here. They don't speak a lot of Dutch as the primary language of this board is English."[20] "Holland" then commented that despite recent cleanups, "there are much lolvids in Holland," referring to sex videos dealing with lolitas, or underage girls.

Although laws have been passed, police are not necessarily enthusiastic about enforcing them or adopting the crusading attitudes that prevail in the United States. There is still resentment that the new prohibitions of child pornography, and particularly of mildly erotic artwork involving children, were imposed under heavy pressure from the "Anglo-Saxon" nations, the United States and Britain. One of the thorniest areas is the hard-line American principle prohibiting simple possession of child porn, which challenges many traditional notions of privacy. The judiciaries of several countries have expressed serious concern about this theory. In 1999, a British Columbia case resulted in a court decision that mere possession was not illegal, invalidating much existing law on the subject, at least in one Canadian province.[21] In 2000, one of Italy's highest criminal courts agreed that some space must be left for private behavior when it decided that taking nude pictures of minors did not of itself constitute child pornography, unless a financial motive was present.[22] Such decisions raise questions about just how long the panic-induced attitudes of the mid-1990s will prevail.

Nor have many countries imitated the stern U.S. policy symbolized by the *Knox* decision, which prohibited erotic pictures of even clothed child subjects. Europeans are freer to possess or post suggestive images of girls in underwear or swimsuits, raising the possibility of conflicts with U.S. regulatory authorities. A photograph of a thirteen-year-old girl wearing only panties is certainly illegal in the United States but probably not in most European countries, as long as no overt sexual overtones are present. If such a picture is posted on a newsgroup (and all newsgroups are, of their nature, international), viewing or saving the image is illegal only for some consumers.

Furthermore, European police forces often have a schizophrenic attitude toward agencies like the FBI, which is envied for its resources and professionalism yet resented for its shameless dabbling in the affairs of other countries. Certainly, the main prosecutions in nations such as Britain have grown directly out of U.S. intervention:

> **G-MAN** > Dutch police is active on the net in a small group. The real risk is US agencies reporting you to local authorities. Most arrests in the Netherlands are made due to mistakes from the arrestees and involve mostly non-Internet related issues.[23]

For the pornographers who are the targets of these operations, anti-Americanism is a predictable response:

> * **Grrrrr** > money rules all. this is why American laws are replacing local laws in all other countries. 'we'll make you rich like us if you ban children's sexuality and green smokable plants while belching more filth into the atmosphere.'[24]

Yet fairly similar views are occasionally heard from European politicians and law enforcement bureaucrats. American heavy-handedness means that international investigations can involve somewhat reluctant alliances.

Beyond the Law

Moreover, outside Western Europe, large areas of the world make virtually no pretense at combating underage sex or child pornography, and from the nature of the Web, there need be only one bandit country to sabotage all international arrangements. In fact, there are dozens of such wayward states, which pay little attention to suppressing child pornography or, much more serious, child prostitution. Former Communist countries tend to be lax in this regard, and much material prohibited elsewhere stems quite freely from Russia, Poland, and the Czech Republic. This trend reflects the extreme weakness of law enforcement in those societies, as well as a common desire to break away from Communist austerity.

The influx of Russian and East European content has revolutionized the child porn world. Nudist sites are prevalent, while many pictures emanating from Russia are unashamedly pornographic and often extremely hard core.[25] They are immensely popular because they depict subjects in contemporary settings and thus form a dramatic contrast to much of the older material, which largely depicted either contemporary Asian girls or Euro-American children in conspicuously dated 1970s settings. Also, and crucially for many fans, the subjects are white: a distaste or even loathing for non-white subjects is a recurrent theme in exchanges. Some astute fraudsters exploit the Russian reputation for corruption by advertising child porn sites with Russian domain names, that is, the suffix *ru*. Foreigners avidly flock to such sites believing they will thereby gain access to utterly uncensored materials, but they are often disappointed, and some *.ru* sites are among the most notorious examples of bogus and deceptive advertising. They offer tantalizing samples, take money, but deliver nothing: in short, they serve spam supreme. In passing, it is one of the great ironies of modern history that the hammer-and-sickle emblem now often serves as a symbol of extreme hedonism and provides a logo for the hardest of hard-core Web sites. Czech sites are also popular. As an enthusiastic board participant wrote in 2000, "Czech Republic liberal! You can search, view and store pedo material without any penalty. For trading is maximum penalty one year." This country is a major source of images of nude young boys, though as in Scandinavia, depicting sexual activity in such contexts is strictly taboo.[26]

The child porn boards offer much advice on how to find countries where underage sex is readily available and where child pornography can easily be obtained or manufactured. The lax morality prevailing in former Communist nations is a common theme:

> * RaNDoM > If you guys are tired of the US why don't you move out.
> . . . I've lived here in Siberia for the past year now and it's absolute Loli-Heaven! You can't go wrong with the former Soviet Union. Or if it's a little out of your budget then consider Mexico. For a few dollars (not pesos) the cops'll look the other way. It's where I used to live.[27]

* **Cross** > I hear Russia is becoming the epicenter of Loliland. Such information in general should help everybody in matters such as proxies, setting up sites, and many more.[28]

* **Greasey** > in Russia be prepared to get mugged and maybe even killed. Russia has no law now, the Russian mafia runs the whole country.
* **TEST_ONE** > if you have enough money, people at the [Moscow] Crime Dept. will drive you to the girls.[29]

In answer to a question about one photo series, G-Man replied:

Looks Rumanian to me. . . . In some places there you can just go to an orphanage and give the adults some money (not a lot—many have not been paid their wages in years!) and you can have your way with some of the kids. . . . The only thing is—the children have never even seen a bath and the beds have never been cleaned. They also shave the heads of the kids, so you'll have to do a bald girl.[30]

After a decade of extreme laissez-faire, some East European countries may finally be undergoing a moral reaction. Czech laissez-faire seems to be weakening as the country becomes ever more closely integrated into the European economic and political order, and there have been major crackdowns in recent months. One recent case involved the arrest and jailing of American and West European visitors who seemed to regard the country as a promising venue for pederastic sex tourism. This affair made international headlines because one of those arrested was Chris Denning, once a popular BBC disc-jockey and music promoter and a famous figure from London's swinging sixties. Poland, too, has recently passed stringent anti-porn legislation, which, if enforced, would suppress most adult soft-core material, but it remains to be seen how far such action would extend to the Internet.[31] Nor is there much likelihood that countries such as Russia and Rumania will return to anything like Stalinist moral discipline in the foreseeable future or succeed in regulating their thriving organized-crime enterprises.

Japan

Having described various nations with notoriously weak law enforcement systems, and weak law enforcement, it can be startling to note that one massive obstacle facing anti-pornography campaigners internationally remains Japan. Unlike countries such as Russia, Japan has an extremely effective and sophisticated law enforcement system and perhaps the most sophisticated electronic technology on the planet. There were 14 million Japanese Net users by 1998, and by 2001, Japan had become the world's largest user of the Internet. Nevertheless, Japan also has very different standards about what constitutes obscenity in the case of children, and the country has a very lively subculture of adult men fascinated by sexy schoolgirls.[32]

Much has been written of the whole *kogal* culture, the Japanese world of, literally, "little girls," often high school girls of fourteen or so, who can make large sums by responding to the sexual whims of grown-ups. Though some actual prostitution enters into this subculture, most of the behavior for sale is milder, including phone sex and soft-core photographs, while used underwear sells at a hefty premium. Also, much Japanese sexual material features adult women posing as schoolgirls or young teenagers. If not exactly respectable, *kogal* culture is not condemned anything like as harshly as manifestations of pedophilia would be elsewhere, and in consequence, Japanese law on visual imagery is relaxed, astonishingly so to Western eyes. Provided genitalia are not actually shown, naked children of more or less any age can be depicted, and often the concealment of the genitals can be very scanty indeed: a blade of grass concealing the vulval cleft will suffice. Nor must there be the slightest hint of sexual activity or interest by the subjects.

Because of the tolerance of *kogal*, soft-core magazines have circulated for years, generally presenting girls alone in dreamy bucolic settings. The contents of these glitzy magazines have been scanned into computers in vast numbers, with the result that Asian nude photos constitute filler on many Western sites, where the enormous volume of "Asian loli" is a recurrent complaint. Japanese animation, *anime* and *manga*, also has a wide Western following. In the child porn world, erotic cartoons and comics known as *hentai* are particularly popular. These might involve schoolgirls in explicit or sadomasochistic settings (including rape scenarios) that would not be tolerated if live models were involved.

Japan's militant reluctance to accept international orthodoxies concerning child porn was long a source of major grievance to the United States and other Western nations, and not until 1999 did Japan pass a new child porn law, in response to massive international pressure. Yet the effects of this change are uncertain. Western anti-porn campaigners often exaggerate the central role of Japan in the child porn trade and consequently overestimate the likelihood that policy changes there might have a major global impact. In the debates surrounding the 1999 law, Interpol suggested that "between 70 percent and 80 percent of the child pornography available on the Internet came from Japanese sources."[33] This statement is so misleading, however, as to raise doubts about the reliability of any other comments on this subject derived from that organization. Japan was indeed the source for soft-core magazines but not for the vast majority of images advertised on the pedo boards, which regularly scorn images of Japanese or other Asian children as pedestrian or boring; while Japan has always penalized hard-core materials as strictly as any other nation. Japan's real importance lies not in its production of images but in its tolerance of the pedo boards themselves, which advertise illicit materials posted on temporary and transient pages on otherwise innocuous servers. These have remained untouched by recent legislation.

The Third World

Despite the attention paid to the former Communist world and Japan, most "bandit" countries are found in the third world nations of Asia and Latin America, where Westerners can readily find underage sex as well as visual depictions of such activity. In coming years, these nations may also host the electronic servers central to the child porn world.

In 1999, one correspondent asked the Maestro community, "Generally speaking—Where do you think the best place to travel to? Does anyone want to come along?"[34] He received numerous replies, most highlighting the third world:

* **FRED THE BED** > I definitely think Brazil is best for lolo!!!!!
* **Ms Knickerworthy** > Israel is a good place for pristine preteen arse. . . . If you're not fussy about skin colour or AIDS then try Fiji, Bali, Jamaica, and similar Third World holes.
* **jo** > Contrary to popular belief the Philippines is still one of the best places to go but you have to be very cautious. Stay away from the tourist areas. The back streets of Manila are a good place to walk around mid afternoon. People are very friendly, and very poor.
* **Pedro Phylle** > As suggested above, stick with the poorer, undeveloped countries such as Latin America, Balkans or preferably S.E. Asia. In Bangkok, go to a red light district named Patpong. . . . Very lax laws and you don't have to worry about getting mugged or killed. To be really safe, talk to a cabbie and some of them will have a photo album of lovelies. Take your pick and he will deliver to your hotel room.
* **Soldo** > By and large, Northern Europe including Scandinavia is very anti-pedo, Holland seems somewhat more tolerant than its neighbors. Southern Europe is more relaxed and a lot of the old Eastern European states don't have many laws in place—and if they do then don't enforce them because of lack of funds. Thailand seems to enforce laws only for the purpose of satisfying western govts, but if you're the one caught then look out. Most other S.E. Asian and Third World countries have far more pressing needs for their funds than stamping out loli material etc.[35]

Among all the recommendations about third world countries, it is startling to find the following advice:

* **UKPEDO** > just come to the UK, get in touch with some loli lvr through the usual channels, and he can introduce you to some pt [preteen] girls and their moms, or you can use intro agencies, just pick moms with nice girls to date, do your movie and move on. All the main cities have some action, the best is London and Edinburgh, seaside towns for boys, just can't miss out, its kinda pricey over here though, bring plenty dollars, if you rent a flat or house rather than live in some

hotel girls will be no problem just gotta be discreet, yeah loads of pt girls do stuff for dollars, no problem.[36]

We sometimes find detailed and specific advice about how to engage in underage sex. In one posting, "Old Timer" asked:

In a few days . . . I will be crossing a border. . . . A geographical one, and a "the-other-type" one. . . . I'm gonna spend a while in a country where it all happens . . . third world, you all know. . . . Still don't know how to manage about taking pictures, what type of cameras and all that. . . . Please, you're welcome to provide your tips.

Elaborate responses told him precisely what equipment to use and how, and concluded:

Take good and many pictures and it is more easy to play them over by Internet connection maybe a laptop than to take it with, plan, if the customs will do a regular check you will grow old in one second, if any pictures made from you are found, you will stay in prison for years.[37]

The easy availability of child sex in many third world nations means that pornographic images are readily obtained, and continuing levels of poverty in these countries suggest that this problem will not be eliminated for many years.

The Future

Far fewer countries today tolerate child pornography than ten or twenty years ago, and at least in official policy, the advanced industrial world now seems to form a united front against this trafficking. Having said this, the nature of the Internet makes it extraordinarily easy for businesses to relocate to other nations with laxer laws, and it is more or less certain that this will be the course of action taken by child pornographers in the coming years.

Some third world countries in particular are notorious for acquiescing in various enterprises forbidden in the West, which may well foreshadow future developments in child porn. Only in 2000, for instance, did Thailand show any signs of responding to impassioned Western pleas to regulate online sales of prescription drugs to American consumers.[38] This trade does not necessarily indicate that Thailand is a major center of pharmaceutical development, but rather that the country sees little point in suppressing such a traffic based on its soil or in forbidding foreigners from setting up shop there. Local police have neither the facilities nor the incentive to combat enterprises that cause no harm locally and, at worst, harm only rich Westerners halfway across the globe.

A similar insouciance permits fraudsters to establish operations in the most unlikely and obscure nations. One common scam in the adult sex world is to offer consumers free software with which they can access pornographic movies online. The program works well enough, but it also routes the viewer to long-distance connections in one of a number of out-of-the-way nations, including Sao Tome, Chad, Vanuatu, Madagascar, and Guyana, so that the customer faces astronomical telephone bills. Such flag-of-convenience nations might also serve as the notional centers of the electronic child porn world. When the Internet eventually booms in what are currently poor African nations, with their strong traditions of public venality, it is likely that these areas will mark the future homes of the international child porn world. We may also see servers in the global south scrambling to build up their business by accepting traffic that can no longer find a ready home in the traditionally advanced countries. These regions would be important if countries like Japan ever cracked down on the servers and boards that are currently so significant in distributing child porn information. The boards would then reopen elsewhere, in Anguilla or Nauru, Madagascar or Uganda.

This "Southern" scenario is already under discussion on the boards. In one illustrative exchange, "Jazzjackass" raised a critical question:

Does anyone believe 'we' (or this board for that matter) really has a future? As someone stated before, the number of on-topic boards is increasing, but yet the hunt has seriously increased in the last five years.

I say this board and all others won't last another 2-5 years, with the new tracking techniques MI5 is planning etc. Feel like we're being cornered more and more, even some ISP's you can't even trust. And posting can be dangerous too nowadays. Just a thought.

But "Visitor1" was more sanguine: "Remember that there are still developing countries in this world. The time may come when we look for an ISP in one of them. Also, a move towards laptops and mobile phones may be the way forward."[39]

In imagining the future of child porn, it is disturbing to observe the very limited success that regulation has enjoyed to date, even in the more advanced Western countries, which tend to respect each other's legal codes and which respond to political or media pressures from their neighbors. Even so, large sections of the Internet remain little regulated, and it is not difficult for users in one country to find, for instance, extremist propaganda that is notionally banned in their own jurisdiction. Copyright issues are just as poorly enforced. The incredible modern expansion of the Internet in Western nations dates back only a decade or so, and it is reasonable to predict that by 2010 there will be comparable growth across the globe, in states that have even less regard for the wishes of the Western international community. Apart from the corruption factor, many emerging countries are deeply sensitive to suggestions of Western pressure or proposals that their laws and mores should automatically bend to reflect those of the United States or of former colonial nations in Europe. Lacking a global moral consensus, there will always be areas of unevenness, fault-lines in moral enforcement, and the child pornographers are likely to survive in those gaps. It remains to be seen whether their operations will continue on their present massive scale, or whether the enterprise can be pruned back to more acceptable dimensions.

NINE

Where Next?

The makers of our Constitution . . . sought to protect
Americans in their beliefs, their thoughts, their emotions
and their sensations. They conferred, as against the government, the right to be let alone—the most comprehensive of rights and the right most valued by civilized men.
>   —Justice Louis Brandeis, dissenting opinion in
>   *Olmstead v. US* (1928)

It is not possible to make a *lasting* compromise between
technology and freedom, because technology is by far the
more powerful social force and continually encroaches on
freedom through *repeated* compromises. . . . Technology
is a more powerful social force than the aspiration for
freedom.
>   —*Industrial Society and the Future*
>   ("The Unabomber Manifesto")

Child pornography is a substantial presence on the Internet, and its potential audience is likely to grow rapidly as Internet usage expands. Given
this fact, what, if anything, can be done? Is it possible to suggest solutions or responses that would not sabotage many of the positive aspects
of the Internet? In other words, is there a cure that is not worse than the
disease? Trafficking in Internet child porn may be so securely protected
that total eradication could be achieved only by means that could not fail
to damage many innocent users. Deciding which means are too severe or
intrusive to combat this problem produces some troubling ethical de-

bates. Briefly, do civil liberties and privacy rights end when one accesses the Internet? Some citizens may well place such a high value on child protection that they would accede to granting police or government the right to observe all Web traffic, to read all mail at random. Most of us, however, would be appalled by such an idea. So what is the proper balance between given technologies being both effective and tolerable?

This is not a simple transaction, a straightforward equation of "how many rights are you prepared to give up to safeguard children?" Repressive new laws theoretically directed against child porn might well cause injustice and inconvenience without having the slightest impact on that traffic. Recognizing a serious problem is one thing: using it as an excuse to implement dangerously bad laws is quite another. The answer to child porn is not to be found by adding ever more legal weapons to an already bulging police arsenal but rather in the proper deployment of existing powers and technologies.

Eliminating Child Porn?

From the outset, we have to realize what goals are achievable, and the total elimination of electronic child porn simply may not be within the bounds of possibility. That does not mean that we have to learn to accept or live with the problem, and we might well achieve a massive reduction of production and availability, on the lines of what was accomplished in the 1980s. The great majority of child porn users are rational enough to be deterred, if the proper methods are applied. If we could achieve, say, a 90 or 95 percent reduction of availability, that would be a massive victory in its own right. The fact that some residual trade will continue indefinitely should not provide grounds for ever-increasing encroachments on the liberties of law-abiding Netizens.

To illustrate just how intractable the child porn problem is, let us imagine a means by which this material could be removed or destroyed entirely. Purely as a fantasy, let us suggest that the Internet should simply be prohibited, along with private communication over computer networks. Such a desperate solution was briefly discussed in Mike Cane's

Computer Phone Book in the mid-1980s, when he reacted angrily to sysops who "resent having the government come into their domain because of systems for child molesters." Cane argued simply, "If there's a choice between most BBS's existing or protecting innocent children, I'll be the first to throw away my modem. How about you?"[1] Nobody was suggesting such a scheme seriously, and that was long before the Internet came to occupy its present hegemonic position in the U.S. economy. Put bluntly, the vast majority of citizens would not be prepared to throw away their modems in the quest for child protection, even if such a scheme were vaguely conceivable. And if a hypothetical government did prohibit computer networks, it still would not eliminate child porn. Such a ban could be enforced only by computers in the hands of police or security forces, and many precedents indicate that these government employees would surreptitiously be sharing pornographic images. If there are computers, there will be computerized child pornography.

To take a marginally less outrageous solution, consider the experience of China, which, like many authoritarian nations, faces a fundamental paradox in its attitudes toward Internet technology.[2] The Chinese want the massive economic benefits of the Net and also realize the military implications of having a computer-literate populace. The ongoing cold war between the People's Republic of China (PRC) and Taiwan is increasingly fought in the form of hacker attacks on each other's electronic installations. At the same time, the PRC's rulers are nervous about the democratic implications of the Internet, the ability of ordinary citizens to form political or cultural groupings online and to circulate information critical of the state. In response to this dilemma, the Chinese government has ordained that all Internet traffic must pass through two portals, both run by the state. The authorities strictly limit what sites can be accessed and keep detailed records of who is visiting what site. All ISPs and Internet users have to register with authorities. Under present arrangements, "Chinese in the People's Republic can now log onto the China Wide Web and find links with the Chinese version of Yahoo, but without the freedom to connect with sites the government does not wish them to see."[3] Even stricter laws have been proposed: under a recent measure, the use of e-mail to transmit what might be regarded as secret information is expressly forbidden. The regulations also put operators of chat rooms on notice that they will be held liable for their content. And Internet sites are required to submit to "examination and approval by the appropriate secrecy work offices," although the rules do not specify what that process involves. . . . A basic principle of the new regulations is that "whoever puts it on the Internet assumes responsibility."[4]

Anyone using encryption technology is required to notify a government agency of that fact. Other countries with comparably strict laws are Singapore, Saudi Arabia, and Vietnam, and one state has taken the principle of control to its logical extent: "Burma [Myanmar] has taken the strongest measures by outlawing the use of the Internet and making ownership of an unregistered computer with networking capabilities illegal."[5]

With such a model, much child pornography could indeed be kept off the Internet and its aficionados rounded up or terrorized into inactivity. The difficulty is that a Western nation would find such a solution unacceptable from a myriad different perspectives, not least because it would hamstring the whole Internet and introduce controls that most members of a democratic society would regard as utterly intolerable. But would it even work? China has an age-old tradition of technological innovation, while successive generations of Chinese dissidents over long centuries have devised ever more imaginative means of outwitting repressive governments and distributing their own propaganda. Not surprisingly, the latest restrictions do not appear too burdensome in practice. Chinese computer users access forbidden sites by means of proxy servers, of which there are far too many to permit concerted government action against them. Users also make extensive use of Internet cafés rather than private machines, so even if authorities note that an unregulated site has been accessed, the odds of detecting a specific individual are slight. The Chinese experience neatly illustrates the remark of Internet pioneer John Gilmore that "the Internet interprets censorship as damage and routes around it."[6] As Ian Buruma notes after describing a recent harsh crackdown on Internet dissidents, "these are desperate measures which cannot stop thousands of others from surfing in forbidden areas."[7] Once again, too, we face the issue of "who guards the guards?" We may wonder what frivolous, decadent, and obscene Web sites are regularly frequented by the guardians of electronic morality in socialist China.

While a Chinese (or Burmese) solution is inconceivable in the West, it is scarcely less Orwellian than some of the ideas that have been floated, however speculatively. Given the nature of the child porn trade, the only policies that might conceivably attempt eradication would involve wide-ranging surveillance of Web traffic by official agencies. This effort might be carried out in a directed way under the approval of court warrants or randomly through general fishing expeditions undertaken against the sort of people thought likely to offend in this particular way. The British example of GTAC and the extravagant powers granted to MI5 indicate that something like this may not be too far away. Yet, as the Chinese example indicates, even such an intolerable set of burdens probably would not eliminate the underlying problem.

Ending Privacy?

If the traffic cannot altogether be eliminated, the next question is how far it can be detected and combated, with a view to suppressing the bulk of the trade and ending the present easy availability of this material. And how far can this be achieved without destroying the privacy rights of law-abiding Net users? When considering this, it is useful to recall just how far the Net has already eroded privacy, and the resentment that such intrusions have already caused. In reaction to current threats, legislators have come under pressure to enact safeguards from electronic snooping, at exactly the same time that the perceived need to combat cybercrime encourages the same lawmakers to enhance official surveillance powers. The result is a strange and fast-moving struggle of priorities, between what might be the irreconcilable values of individual privacy and public security.[8]

One obvious privacy danger emerges from the linking of databases, permitting agencies or individuals, with or without authorization, to gather an astonishingly rich picture of the intimate lives of ordinary citizens. Personal, financial, and medical records thus become available to virtually anyone with a desire to investigate them. In Canada, for instance, virtually everyone who has ever had contact with an official agency has unwittingly volunteered to become the subject of an exceedingly detailed secret file, the like of which would have been beyond the wildest dreams of most traditional police states:

> A government database . . . contains highly personal information about more than 30 million Canadians. The Longitudinal Labor Force File, maintained by Canada's federal government, contains information on individuals collected from tax returns, child tax benefit payments, welfare files, federal job programs, job training and employment services, employment insurance files and the nation health insurance master file. . . . There are pending proposals to include data from other government programs, including Canada's Student Loan Program, the Canada Pension Plan and the Old Age Security Program.[9]

The obvious response, whether in Canada or elsewhere, is to place severe restrictions on access to such information, confining it to authorized agencies working under court warrants, which (unlike too much current practice) would be granted only in the rarest and most pressing of circumstances. Yet, as we will see, the demand to combat child porn and other cybercrime tends to expand rather than shrink the circumstances under which agencies can gain expedited access to information, often without troubling with the formalities of a judicial hearing.

Apart from official databases, anyone who uses the Internet, anywhere in the world, is likely to be assembling for him/herself a still more thorough dossier, revealing aspects of individual taste and preference, political, economic, literary, musical, and sexual. Some of the methods used are quite well known, such as the cookies sent by a site to the computer that accesses it, which can be recognized by that or other servers. The implications are bothersome, to say the least. To take a simple example cited by journalist Mark Boal, imagine that the cookie evidence records that you visited *Koop.com* for cancer information and then went to the site of your insurance company. Does the linkage send up a red flag that leads the company to cancel your insurance? In a recent Texas lawsuit, a plaintiff protested that cookies violated the state's law against stalking and trespass. Clearly, this practice was not what legislators had in mind when they passed anti-stalking laws, but on reflection, what cookies do may well violate the letter of a law designed to protect individual privacy against persistent snooping.[10]

Scandals have recently erupted over the techniques of certain companies to gather market data—or, as we might rephrase it, to engage in unauthorized snooping. One instance involved the company RealJukebox, a music server with some 30 million users, which reported to its parent company about the music downloaded by each user, who was matched with a unique identifying number signifying the person's real-world identity. In a similar affair, the online advertising company DoubleClick was attacked for a scheme to connect personal information to surfing data collected from consumers on the Internet. Perhaps the most terrifying prospect in the new networked world is the growth of so-called GUIDs, globally unique identifiers, which link to every document a person creates, every message one e-mails, every chat posted.[11]

News stories such as these have understandably caused public alarm, all the more so as millions more consumers begin regarding the Internet as an everyday part of life. Successive inquiries indicate that private corporations have largely failed to exercise any significant degree of self-regulation, leading official agencies like the Federal Trade Commission to demand much tougher legal safeguards. Moreover, as e-mail use grew exponentially from the mid-1990s onward, it became apparent that the privacy of such communications was severely limited, and there were demands for protection. By 2000, the privacy issue was emerging as a powerful political theme, which legislators neglected at their peril: to quote one Republican Party pollster, "It tests off the charts!" A broad political consensus now calls for tight constraints on the ability of either public agencies or private corporations to track individuals without explicit judicial permission. Until official protections become available, demand grows for technologies that individuals can use to safeguard their privacy, which might mean encryption or means of evading corporate surveillance.[12]

Yet one clear political trend seems to be flatly contradicted by another, namely, the urge to combat cybercrime, a collection of concerns among which child pornography is prominently represented. As judges and legislators seek to defeat child porn, they are often enhancing the very threats to privacy and individual rights that, rhetorically, they are pledged to curb. In the process, tactics that might legitimately be applied against child pornographers (or spies, druglords, or terrorists) come to be applied to the vast majority of ordinary, law-abiding citizens. To put this in context, the attempt to suppress the misdeeds of (at a maximum) a hundred thousand people in the child porn subculture becomes the means of destroying the liberties of several hundred million others. This is a classic illustration of the adage that "hard cases make bad law."[13]

As an ultimate evil, child porn has already justified various enhancements of law enforcement powers. Nations such as Britain historically have had a low regard for individual rights in the face of police powers, but disturbing legal precedents have also arisen in the United States. For example, most American states have laws against wiretapping, strictly regulating the circumstances in which authorities can gain access to private communications; but do such laws apply to accessing e-mail? This question often arises in cases involving threats to the young, and the need to protect the innocent encourages courts to find for the authorities. In a recent Pennsylvania cyberstalking prosecution, a judge determined that the state's wiretap law did not apply to the Internet. One wonders if judicial logic might have operated differently had the case at issue been less emotive, if sexual threats to children were not involved.[14] A similar dynamic can be observed at the federal level. Armed with powers granted by the federal Sexual Predator Act of 1998, the FBI hopes to gain quicker access to online pornographers and pedophiles by subpoenaing online accounts directly, without court orders or grand-jury subpoenas.

Repeatedly, we find child porn and other sensational crimes used to justify expanding police powers over the electronic world, though it is difficult to see just what effect these measures have had, or could have, on the subculture itself. Encryption is an obvious example. Over the last decade, police agencies have expressed alarm at the spread of technologies that permit private citizens to send messages impervious to decoding by any outside party. The virtues of such encryption are obvious, as are the countless lawful circumstances in which people might wish to avoid prying eyes. A convincing case can also be made that the source code involved in encryption represents a form of constitutionally protected speech, in that it conveys a meaningful message much as musical notation does.[15] Yet the spread of effective encryption has been delayed by the protests of law enforcement, particularly the FBI, who cite the dangers from terrorism, espionage, and child pornography. In 1997, FBI director Louis Freeh told a Senate investigative hearing:

> Law enforcement is already encountering the harmful effects of non-recoverable encryption in many important investigations today. For example: convicted spy, Aldrich Ames, was told by the Russian Intelligence Service to encrypt computer file information that was to be passed to them; an international terrorist was plotting to blow up eleven U.S.-owned commercial airliners in the far east. His laptop computer which was seized during his arrest in Manila contained encrypted files concerning this terrorist plot; a subject in a child pornography case used encryption in transmitting obscene and pornographic images of children over the Internet; a major international drug trafficking subject recently used a telephone encryption device to frustrate court-approved electronic surveillance.[16]

Freeh's list of menaces is a remarkable juxtaposition, since it implies that kiddie porn is a threat to national security comparable to the more obvious dangers of subversion and armed violence.

In consequence, the United States has fought a long war to prevent the spread of various encryption programs, to the extent that posting them on the Internet has prompted charges of exporting sensitive military technology. In 1993, the FBI and other federal agencies were demanding that so-called clipper chips be installed in all computers and other forms of electronic communication, in order to give federal agencies the capacity to exercise surveillance. In effect, this would have required all users of encryption to hand over the keys to the government, and the proposal was withdrawn after widespread protests. Nevertheless, similar efforts ensued over the next few years, notably in attempts to dumb down telecommunications technology in order to permit wiretapping or to create "surveillance-friendly" e-mail systems. Since police agencies rarely possess the best or most advanced electronic technology, such proposals perforce open private communications to surveillance by many other unauthorized groups and individuals. The FBI has recently been clamoring for a proposed Cyberspace Electronic Security Act to give police access to codes to unscramble encrypted communications.[17]

Law enforcement has similarly fought against other techniques intended to avoid electronic surveillance, whether by government or marketers. One example of such a technique is the "Freedom" technology, which is designed to evade cookies by providing users with various fake identities, or "nyms": "Activate a nym before browsing, and cookies will be contained in that nym's own Cookie Jar. Even the smartest cookie can only reference the browsing history of the nym itself. . . . The specter of these foolproof fake IDs is precisely what interests our three-letter spy agencies. If such software were widely used, the Internet would change from a place where everybody leaves a data trail to one where newbies, pedophiles, and terrorists are equally cloaked."[18] The development of "Freedom" has been possible only because the company involved is based in Canada. It is a telling commentary on the effects of police-inspired restrictions that much of the recent development of encryption has had to take place off American soil. Equally troubling is the underlying message that individuals should not be able to shield themselves against corporate exploitation because they would be using a technology that might, conceivably, be used by criminals.

As a rhetorical tactic, the argument made by the FBI and other "spy agencies" is superb, as it suggests that those who oppose restrictions on encryption must be, innocently or otherwise, favoring the interests of spies, terrorists, and child porn merchants. On closer examination, though, the arguments made by law enforcement have obvious flaws. Just to take the area of child porn, has there ever been a single investigation or prosecution that was stymied by lack of adequate legal powers or thwarted by encryption? When? Where? I have never heard of one and feel sure that the FBI would have trumpeted any such instance as part of its war against effective public access to encryption. Just to cite Freeh's example, if the images sent by the suspect could not be decrypted, how does the FBI know they constituted child porn? Did the agency decipher them in the end? Or, more likely, did they have so much other evidence to justify prosecution in this case that it mattered not a whit that a few suspect images remained unavailable?

Apart from their intrinsic dangers, enhanced police powers are largely irrelevant to the fundamental child porn problem. As we have seen repeatedly, the failure to suppress child porn has not resulted from a shortage of such powers, nor from a shortage of adequate technology, since even with existing resources, significant victories have been achieved. There have been mass raids and arrests, some of which have broken up major child porn rings, and operations have demonstrated an impressive degree of international coordination. As one pedo board participant writes, with not too much exaggeration:

> I think the US-Gov would do anything to get us. . . . LEA has strict rules there, but when US-gov considers us the enemy, bending and breaking the rules may be an everyday thing. . . . The US has laws that loop and bend-over-backwards, all in the name of justice . . . you'd be surprised at what they would do to get anyone, anywhere, without creating too much attention.[19]

Over the last two years, server administrators, too, have cooperated much more closely with authorities to prevent the proliferation of temporary CP Web sites, and some once-preferred sites such as *angelfire* and *sexhound* are now off limits. Presumably, other servers will react more quickly if they find themselves being used by child porn merchants. Once they are aware of the danger, improving technology should make it much easier and quicker for search robots to identify and remove child porn postings. Many ISPs have shown themselves willing to report and suppress any child porn activity that comes to their attention. Most telling, hackers and private enterprise anti-pedophile groups have emerged as a serious challenge to the subculture, in a way that may well shift the balance in the ongoing struggle to the side of the authorities. No number of new laws or new police powers, no new restrictions on encryption, would fundamentally change this situation.

Enforcing the Law?

The biggest single problem facing police is simply recognizing and understanding the nature of the child porn world on the Net. Despite all the enforcement efforts of recent years, it is still remarkably easy for any reasonably discreet person to pursue this highly illegal conduct indefinitely, as long as obvious traps are avoided. This does not mean that police have been lackadaisical or incompetent, still less that their hands have been tied by legislators. Hitherto, law enforcement agencies and their political masters have just had a very poor idea of the organization and mechanisms of the child porn subculture, and above all, of its critical institutions such as the newsgroups and bulletin boards. To take a glaring example, given the public loathing of child porn and the support that could be mobilized against it, it is incredible that virtually nobody outside the subculture itself has ever heard of *abpep-t*: the name barely appears in searches of media databases.

In observing this neglect, we might make the analogy to illegal drugs, in which there is both a supply side (manufacturers and importers) and a demand side (street-level users). Current efforts against child porn parallel what would happen if anti-drug policing were solely confined to arresting users and addicts, ignoring organized rings and suppliers. In this fantasy world, no attention would be given to tracing the origin of supplies of cocaine, and the assumption would be that the substance "just grew" or perhaps appeared naturally in neighborhood gardens. Police would remain blissfully unaware of potent names such as Colombia.

Such an approach might result in numerous arrests and convictions, but it could never make a dent in illicit drug supplies; nor does a pure demand-side approach work for child porn. This needs to be emphasized because the occasional attempts to outline anti-child porn strategies concentrate entirely on intimidating ordinary users. In 1995, for instance, Barry Crimmins told a congressional hearing on child porn: "People need to see their neighbors (who have participated in these criminal acts) taken away, jailed, and stigmatized as 'perverts.' If this is done in a public, no-nonsense manner, it should seriously reverse the crisis that is destroying countless innocent children." Filling the prisons with child porn users is likely to be as ineffective as the zero-tolerance drug strategy that has incarcerated hundreds of thousands of small-time consumers, combining minimal deterrence with maximum social devastation.

If there is to be major progress against the core of the subculture, as opposed to its fringes, it has to focus on organizational aspects, which means suppressing the newsgroups, above all *abpep-t*, as well as the bulletin boards. The results of such a prohibition or disruption of groups and boards would be sweeping. Hard-core users would still produce and circulate materials, but these would only with the greatest difficulty become available to a mass audience, as they do regularly at present. It would also be much more difficult for casual or curious visitors to be drawn into the subculture. Child porn activity would thus be driven deep into the shadows, perhaps into a new range of elite, closed networks. Though it will never be eliminated, the problem will be reduced to trivial proportions.

Such an approach would require action at a political level, rather than a simple law enforcement response. In the case of the boards, one key issue is that these are doing nothing contrary to the laws of any major country, since they are only providing the facility for individuals to post information such as URLs. But even though their activities are not illegal, they are so intimately bound up with criminal activity that the nations and ISPs that tolerate the pedo boards might be induced to regulate them by international demand. Though it took a very long effort, this was how Japan was eventually persuaded to pass a more effective child pornography law in 1999. As we have seen, the likelihood is that the boards would then move to other nations less susceptible to Western pressure, but we might have to face the reality that suppression will be a long, drawn-out process, which might need to be dealt with country by country.

Newsgroups such as *abpep-t* are a still thornier issue, since they exist only on the Net and have no fixed home. Still, groups are harmful only as long as they can be accessed, and the problem for political leaders, far more than for law enforcement, is to exercise pressure on nations and corporations to prevent servers from carrying these groups. Again, this is not an easy task, and it raises many political and ethical questions. I quote from a security FAQ often cited on the boards, which makes some shrewd and undeniable observations:

> The reason why news servers are legally protected for the content they carry is because something that is illegal in one country can be legal in another, and due to the way in which news is designed, each good news server needs to carry all the standard groups. . . . As an example, discussions on Christianity are illegal in many countries. However, it is definitely legal in others, and so there is no rationality in censoring out any talk about Christianity in newsgroups just because some countries don't allow it. If that were the case, the Internet would have almost nothing, because a large number of things are illegal in at least one country (you'd be surprised at what is illegal in some countries).

If a global standard is to be applied to enforcing Internet content, the obvious question is, which standard? Why that of the United States and the United Kingdom and not that of, say, Iran or Saudi Arabia? And if other countries are forced to observe America's stringent standards concerning youth sexuality, why should the United States not accede to pressure from its European allies and suppress so-called hate speech and extremist propaganda on the Net, even though such expressions are protected under the U.S. Constitution? European countries such as France and Germany desperately want to prevent firms like Yahoo from hosting auction sites on which collectors trade Nazi memorabilia, but can one nation-state really succeed in blocking itself off from a global traffic? On all these issues, the danger is that the international community might be forced to follow the standards prevailing in the most repressive and over-protective member state.

By now, it should be apparent that no magic bullet exists to suppress child porn on the Internet. Still, the approach outlined here would begin the crucial process of dismantling the institutions on which the traffic re-lies, and without destroying the civil liberties of the vast majority of Net users. It will be a long and difficult process, but as with all such endeav-ors, the best way to achieve success is to begin, to take the first step.

Changing the Law?

Whether the policies outlined here would work is open to debate, but we can be confident in saying that other obvious approaches would not have any real effect and might do more harm than good. In particular, legis-lators need to be aware that piling on additional punishments is useless, since, hitherto, the traditional strategies for deterrence have had little im-pact on this area. Short of imposing capital punishment or mutilation, it is difficult to conceive of penalties harsher than those already prevailing for child pornography, and harsher penalties simply are not necessary. Users know that the mere fact of a child porn conviction would mean os-tracism and social ruin, so it really matters little whether the prison time they face is two years or eight. Everyone in the child porn world is well aware of "bubba"; they just don't think they will end up in his care. The answer is to be found in neither new prohibitions nor new penalties but in trying to enforce existing laws.

All too often, "get tough" campaigns garner rich publicity by appear-ing to be striking at the problem enthusiastically, but the effects are min-imal if not counter-productive. Furthermore, the horror inspired by child pornography naturally inspires politicians to try to "do some-thing," but the "something" in question has nothing to do with the issue at hand. Though child porn is harrowing enough in its own right, the massive reaction to Web-based obscenity by politicians and media un-

doubtedly reflects a sense of loss of control in the face of Internet technology, augmented by a recognition of the fragility of international
boundaries and laws. So deep is this unfocused concern that it all too
readily justifies legal efforts directed not against the genuinely harmful
area of child pornography but against far milder forms of adult-themed
indecency, explicit images, and even language. Hence the instant appeal
of successive high-octane campaigns against cyberporn, none of which
would have the slightest impact on the real world of child pornography.
When misdirected laws fail to suppress child porn, the predictable result
is to pass still more laws of the same hue, and so the cycle continues.
Agreeing unhesitatingly that child porn is an unqualified evil should not
mean acceding to every measure proposed, however tenuously, under an
"anti–child porn" rubric. When passing laws, it is useful to recall the
opening words of the Hippocratic Oath: "First, do no harm."

Examining the child pornography laws of the 1980s and 1990s, one
can make the case that some, at least, have gone too far. This is a
deeply controversial area, since the thought of weakening laws against
child pornography is politically intolerable. If "just looking" were to
be legalized, that would itself generate demand for new materials, and
children would be victimized in the process of manufacture. In a few
areas, though, limited liberalization is indicated. While agreeing completely that child pornography should—must—remain prohibited,
there is space for rethinking just what "pornography" is in this context. Eliminating overkill provisions would have many benefits, not
least in making it clear that the laws were directed against authentic
child exploiters, such as those who made and still circulate hel-lo and
KX. Some sane legal changes would seriously limit the number of ambiguous or controversial prosecutions. It would also make it vastly easier to form an international consensus about enforceable child pornography laws and end the impression that Americans are simply trying to export their puritanical obsessions.

Judging by the consensus of American state laws and the codes of
most advanced nations, for instance, eighteen is too high a minimum age
at which individuals can be depicted in sexual contexts, and sixteen

would be more sensible. This was the age established by U.S. law under the restrictive 1978 anti–child porn law, and it is closely in tune with the ideas prevailing in most advanced European states. Seventeen-year-olds are not children, and it is ludicrous to try to impose upon them the same limitations that apply to seven-year-olds. We might consider a kind of sliding scale of seriousness, so that offenses involving younger children are treated severely while official reaction diminishes as the age of the subject increases. We cannot carry on pretending that sexuality is a mysterious force that descends on a person suddenly on his or her eighteenth birthday, prior to which the individual remains in pristine innocence.

Also, the current strict liability system ("you possess it, you're guilty") might be replaced with a more flexible model that acknowledges intent and reverses some of the legislation derived from the peak child-abuse panic years of the mid-1980s. This would remove the ludicrous situations that result in parents being prosecuted for taking bathtime pictures of children or art books being confiscated from store shelves. In case this seems like a license for pornographers, it might be useful to illustrate other examples in which child protection laws have gone much too far and have needed to be pruned back. In 1996, a Child Pornography Prevention Act prohibited depictions of sex or suggestive situations by persons who are or who *appear to be* below the age of eighteen. But—appear to whom? Some years ago, millions of people worldwide saw the film *Titanic*, in which Kate Winslet plays a seventeen-year-old girl who has sex during the course of the story. Nobody was troubled by this incident, as the actress herself is well over the age of consent, but the film probably violated the 1996 act by simulating a sex act by someone presented, plausibly or not, as a minor. Other recent films, such as *Lolita* and *American Beauty*, have faced similar dangers. Not surprisingly, a federal court struck down the 1996 act, as it produced results that were unjust and, often, silly. Other aspects of the existing child porn code could be targeted on similar grounds of overbreadth.[20]

Much more significant would be to recognize a journalistic exemption to the law, permitting access to child porn materials in the course of a legitimate news-gathering venture. Opening this avenue would

raise the possibility of better exposing the trade, raising public awareness of its major institutions, and placing pressure on politicians to act
against suppliers rather than just consumers. The change would, in
short, end the monopoly currently enjoyed by law enforcement agencies in defining the problem and open the quality of police work to
public examination and criticism. Above all, it would end the dangerous delusion that tracking down online stalkers is making the slightest
contribution to confronting electronic child porn. As Tim Tate has
justly remarked, "The greatest single obstacle to the fight against child
pornography is that too few people ever see it."[21] This remark is all the
more notable because Tate himself is a fanatical opponent of child exploitation in all its forms, and his hatred of all pornography, including
adult material, goes far beyond mine.

Democratizing Sex

In listing the dangers of overreaction to child porn, we naturally focus on
the most pressing threat, namely, that the Internet becomes a tool for
Big Brother; yet other perils should not be dismissed. Civil libertarians
rightly cite the many beneficial features of the Internet that would be en-
dangered by restrictive legislation, for example, how laws against "indecent" material might stifle sites devoted to health education or AIDS
prevention. But we need not always frame our defenses in purely utili-
tarian terms. It would be tragic if zeal against child exploitation were
used to justify suppressing adult sexual material on the Internet, which
so many people enjoy in private, without causing harm to others. Unpopular as this statement might be in what often seems an increasingly
puritanical America, a case can be made that pornography contributes
positively to sexual frankness, freedom, experimentation, and pleasure:
there is such a thing as good, clean, healthy smut.

It is vital to draw a sharp line between child pornography and
adult material. No matter what anti-smut activists claim, cyberporn is
not the same as child porn. Such confusion emerges from interviews
with the leaders of the Cyber Angels, a vigilante group that "patrols"

the Internet with the worthy goal of detecting and deterring online pedophiles:

> In their metaphors, something bad often becomes something much worse; something legal they happen to dislike becomes tainted with a miasma of unlawfulness. Curtis and Colin believe that people who swap child porn are also predators and child molesters—and the Angels will casually mention them in the same breath as serial killers. When Colin got into an online discussion about smut with one of his critics, he praised a new European access provider for offering a porn-free environment and sneered: "You may choose to live in a cyber-neighborhood infested with child pornographers and other criminals." Note how the subject of legal adult material, which was at issue, is suddenly equated with (illegal) child porn.[22]

The positive aspects of such "legal adult material" should be stressed. Indeed, the recent boom in child pornography has occurred because of the powerful democratizing effect of new technology, which in other ways has been an unqualified good. Though moralists complain about the proliferation of adult and sexual material on the Internet, this outpouring just reflects the fact that, for the first time in history, ordinary people can publish to the world anything they wish, and many men and women have a deep interest in sex. Contrary to most denunciations of Net pornography, a huge amount of this material is not commercial, is not for profit, and is done, dare we say, for love. (I dispute the recent argument by Frederick Lane that the quantity of amateur material is far less than is popularly believed, though both of us are relying on subjective impressions rather than solid, quantitative evidence. I would suggest that factoring in Usenet groups massively raises the proportion of undeniably amateur images.)[23]

We can, in fact, argue that the highly democratic and easily accessible nature of sex on the Internet creates a social benefit by so frequently depicting real people, with all their visible flaws and imperfections, rather than the distorted and overidealized imagery that so long characterized X-rated magazines and movies. The amateur quality of much Internet material serves to undermine one of the major arguments against pornography. According to feminist critics, the traditional depictions of female nudity found in publications such as *Playboy*, *Penthouse*, and *Hustler* were simply too perfect, the women too slim and wrinkle free. The proliferation of such idealized imagery had a pernicious effect on women in the real world, who were coerced into seeking unattainable body shapes, with all the familiar consequences of depression, eating disorders, and unnecessary cosmetic surgery. (The feminist indictment of pornography has many other aspects, of course, but this is the complaint that attracts the broadest consensus.)[24] Contrary to the pornographic dream, the vast majority of women look nothing like supermodels and never could do so. In contrast, many of the sexually oriented sites on the Web portray real women, with scant resemblance to *Playboy* models. They can be overweight or skinny and range in age into their sixties and beyond. Both men and women depicted generally look like a cross section of the real-world population, and yet these images are immensely popular, and the women in question attain the status of global sex stars. On *egroups.com*, almost five hundred groups are now devoted to BBWs, "big beautiful women." Possibly, the preference for older women reflects the graying of the baby boom generation, as the large cohort of men entering their forties and fifties appreciate the sexuality of women around their own age.[25]

Whatever the reason, some of the new generation of Internet porn stars would have startled an earlier generation of viewers, both in their appearance and in the astonishing public reaction. One is "SassySally," who introduces herself on her Web site as "a 5 foot, 10 inch, 210 pound, 47 year old, midwestern housewife with 38D breasts." Another subject often seen on adult sites is "Shea," a thirty-seven-year-old Wyoming nurse. Though she is undoubtedly attractive, there are countless reasons why Shea would not have appeared in any traditional pornography. By conventional standards, she is at least a decade too old for such productions; her hips are too large; her belly has pronounced stretch marks; and who in the adult magazine world could imagine a mother being sexy? Yet, after her pictures started appearing on amateur sex sites, the clamor for more resulted in her establishing her own popular Web site, which continues to flourish.[26] In another case, a South Carolina woman who had long regarded herself as seriously overweight was cast into grave depression after the birth of her third child, an experience that, in her view, left her looking hopelessly undesirable. Her husband had the idea of posting some nude photographs of her on the Internet, which within months made her an international sex symbol whose site attracted tens of thousands of visitors each day. This global interest permitted her to develop a lucrative business selling photographs and videos by mail. Though she remains baffled by her stardom, her self-image has vastly improved.[27] Among all the jeremiads about the "torrent of smut" on the Internet, it's useful to recall that a lot of men and women seem to be enjoying it immensely and may even be enjoying better sex lives as a result.

While cases like this are by no means typical and can scarcely be claimed as a feminist Horatio Alger success story, these stories do indicate that the democratization of pornography on the Internet has affected ideals of female beauty, and in a way that many observers would consider highly positive. The fact that the spectrum of Internet pornography also includes the loathsome KX should not discredit the medium as such, any more than the printing press should be condemned because it was used to produce *Mein Kampf.* Using child pornography to attack Internet sex is illogical and dishonest.

When we consider the thriving kiddie porn culture on the Internet, we might recall the Maoist dictum that guerrillas move among the people as fish swim in the sea. While I have no desire to dignify these individuals by comparing them to guerrillas, the analogy holds to the extent that child pornographers indeed travel the Internet like the proverbial swimming fish, and there is no easy way to catch the fish without draining or poisoning the entire sea. We have to find means of killing or crippling the subculture without destroying the Internet, with which so much good can be accomplished.

ABBREVIATIONS

ABA	American Bar Association
AP	Associated Press
BG	*Boston Globe*
GPO	Government Printing Office
HC	*Houston Chronicle*
LAT	*Los Angeles Times*
MB	Maestro board, pseudonymous Web site
NCMEC	National Center for Missing and Exploited Children
NYT	*New York Times*
RB	R-board, pseudonymous Web site
WP	*Washington Post*
WSJ	*Wall Street Journal*
www	World Wide Web

NOTES

Notes to Chapter 1

1. The quote is from "Helena Lover" on the main discussion board (BBS2) of the Maestro Web site, February 6, 2000. As I will explain, "Maestro" is a pseudonym, and I will not publish the actual URL of this site. Henceforward, all quotations from this site will be introduced with the prefix MB.

2. MB: "Don't Know," October 29, 1999.

3. *New York v. Ferber*, 458 U.S. 747, 1982.

4. A large and growing literature deals with the legal and constitutional challenges involved in regulating the Internet. See, for example, William S. Byassee, "Jurisdiction of Cyberspace," *Wake Forest Law Review* 30 (1995): 197–220; J. Q. Crews, "Regulating Pornography on the Internet," *Law and Psychology Review* 20 (1996): 179–195; Lilian Edwards and Charlotte Waelde, *Law and the Internet* (Oxford: Hart, 1997); Lesli C. Esposito, "Regulating the Internet," *Case Western Reserve Journal of International Law* 30 (1998): 541–565; Mark J. Stefik, *The Internet Edge* (Cambridge, MA: MIT Press, 1999); Jean Hellwege, "Law Enforcement, Legislators Grapple with Child Sexual Exploitation on the Net," *Trial*, March 2000, 13–16; S. J. Drucker and G. Gumpert, "CyberCrime and Punishment," *Critical Studies in Media Communication* 17 (June 2000): 133–158.

5. Ian Hacking, *The Social Construction of What?* (Cambridge, MA: Harvard University Press, 1999); Philip Jenkins, "Fighting Terrorism as if Women Mattered," in Jeff Ferrell and Neil Websdale, eds., *Making Trouble* (Hawthorne, NY: Aldine de Gruyter, 1999), 319–346; Philip Jenkins, *Synthetic Panics* (New York: New York University Press, 1999).

6. Philip Jenkins, *Moral Panic* (New Haven, CT: Yale University Press, 1998), 209–213; Jim Exon, "At Issue: Should the Government Crack Down on Pornography on the Internet?" *CQ Researcher* 5 (24), June 30,

1995; *Cyberporn and Children: Hearing before the Committee on the Judiciary, US Senate, 104th Congress, 1st session . . . July 24, 1995* (Washington, DC: GPO, 1995); *Cyberporn: Protecting Our Children from the Back Alleys of the Internet. Joint Hearing before the Subcommittee on Basic Research and the Subcommittee on Technology of the Committee on Science, US House of Representatives, 104th Congress, First Session, July 26, 1995* (Washington, DC: GPO, 1995). The cyberporn issue by no means died with the CDA. See, for instance, *Internet Indecency: Hearing before the Committee on Commerce, Science, and Transportation, US Senate, 105th Congress, Second Session, February 10, 1998* (Washington, DC: GPO, 1999); *Legislative Proposals to Protect Children from Inappropriate Materials on the Internet: Hearing before the Subcommittee on Telecommunications, Trade, and Consumer Protection of the Committee on Commerce, House of Representatives, 105th Congress, Second Session, . . . September 11, 1998* (Washington, DC: GPO, 1998); "More People Named to Panel for Curbs on Web Pornography," *WSJ*, October 20, 1999; Jeri Clausing, "Commission Will Work to Protect Children after Legislation Fails," *NYT*, March 7, 2000.

7. Yaron Svoray and Thomas Hughes, *Gods of Death* (New York: Simon and Schuster, 1997).

8. *Use of Computers in the Sexual Exploitation of Children* (Washington, DC: U.S. Dept. of Justice, Office of Justice Programs, Office of Juvenile Justice and Delinquency Prevention, 1999).

9. LeRoy G. Schultz, *"Kiddie Porn": A Social Policy Analysis* (Morgantown, WV: School of Social Work, West Virginia University, 1977); Shirley O'Brien, *Child Pornography* (Dubuque, IA: Kendall Hunt, 1983); Kenneth V. Lanning and Ann W. Burgess, *Child Pornography and Sex Rings* (Washington, DC: FBI, U.S. Dept. of Justice, 1984); Ann W. Burgess and Marieanne L. Clark, eds., *Child Pornography and Sex Rings* (Lexington, MA: LexingtonBooks, 1984); Howard A. Davidson and Gregory A. Loken, *Child Pornography and Prostitution* (Washington, DC: NCMEC, 1987); Patricia N. Chock, "The Use of Computers in the Sexual Exploitation of Children and Child Pornography," *Computer Law Journal* 7 (1987): 383–407; D. Campagna and D. Poffenberger, *The Sexual Trafficking of Children* (Dover, MA: Auburn House, 1988); Kenneth V. Lanning, *Child Sex Rings* (Washington, DC: NCMEC, 1989); Tim Tate, *Child Pornography* (London: Methuen, 1990); Jan Schuijer and Benjamin Rossen, "The Trade in Child

Pornography," *Issues in Child Abuse Accusations* 4 (1992): 55–107. For more up-to-date studies, see Carl Goran Svedin, Kristina Back, and Radda Barnen, *Children Who Don't Speak Out* (Stockholm, Sweden: Swedish Save the Children, 1996); Ronald Weitzer, ed., *Sex for Sale* (New York: Routledge 1999); Anna Grant, Fiona David, and Peter Grabosky, "Child Pornography in the Digital Age," in Phil Williams, ed., *Illegal Immigration and Commercial Sex* (London: Frank Cass, 1999), 171–188; Yaman Akdeniz, *Sex on the Net* (London: South Street, 1999). For contemporary European writing, see, for instance, Gisela Wuttke, *Kinderprostitution, Kinderpornographie, Tourismus* (Gottingen: Lamuv, 1998); Detlef Drewes, *Kinder im Datennetz: Pornographie und Prostitution in den neuen Medien* (Frankfurt am Main: Eichborn, 1995). Carlos A. Arnaldo, ed., *Child Abuse on the Internet* (New York: Berghahn Books, 2000).

10. Laurie J. Flynn, "Guardian Angels Now Patrol the Net" *NYT,* March 16, 1996; *Cybersex Cop,* documentary program broadcast on A&E network, 1998. Keith A. Schroeder and Julie Ledger, eds., *Life and Death on the Internet* (Supple Publishing, 1998); Deborah Boehle, "Terrorized on the Internet," *Woman's Day,* March 9, 1999, 22–27; Stephanie Mansfield; "The Avengers Online," *Good Housekeeping,* June 1999, 122–125+; Sean Kelly and Karen E. Crummy, "Netting Sexual Predators," *Denver Post,* November 8, 1999; Catherine Edwards, "Pedophiles Prowl the Internet," *Insight on the News,* February 28, 2000; "Gumshoe Mom Helps Collar Criminals On Line," *Centre Daily Times* (State College, PA), March 13, 2000; Katherine Tarbox, *Katie.com: My Story* (New York: E. P. Dutton, 2000); Anita Hamilton, "Chatting with the Enemy," *Time,* May 8, 2000, 95; Peter A. Carlin and Barbara Surk, "Cyber Survivor," *People Weekly,* May 29, 2000, 95–96; Michelle Malkin, "Parental Neglect Leads Teen-agers to Be Seduced on the Internet," *Insight on the News,* June 5, 2000; Debra West, "Aftermath of Internet Pedophilia Case," *NYT,* July 12, 2000.

11. Wendy Grossman, *Net.Wars* (New York: New York University Press, 1997), 201, 99; James R. Kincaid, *Erotic Innocence* (Durham, NC: Duke University Press, 1998), 170–172; Frederick S. Lane, *Obscene Profits* (New York: Routledge, 2000), 64, 125–127, 234; Laurence J. O'Toole, *Pornocopia,* 2d ed. (London: Serpent's Tail, 1999), 262.

12. The Glitter story is from Mark Rowe, "Law Outdated, Say Ministers," *The Independent* (London), November 14, 1999. From many recent

news reports, see, for example, Robin Wilson, "Yale to Fire Professor for Child Pornography," *Chronicle of Higher Education*, March 10, 2000, A20; "Teacher Charged with Owning Child Porn," *LAT*, March 17, 2000; "Fifty Year Porn Sentence," *HC*, May 23, 2000; Marcella Bombardieri, "Police Remove Files from Woburn Church," *Boston Globe*, August 27, 2000; David W. Chen, "Bronx Principal Arrested in Child Pornography Investigation," *NYT*, September 8, 2000. "Vice Principal Accused of Sending Child Pornography," *Los Angeles Times*, November 14, 2000: *http://www.latimes.com/news/state/20001114/t000109216.html*.

13. MB: Godfather Corleone, November 10, 1999.

14. MB: Granpa Bob, January 28, 2000.

15. Benjamin Wallace-Wells, "Man Charged with Possession of Child Pornography in Revere," *BG*, February 26, 2000; Henry K. Lee, "Bail Set in Child Pornography Case," *San Francisco Chronicle*, March 11, 2000; Stephen Brewer, "Two Life Terms Given to Man for Abusing Grandchild," *HC*, March 14, 2000. For public libraries, see Michael Rogers and Norman Oder, "Child Porn Arrest in Public Library," *Library Journal*, July 1999, 20–22; "Child Porn Suspect Surrenders," *American Libraries*, May 2000, 31.

16. Barry F. Crimmins, *Testimony before Congressional Hearing on Child Pornography on the Internet, 24 July 1995, Senate Judiciary Committee, 104th Congress, U.S. Senate* (Washington, DC: GPO, 1995).

17. MB: exchange on May 31, 2000.

18. *Proliferation of Child Pornography on the Internet: Hearing before a Subcommittee of the Committee on Appropriations, U.S. Senate, 105th Congress, First Session, Special Hearing* (Washington, DC: GPO, 1997); *Preventing Child Exploitation on the Internet: Hearing before a Subcommittee of the Committee on Appropriations, U.S. Senate, 105th Congress, Second Session, Special Hearing* (Washington, DC: GPO, 1998).

19. Keith F. Durkin and Clifton D. Bryant, "'Log On to Sex': Some Notes on the Carnal Computer and Erotic Cyberspace as an Emerging Research Frontier," *Deviant Behavior* 16(3) (1995): 179–200.

20. Advertising material for Jeff Ferrell and Mark S. Hamm, eds., *Ethnography at the Edge* (Boston: Northeastern University Press, 1998); Delos H. Kelly, ed., *Deviant Behavior*, 5th ed. (New York: St. Martin's Press, 1996); Laud Humphreys, *Tea Room Trade* (New York: Aldine, 1975).

21. Alicia G. Shepard, "Journalistic Research or Child Pornography?" *American Journalism Review* 21(4) (1999): 18–19.

22. Kincaid, *Erotic Innocence*, 172.

23. MB: Snagglepuss and Godfather Corleone, November 10, 1999.

24. I should add one exception here. As I explain further in chapter 3, in response to the recent proliferation of child porn sites on *egroups.com*, I did alert that firm's complaint staff to blatant sites that I encountered there.

25. MB: Dad, December 28, 1999.

Notes to Chapter 2

1. Philip Jenkins, *Moral Panic* (New Haven, CT: Yale University Press, 1998); James R. Kincaid, *Child-Loving* (New York: Routledge, 1994).

2. *R. v. Sharpe*, BCCA 1999 416, June 30, 1999, at *http://www.courts.gov.bc.ca/jdb-txt/ca/99/04/c99-0416.html*.

3. Philip Jenkins, *Pedophiles and Priests* (New York: Oxford University Press, 1996).

4. Stephen Lemons "Thank Heaven for Little Girls," *Salon*, December 4, 1999, online at *http://www.salon.com/health/sex/urge/1999/12/04/underage*.

5. For discussions of pedophilia, see William Kraemer, ed., *The Forbidden Love* (London: Sheldon Press, 1976); Jay R. Feierman, ed., *Pedophilia: Biosocial Dimensions* (New York: Springer Verlag, 1990); Kenneth Lanning, *Child Molesters* (Arlington, VA: NCMEC, 1992); Dennis Howitt, *Pedophiles and Sexual Offenses against Children* (New York: J. Wiley, 1995); Bruce Golding, "Prosecutors Put Sting into Online Search for Pedophiles," *Daily Item* (Gannett Suburban Newspapers), April 13, 1998; Elsa Brenner, "Tracking Down Pedophiles Gains Impetus," *NYT*, October 17, 1999.

6. For the content of adult Web sites, see Frederick S. Lane, *Obscene Profits* (New York: Routledge, 2000).

7. Michael Pearson, *The Age of Consent* (Newton Abbot, UK: David and Charles, 1972); for the Los Angeles scandal, see Cecilia Rasmussen, "D.A. Fitts Was Good Match for Scandalous '30s," *LAT*, September 19, 1999.

8. Walter Kendrick, *The Secret Museum* (New York: Viking 1987); Lynn Avery Hunt, ed., *The Invention of Pornography* (Cambridge, MA: Zone Books, 1993); Jay A. Gertzman, *Bookleggers and Smuthounds* (Philadelphia: University of Pennsylvania Press, 1999).

9. Jenkins, *Moral Panic*; Anne Higonnet, *Pictures of Innocence* (London: Thames and Hudson, 1998); Kincaid, *Child-Loving*. For the Victorian erotic photographic tradition, see, for example, Baron Wilhelm Von Gloeden, *Taormina* (Altadena, Calif.: Twelvetrees Press, 1990).

10. MB: "Looking Back," January 3, 2000. For the easy availability of child porn in the 1970s, see Tim Tate, *Child Pornography* (London: Methuen, 1990); Laurence J. O'Toole, *Pornocopia*, 2d ed. (London: Serpent's Tail, 1999), 217–272.

11. For the changing availability of child porn, see again Tate, *Child Pornography*; Jan Schuijer and Benjamin Rossen, "The Trade in Child Pornography," *Issues in Child Abuse Accusations* 4 (1992): 55–107.

12. Jenkins, *Moral Panic*, 121–127; Laurence A. Stanley, "Hysteria over Child Pornography," in Joseph Geraci, ed., *Dares to Speak* (Swaffham, England: Gay Men's Press, 1997), 179–206; David Sonnenschein, *Pedophiles on Parade*, 2 vols. (San Antonio, TX: privately printed, 1998); Judianne Densen-Gerber, "What Pornographers Are Doing to Children," *Redbook*, August 1977, 86+

13. *Sexual Exploitation of Children: Hearings before the Subcommittee on Crime of the Committee on the Judiciary, U.S. House of Representatives, 95th Congress, First Session* (Washington, DC: US GPO 1977); Committee on Education and Labor, Subcommittee on Select Education, *Teenage Prostitution and Child Pornography: Hearings before the Subcommittee on Select Education of the Committee on Education and Labor, U.S. House of Representatives, 97th Congress, Second Session* (Washington, DC: GPO, 1982); *Child Pornography: Hearings before the Subcommittee on Juvenile Justice of the Committee on the Judiciary, U.S. Senate, 97th Congress, Second Session* (Washington, DC: GPO, 1983); *Child Pornography and Pedophilia: Hearings before the Permanent Subcommittee on Investigations of the Committee on Governmental Affairs, U.S. Senate, 98th Congress, Second Session* (Washington, DC: GPO, 1985); *Child Pornography and Pedophilia: Report Made by the Permanent Subcommittee on Investigations of the Committee on Governmental Affairs, U.S. Senate* (Washington, DC: GPO, 1986).

14. These allegations are quoted from Jenkins, *Moral Panic*, 145–156; see also James R. Kincaid, *Erotic Innocence* (Durham, NC: Duke University Press, 1998).

15. Media and political claims are quoted and discussed in Jenkins, *Moral*

Panic, 144–163; for the Meese report, see *Attorney General's Commission on Pornography, Final Report* (Washington, DC: U.S. Dept. of Justice, 1986).

16. The recent author quoted on the supposedly vast scale of the porn industry is Kimberly A. McCabe in "Child Pornography and the Internet," *Social Science Computer Review* 18 (2000): 73–76; for the Illinois report, see Anne Higonnet, "Conclusions Based on Observation," *Yale Journal of Criticism* 9(1) (1996): 1–18.

17. "Man Faces Prison for Nude Photos," *Detroit News*, November 12, 1999. Yaman Akdeniz's excellent comparative survey of the "Regulation of Child Pornography on the Internet," can be found at: *http://www.cyber-rights.org/reports/child.htm*. See also *http://www.cyber-rights.org/reports/uscases.htm*; *http://www.cyber-rights.org/reports/interdev.htm*; *http://www.cyber-rights.org/reports/ukcases.htm*. It still reads oddly when the media report a "child porn" case featuring young people of seventeen: see, for example, "Two Men Arrested in Child Porn Case," *LAT*, July 1, 2000.

18. For the Knox and Dost cases, see *US v. Knox*, 32 F.3d 733, 746n. 10 (3rd Cir. 1994); *US v. Dost*, 636 F.Supp. 828 (S.D. Cal. 1986), aff'd, 812 F.2d 1231 (9th Cir. 1987); "Private Possession of Expressive Material— Child Pornography," *Harvard Law Review* 104 (1990): 237–247; Robert R. Strang, "She Was Just Seventeen: Child Pornography and Overbreadth," *Columbia Law Review* 90(6) (1990): 1779–1803; John Quigley, "Child Pornography and the Right to Privacy," *Florida Law Review* 43(2) (1991): 347–358. Lisa S. Smith, "Private Possession of Child Pornography," *Annual Survey of American Law* 4 (1991): 1011–1045.

19. *Child Protection and Obscenity Enforcement Act and Pornography Victims Protection Act of 1987: Hearing before the Committee on the Judiciary, U.S. Senate, 100th Congress, Second Session . . . June 8, 1988* (Washington, DC: GPO, 1988); *Child Protection and Obscenity Enforcement Act of 1988: Hearings before the Subcommittee on Crime of the Committee on the Judiciary, U.S. House of Representatives, 100th Congress, Second Session* (Washington, DC: GPO, 1989); Linda Greenhouse, "Supreme Court Upholds Government's Ambiguously Written Child Pornography Law," *NYT*, November 30, 1994; John Simons, "Internet Child-Pornography Peddlers, Sex Predators Targeted by White House," *WSJ*, December 3, 1997; Lizette Alvarez, "House Passes Bill to Curb Internet as Pedophiles' Lure," *NYT*, June 12,

1998; Pamela Mendels, "States Just Won't Give Up on Online Pornography Laws," *NYT*, October 8, 1999; Karina Bland, "Pedophiles Stay Ahead of State Law for Internet," *Arizona Republic*, January 26, 2000.

20. Harris Mirkin, "The Forbidden Image," in James Elias, Veronica Diehl Elias, Vern L. Bullough, Gwen Brewer, Jeffrey Douglas, and Will Jarvis, eds., *Porn 101* (Amherst, NY: Prometheus Books, 1999), 501–520; "Cynthia Stewart's Ordeal," *The Nation*, May 1, 2000; James R. Kincaid, "Is This Child Pornography?" *Salon*, January 31, 2000; Bill Andriette, "Are You a Child Pornographer?" *Playboy*, September 1991. For some of the controversies over artistic photography, see Laura U. Marks, "Child Pornography and the Legislation of Morality" *Afterimage* 18(4) (November 1990): 12; Doreen Carvajal, "Bookstore Chain Undaunted by Obscenity Indictments," *NYT*, February 20, 1998; Richard Goldstein, "The Eye of the Beholder," *Village Voice*, March 10, 1998, 31–36; Jock Sturges, *The Last Day of Summer*, 8th ed. (New York: Aperture, 1998); David Hamilton, *David Hamilton: Twenty Five Years of an Artist* (London: Aurum Press, 1998); James Christen Steward, "The Camera of Sally Mann and the Spaces of Childhood," *Michigan Quarterly Review* 39 (2000): 365–375; Michael Rogers and Norman Oder, "Judge: Books Are Pornographic," *Library Journal*, May 15, 2000: 16. Terry is quoted from "Protesters Escalate Campaign; ABFFE Decries Book Destruction," *Bookweb*, *http://www.bookweb.org/news/*, September 22, 1997.

21. Claudia Puig, "'Happiness' Has a Dark Side," *USA Today*, October 21, 1998; Bob van Voris, "Lawyers Were Forced to Cut Scenes from Lolita because of Vagueness in Obscenity Laws," *National Law Journal*, August 17, 1998, at *http://www.anusha.com/loli-cut.htm*; Reynolds Holding, "Fallout from Child Pornography Act," *San Francisco Chronicle*, August 3, 1997. For advertising, see Andy Newman, "Calvin Klein Pulls Ads for Children's Underwear," *NYT*, February 18, 1999; Richard Marusa, "American Prudery, and Its Opposite," *NYT*, February 19, 2000. For the *Tin Drum* controversy, see *http://www.state.ok.us/~odl/fyi/ifreedom.htm*.

22. Lane, *Obscene Profits*, 33, for the growth of videotaping; U.S. Customs Service, Child Pornography and Protection Unit, *The Child Pornography Enforcement Program* (Washington, DC: Treasury Dept., 1987); *Child Pornography, Obscenity and Sexual Oriented Advertisements*, U.S. Postal Inspection Service, *http://www.framed.usps.com/postalinspectors/*; Mary

Thornton, "US Customs: Crusaders in the Child Pornography War," *WP* Weekly Edition September 8, 1986.

23. Compare Stanley, "Hysteria over Child Pornography," 186–187; Tate, *Child Pornography*, 81; Jack M. Weatherford, *Porn Row* (New York: Arbor House, 1986).

24. Lane, *Obscene Profits*, 62–72; Howard Rheingold, *Virtual Community* (New York: Harper Perennial, 1993).

25. Mike Cane, *The Computer Phone Book*, rev. and expanded ed., 2 vols. (New York: New American Library, 1986); compare Jay M. Shafritz and Louise Alexander, *The Reston Directory of On-Line Databases* (Reston, VA: Reston Pub. Co., 1984).

26. Cane, *Computer Phone Book*, xiv.

27. Cane, *Computer Phone Book*, 11.

28. For the early charges about pedophile use of computers, see Tate, *Child Pornography*, 212; compare Cane, *Computer Phone Book*, 286; Carol McGraw, "Child Smut Business Going Underground," *LAT*, September 16, 1985; Meese is quoted from Tate, *Child Pornography*, 209; O'Toole, *Pornocopia*, 261.

29. Quotes in this paragraph are from George Johnson, "From Two Small Nodes, a Mighty Web Has Grown," *NYT*, October 12, 1999.

30. William Gibson, *Neuromancer* (New York: Ace Books, 1984).

31. These quotes are all from MB: "Hey, I remember things" is from Scorch, March 18, 2000; "Twenty years ago" is from Infoo, March 18, 2000; "Master Blaster" wrote on February 25, 2000; Zapper wrote on May 25, 2000.

32. Barry F. Crimmins, *Testimony before Congressional Hearing on Child Pornography on the Internet, 24 July 1995, Senate Judiciary Committee, 104th Congress, U.S. Senate* (Washington, DC: GPO, 1995); idem, "Child Pornography," *BG*, July 29, 1995, 17:3.

33. The account of the Rimm study and all quotes in this paragraph are from Jenkins, *Moral Panic*, 210–211.

Notes to Chapter 3

1. MB: Godfather Corleone, March 21, 2000.

2. The remarks about the volume of material on *abpep-t* are taken from a

FAQ posted by Godfather Corleone. Compare Jamie Doward and Andrew Smith, "Exposed: Where Child Porn Lurks on the Net," *The Observer* (London), March 19, 2000; Neil Bennett, "Netting the Pornographers," November 12, 1999, BBC News Online at *news.bbc.co.uk/hi/english/uk*; Anna Grant, Fiona David, and Peter Grabosky, "Child Pornography in the Digital Age," in Phil Williams, ed., *Illegal Immigration and Commercial Sex* (London: Frank Cass, 1999), 171–188. For adult materials on the newsgroups, see Denna Harmon and Scot Boeringer, "A Content Analysis of Internet-Accessible Written Pornographic Depictions," *Electronic Journal of Sociology* 3(1) (1997). For recent trends, see Lynn Burke, "The Mainstreaming of Kiddie Porn," *Wired* magazine online, August 24, 2000.

3. MB: Me, October 24, 1999.

4. MB: Picmazter, May 30, 2000.

5. MB: Angus, March 4, 2000.

6. Stephanie Mansfield, "The Avengers Online," *Good Housekeeping*, June 1999, 122–125+; compare Parry Aftab, *The Parent's Guide to Protecting Your Children in Cyberspace* (New York: McGraw-Hill, 2000); Parry Aftab, "ALA and the UNESCO Initiative to Combat Child Porn," *American Libraries* 30(9) (October 1999): 9. More recently, Aftab has publicized another dramatic-sounding statistic, the foundations for which are highly questionable. In 2000, she "told a congressional commission that three thousand children were kidnapped in the US last year because of online messages posted by their abductors." Aravind Adiga, "Internet Kidnap Warning," *Financial Times*, June 9, 2000.

7. MB: Godfather Corleone, May 30, 2000.

8. MB: FAQ by Godfather Corleone, June 7, 2000; Pirra8, November 8, 1999.

9. MB: G-Man, October 5, 1999; though for the value of such claims, see Joseph Menn, "Web Firms May Vastly Inflate Claims of Hits," *LAT*, April 17, 2000.

10. MB: GEN, January 15, 2000; Tomcat, April 30, 2000; Zep, May 1, 2000. Interpol is quoted from Lesli C. Esposito, "Regulating the Internet," *Case Western Reserve Journal of International Law* 30 (1998): 541–565. For the U.S. Customs figures, see Ron Scherer, "US Spins Wider Web to Halt Child Porn Online," *Christian Science Monitor*, October 5, 2000.

11. Michael Grunwald, "Global Internet Child Porn Ring Uncovered,"

WP, September 3, 1998; David Stout, "Internet Pornography Group Is Seized in U.S. and Abroad," *NYT* September 3, 1998; Elaine Shannon, "Main Street Monsters," *Time*, September 14, 1998, 59; "Eight in Court over Internet Porn," BBC News Online, January 7, 1999; Tim Bryant, "Prosecutor Tells How Child Pornography Ring Unraveled," St. *Louis Post-Dispatch*, February 20, 1999. Nick Davies and Jeevan Vasagar, "Global Child Porn Ring Broken," *Guardian* (London), January 11, 2001.

12. MB: Jayjay, January 6, 2000. For women and child porn, see, for instance, Nathan Collins "Teen Girl Caught in Porn Sting," *Detroit News*, May 5, 2000; Rummana Hussain, "Professor Is Guilty in Child Porn Case," *Chicago Tribune*, October 6, 2000. Compare Bosah Ebo, ed., *Cyberghetto or Cybertopia? Race, Class, and Gender on the Internet* (Westport, CT: Praeger, 1998).

13. MB: G-Man, November 27, 1999.

14. MB: AnonAmos, February 16, 2000; Jethro Tull, February 25, 2000.

15. MB: Smile, January 15, 2000, emphases in original; Anon, December 31, 1999.

16. MB: PussyPig, October 13, 1999.

17. Shannon, "Main Street Monsters."

18. MB: PussyPig, October 13, 1999.

19. MB: Dune Atried, January 2, 2000.

20. Adam Cohen and Chris Taylor, "The Infoanarchist," *Time*, June 26, 2000, 46; Don Tapscott; "Freenet May Make the Internet a Wilder Place," *Computerworld*, May 22, 2000, 32; Thomas E. Weber, "Maverick Programmers Prepare to Unleash Anarchy on the Web," *WSJ*, March 27, 2000. Darkstar is quoted from MB: January 4, 2000.

21. "Nudist Hall of Shame," at *http://www.nostatusquo.com/ACLU/ NudistHallofShame/index.html*. See also Christine Wicker, "Kids May Be at Risk in Nudist Camps," *Dallas Morning News*, March 29, 1992; Art Barnum, "Summer Camp Leader Guilty of Sexually Abusing Two Boys," *Chicago Tribune*, February 24, 1989.

22. MB: Admin, May 26, 2000.

23. For the discussion of snuff films, see Shannon, "Main Street Monsters."

24. MB: Darkstar, February 2, 2000; Lord High Executioner, May 29, 2000, emphasis in original.

25. MB: The exchange occurred on November 20, 1999.

26. MB: BoBo, February 4, 2000 (rape); Boricua, February 5, 2000 (ted-dybears); Uncle, February 6, 2000 (dolls); Anon, January 31, 2000 (hair washing); Syberdude, January 26, 2000 (pregnant); Superman, April 11, 2000 (lingerie); January 30, 2000 (Catholic girl).

27. MB: Jose, January 31, 2000.

28. MB: Adolf Eichmann, March 5, 2000; Another Aryan, March 5, 2000.

Notes to Chapter 4

1. Joel Best and David F. Luckenbill, *Organizing Deviance*, 2d ed. (Englewood Cliffs, NJ: Prentice Hall, 1994), 24.

2. Ibid.

3. MB: The exchange occurred on December 28–29, 1999.

4. MB: November 9, 1999.

5. MB: February 6, 2000.

6. MB: November 24, 1999.

7. MB: Darkstar, October 6, 1999; Pirra8, January 17, 2000.

8. MB: Jayjay, January 6, 2000.

9. MB: Count Dracula, February 21, 2000.

10. The literature on the culture and social psychology of the Internet is already substantial and growing rapidly. See Howard Rheingold, *Virtual Community* (New York: Harper Perennial, 1993); David Porter, ed., *Internet Culture* (New York: Routledge, 1997); Sara Kiesler, ed., *Culture of the Internet* (Mahwah, NJ: Lawrence Erlbaum Associates, 1997); S. Jones, ed., *Virtual Cultures: Identity and Communication in Cybersociety* (London: Sage, 1997); Richard Holeton, *Composing Cyberspace* (New York: McGraw Hill College Division, 1997); Marc A. Smith and Peter Kollock, eds., *Communities in Cyberspace* (New York: Routledge, 1998); Stacy Horn, *Cyberville* (New York: Warner Books, 1998). For online deviance, see particularly Matthew Williams, "Virtually Criminal: Discourse, Deviance and Anxiety within Virtual Communities," *International Review of Law, Computers and Technology* 14(1) (2000) 95–99.

11. Beth Lipton Krigel, "ISP Attacked after Finding Child Porn," *CNET News.com*, April 6, 1998.

12. Kimberly A. McCabe, "Child Pornography and the Internet," *Social Science Computer Review* 18 (2000): 73–76.

13. For the San Diego case, see John Gibeaut, "Image Is Everything," *ABA Journal* 86 (May 2000): 20–21; Tim Jones, "Paedophile Jailed for Thirty Months," *The Times* (London), January 24, 2000.

14. MB: Loko, May 25, 2000; Dad, June 11, 2000

15. MB: Sweetsnatch, January 10, 2000.

16. Laurence Zuckerman, "Studying the Ageless Need to Amass Collections," *NYT*, January 22, 2000. See also Mitch Tuchman, *Magnificent Obsessions* (San Francisco: Chronicle Books, 1994); Russell W. Belk and Susan M. Pearce, eds., *Collecting in a Consumer Society* (New York: Routledge, 1995); A. D. Olmsted, "Morally Controversial Leisure: The Social World of Gun Collectors," *Symbolic Interaction* 11 (1988): 277–287.

17. MB: Lum, March 27, 2000.

18. MB: Dad, June 11, 2000.

19. MB: Led Zeppelin, May 28, 2000.

20. MB: Darkstar, February 2, 2000.

21. MB: Darkstar, March 10, 2000.

22. MB: Pirra8, January 14, 2000.

23. MB: The exchange was posted on April 30, 2000.

24. MB: Milky Way, April 13, 2000.

25. MB: January 1, 2000.

26. MB: Owl, January 19, 2000.

27. MB: March 6, 2000.

28. See the Web site sponsored by Dr. Kimberly Young at *http://www.netaddiction.com/clinic.htm;* Dori Jones Yang, "Craving Your Next Web Fix," *US News and World Report*, January 17, 2000; John Markoff, "Portrait of a Newer, Lonelier Crowd Is Captured in an Internet Survey," *NYT*, February 16, 2000; Jane E. Brody, "First Step Is Recognizing the Signs of Internet Abuse" and "Cybersex Gives Birth to a Psychological Disorder," *NYT*, May 16, 2000. For skepticism about "cybersex addiction," see R. W. Greene, "Internet Addiction," *Computerworld*, September 21, 1998, 78–79; Richard Goldstein, "Modem Madness," *Village Voice*, June 13, 2000; Patricia M. Wallace, *The Psychology of the Internet* (Cambridge: Cambridge University Press, 1999).

29. MB: Lookangle, September 24, 1999.

30. MB: Rakjing, November 20, 1999.

31. MB: Darkstar, April 23, 2000.

32. MB: Sleeper, January 4, 2000.

33. MB: Scooby, January 10, 2000.

34. MB: Mr. Bungle, March 17, 2000.

35. MB: This exchange is from October 24, 1999.

36. MB: The Detective, April 5, 2000.

37. MB: Bummer, May 16, 2000.

38. MB: Joel the Troll, October 25, 1999.

39. MB: The postings are from December 5, 1999.

Notes to Chapter 5

1. This discussion of criminological theory is drawn from George B. Vold, Thomas J. Bernard, and Jeffrey B. Snipes, *Theoretical Criminology*, 4th ed. (New York: Oxford University Press, 1997); David Matza, *Delinquency and Drift*, reprint (Transaction Pub., 1990).

2. This observation is based on Tim Tate, *Child Pornography* (London: Methuen, 1990).

3. MB: Nate, December 28, 1999; replies followed on the same date.

4. MB: Humbert Humbert, February 27, 2000.

5. MB: Absolutely Correct, January 14, 2000.

6. MB: Baldpubes, January 18, 2000.

7. MB: Stiffbizkit, May 1, 2000.

8. MB: Dad, May 1, 2000.

9. MB: _we, May 1, 2000.

10. MB: Love2See, May 1, 2000.

11. MB: J. L. Byrd, October 24, 1999.

12. MB: A pedophile, May 1, 2000.

13. MB: Comiskey, January 3, 2000.

14. MB: Sikk, January 12, 2000.

15. MB: This exchange is from October 24, 1999.

16. MB: This exchange is from January 12, 2000. Since the 1970s, numerous writers have tried to present a case for pederast/pedophile rights, usually framed in the context of the sexual liberation of young people; lovers of boys have been far more publicly active than those preferring girls. From

a substantial literature, see, for example, Parker Rossman, "The Pederasts," in Erich Goode and Richard R. Troiden, eds., *Sexual Deviance and Sexual Deviants* (New York: Morrow, 1974), 396–409; Tom O'Carroll, *Pedophilia: The Radical Case* (London: Peter Owen, 1980); Glenn D. Wilson and David N. Cox, *The Child-Lovers* (Boston: Peter Owen, 1983); Edward Brongersma, *Loving Boys* (New York: Global Academic, 1986); Theo Sandfort, *Boys on Their Contacts with Men* (Elmhurst, NY: Global Academic, 1987); Frits Bernard, *Persecuted Minority* (Amsterdam: Southernwood, 1989); Theo Sandfort, Edward Brongersma, and Alex Van Naerssen, "Man-Boy Relationships," *Journal of Homosexuality* 20 (1991): 5–12; Edward Brongersma, "Boy-Lovers and Their Influence on Boys," *Journal of Homosexuality* 20 (1991): 145–174; Mark Pascal, *Varieties of Man/Boy Love* (New York: Wallace Hamilton, 1992); "Trobriands Collective," in *Crimes without Victims: Documents on Pedophilia* (New York: Global Academic, 1992); Mark Blasius and Shane Phelan, *We Are Everywhere* (New York: Routledge, 1997), 459–468; Michael Davidson, *The World, the Flesh and Myself* (Swaffham, England: Gay Men's Press, 1997); Joseph Geraci, ed., *Dares to Speak* (Swaffham, England: Gay Men's Press, 1997).

17. MB: This exchange was posted November 24, 1999.

18. MB: This exchange is from October 23, 1999.

19. MB: Spider Man, April 4, 2000; the responses were posted the same date.

20. MB: Gingerbread Man, November 24, 1999.

21. MB: Adolph, October 24, 1999.

22. MB: Duke, March 15, 2000.

23. MB: Dr. Who, September 23, 1999.

24. MB: October 27, 1999.

25. MB: This exchange is from March 16, 2000.

26. MB: These responses are from October 31, 1999.

27. Tim Jones, "Paedophile Jailed for Thirty Months," *The Times* (London), January 24, 2000.

28. MB: Norman, May 8, 2000.

29. MB: Dr. Who, September 24, 1999.

30. MB: Lomalee, September 24, 1999.

31. MB: Newbee, September 23, 1999.

32. MB: This exchange is from November 9, 1999.

33. MB: This question was posted December 11, 1999.

34. MB: The responses were posted December 12, 1999.

35. MB: Teddybear, March 15, 2000.

36. MB: Blind, Crippled, Crazy, December 28, 1999.

37. MB: Nikostealth, November 24, 1999.

38. MB: Dracula, January 23, 2000; Soul-less, November 23, 1999.

39. MB: RockfordFosqate, December 27, 1999.

40. The Marion correspondence is taken from MB: January 14, 2000. See "Internet als 'pornografischen Kontakthof' missbraucht," *Der Spiegel*, January 19, 2000.

41. MB: These responses are from January 20, 2000.

42. MB: Froonobulax, January 19, 2000.

43. MB: Lurker Newbie, November 10, 1999.

44. MB: Tomcat, May 1, 2000.

45. For the "pinning" controversy, see MB: December 23, 1999; for Natasha, see MB: May 8–9, 2000.

46. MB: These responses are from February 5, 2000.

47. MB: Knightshade, September 24, 1999; the responses by LEA Mole and Darkstar appeared on the same date.

48. MB: Farfhad, September 25, 1999.

49. MB: This exchange is from December 9, 1999.

50. MB: November 16, 1999.

51. MB: October 7, 1999

52. MB: November 16, 1999.

Notes to Chapter 6

1. MB: These reactions appeared on January 12, 2000.

2. MB: This discussion took place on November 10, 1999.

3. Charles L. Lindner "Separating Internet Fantasy from Reality," *LAT*, January 9, 2000; Brad Stone, "A High-Technology Crash," *Newsweek*, October 4, 1999, 54; Nadya Labi, "Cooling Off Hotseattle," *Time*, October 4, 1999; Greg Miller, "Careers: FBI Agent Surfs the Dark Side of the Internet," *LAT*, March 27, 2000. For comparable recent cases, see Edythe Jensen, "Ex-Official Admits Child-Rape Attempt," *Arizona Republic*, July 29, 2000.

4. Scott Sullivan, "Policing the Internet," *FBI Law Enforcement Bulletin* 68(6) (1999): 18–21; Sean Kelly and Karen E. Crummy, "Netting Sexual Predators," *Denver Post*, November 8, 1999; T. Lesce, "Pedophiles on the Internet," *Law and Order* 47(5) (1999): 74–78; K. F. Durkin, "Misuse of the Internet by Pedophiles," *Federal Probation* 61(3) (1997): 14–18; David E. Kaplan, "New Cybercop Tricks to Fight Child Porn," *US News and World Report*, May 26, 1997.

5. "Internet Crimes against Children Task Force Training and Technical Assistance Program," *http://www.ojjdp.ncjrs.org/fedreg/081799.txt*; Manny Frishber, "Northwest's Plans vs. Cybercrime," *Wired* magazine online, April 28, 2000.

6. Rafer Guzman, "AOL Case Will Test ISP Liability," *WSJ*, August 18, 1999; T. E. Blair, "How Do 'Constitutional Rights' Apply to the Internet?" *The Harbinger*, November 3, 1998, at *http://entropy.me.usouthal.edu/harbinger/xvii/981103/blair.html*.

7. Michael Grunwald, "Police Probe America Online–Pornography Link," *BG*, January 18, 1995; Jared Sandberg, "FBI Crackdown on Child Pornography Opens Hornet's Nest, Stinging America Online," *WSJ*, September 15, 1995; MB: September 21, 1999. See the discussion in Philip Jenkins, *Moral Panic* (New Haven, CT: Yale University Press, 1998), 209–212.

8. Matt Schwartz, "Computer Child Porn Raid Targets Home in Houston," *Houston Post*, March 5, 1993; Jordana Hart, "Child Pornography via Computer Is Focus of Federal Sweep," *BG*, March 7, 1993; Ronald J. Ostrow, "Fight against Child Pornography Waged on New Front: Computers," *LAT*, September 1, 1993; Sebastian Rotella, "Computerized Child Porno Ring Broken," *LAT*, September 24, 1994; John Larrabee, "Cyberspace a New Beat for Police," *USA Today*, April 26, 1994; Dwight Silverman, "Pornography in Cyberspace Poses Dilemma," *HC*, July 21, 1995; Kara Swisher, "On-line Child Pornography Charged as Twelve Are Arrested," *WP*, September 14, 1995; David Johnston, "Use of Computer Network for Child Sex Sets Off Raids," *NYT*, September 14, 1995; Laura Evenson, "FBI Raid on Cyberporn Heightens Concern about Children Online," *San Francisco Chronicle*, September 15, 1995; John W. Fountain, "Federal Agents Baited 'Net in Child Pornography Case," *WP*, November 9, 1995; Judy Rakowsky, "Computers from N.E. Analyzed for Child Porn," *BG*,

September 19, 1995; David Stout, "Forty-five Arrested in a Nationwide Child Pornography Ring, US Says," *NYT*, May 10, 1996; "A Twenty City Search in Child Pornography Inquiry," *NYT*, December 12, 1996.

9. MB: Curious George, September 21, 1999.

10. MB: Methusla, January 18, 2000.

11. MB: AOL refugee, January 11, 2000.

12. MB: Fnord is from January 15, 2000; the remaining posts are from an exchange that occurred on September 21–22, 1999.

13. Many of these principles also apply to legitimate Web users who wish to avoid leaving a trail of evidence to be exploited by advertisers; see Matt Lake, "Stealth Surfing," *PC World*, June 2000, 121–136.

14. MB: Lord High Executioner, December 30, 1999.

15. BBC News Online, September 3, 1998; Elaine Shannon, "Main Street Monsters," *Time*, September 14, 1998: 59; Gary Marx, *Undercover* (Berkeley: University of California Press, 1988).

16. Carl S. Kaplan, "Report Questions Government Efforts against Computer Crime," *NYT*, August 20, 1999.

17. David Stout, "Internet Pornography Group Is Seized in U.S. and Abroad," *NYT*, September 3, 1998.

18. MB: Darkstar, March 17, 2000.

19. The ACLU quote is from *http://www.aclu.org/echelonwatch/index .html*; Suzanne Daley, "French Prosecutor Investigates US Global Listening System," *NYT*, July 5, 2000; Tom Raum, "NSA Denies Spying on Americans," *AP*, April 12, 2000.

20. Wendy M. Grossman, "Are British Bobbies Reading Your E-mail?" *Salon* magazine online, August 23, 2000; Jamie Doward, "Climbdown on E-snooping Bill," *The Guardian*, July 2, 2000; J. Michael Waller and Jamie Dettmer, "Britain's Email Scandal Heats Up," *Insight on the News*, May 29, 2000; Philip Willan, "Cyberspook Tomlinson Defiantly Speaks His Mind," *Computerworld*, May 29, 2000, 26; Mark Ward, "Watching While You Surf," BBC News Online, May 25, 2000, at *news.bbc.co.uk/hi/english/sci/ tech*; Chris Nuttall, "UK Customs Check for Laptop Porn," BBC News Online, August 13, 1998.

It was frequently remarked that MI5 had a powerful bureaucratic self-interest in portraying itself as the vanguard in the struggle against cybercrime. See, for instance, these comments from a recent British newspaper account:

"Following the end of the Cold War and IRA ceasefires, MI5 lobbied fiercely within Whitehall to be given other work to justify its existence. In 1996, its activities were extended to support police in the prevention and detection of serious crime." Rob Evans and David Hencke, "Gag on Spies' Role in Noye Case," *The Guardian*, July 22, 2000.

21. MB: Smile, March 18, 2000.

22. MB: Qwert345, March 18, 2000.

23. MB: NickNack, March 19, 2000.

24. MB: Pirra8, March 3, 2000.

25. MB: Godfather Corleone, December 5, 1999.

26. "Reno and Freeh Testify on Internet Security " AP story, in *NYT*, February 16, 2000.

27. MB: G-Man, May 26, 2000.

28. MB: Roman Polanski, June 5, 2000.

29. Cynthia Perez, "US v. Jacobson: Are Child Pornography Stings Creative Law Enforcement or Entrapment?" *University of Miami Law Review* 46(1) (1991): 235–249; Ruth Marcus, "Fair Sting or Foul Trap? Child Pornography Investigation Challenged," *WP*, November 6, 1991. For more recent cases, see Eric Miller, "Online Tour Ad Aids Crackdown on Sex Crimes," *Arizona Republic*, March 26, 1998; Tracy Wilson, "Officer Surfs the Net for Sexual Predators . . . Defense Attorneys Call It Entrapment," *LAT*, November 21, 1999.

30. The quote is from David Rosenzweig, "Internet Sex Probe Was a Trap, Court Says," *LAT*, June 30, 2000; Carl S. Kaplan, "Court Says Agents Went Too Far in Online Sting," *NYT*, July 7, 2000; Debra Baker, "When Cyber Stalkers Walk," *ABA Journal* (December 1999): 50–54.

31. "Teacher Charged with Owning Child Porn," *LAT*, March 17, 2000; Lee Condon, "Teacher Pleads Not Guilty in Abuse Case," *LAT*, May 27, 2000. All the posted remarks quoted on the case are from MB: March 18, 2000.

32. Darkstar is quoted from MB: January 9, 2000.

Notes to Chapter 7

1. MB: December 30, 1999.

2. MB: December 30, 1999.

3. MB: Sleeper, March 3, 2000.

4. MB: May 24, 2000.

5. MB: Licker, May 24, 2000.

6. Stephanie Mansfield, "The Avengers Online," *Good Housekeeping*, June 1999, 122–125+

7. Sascha Segan, "For the Kids: Hacker Groups Attack Net Child Porn," ABC News online, June 16, 2000.

8. Matt Richtel; "In the Pursuit of Cybercriminals, Real Detectives Rely on Amateurs," *NYT*, May 17, 2000; Deborah Radcliff; "Vigilante group targets child pornography sites," *Computerworld*, January 17, 2000, 40.

9. Segan, "For the Kids"; *http://www.antichildporn.org/cgi-bin/hq/*.

10. Segan, "For the Kids."

11. MB: Anon, June 4, 2000.

12. Daniel Sieberg, "Naked Eye," *Salon*, December 22, 1999, at *http://www.salon.com/tech/feature/1999/12/22/hacked*.

13. MB: Darkstar, January 18, 2000.

14. MB: Lord High Executioner, May 31, 2000.

15. MB: Argono, March 1, 2000.

16. MB: LeRoin, June 24, 2000.

17. R-board [pseudonym]: Lunar 7, June 28, 2000. Henceforth, I refer to this board as "RB."

18. RB: Darkstar, June 18, 2000.

19. This correspondence is from MB: June 23, 2000.

20. RB: Anon, June 25, 2000.

21. RB: Concerned, June 19, 2000.

22. RB: June 23, 2000.

23. RB: This exchange is from June 19, 2000.

24. MB: This exchange is from June 22, 2000.

25. RB: J. L. Byrd, July 8, 2000.

26. RB: Danube, June 28, 2000; Admin, June 26, 2000; Morgoth, June 25, 2000.

27. MB: June 23–24, 2000.

28. RB: July 7–8, 2000.

29. RB: June 26, 2000.

30. RB: Johnboy, July 1, 2000.

31. RB: Kidflash, June 22, 2000.

Notes to Chapter 8

1. Clifford Krauss, "Eight Countries Join in an Effort to Catch Computer Criminals," *NYT*, December 11, 1997; "New War on Internet Porn: Paedophile Networks Are a Global Problem, Says Unesco," BBC News online, January 18, 1999, at news.bbc.co.uk/hi/english/sci/tech; "Unesco steps up fight against Internet paedophiles," BBC News online, June 16, 1999, at *news.bbc.co.uk/hi/english/sci/tech*; Cynthia Guttman, "The Darker Side of the Net," *Unesco Courier*, September 1999, 43–45.

2. Fredric Jameson and Masao Miyoshi, eds., *The Cultures of Globalization* (Durham, NC: Duke University Press, 1998); Arjun Appadurai, *Modernity at Large* (Minneapolis: University of Minnesota Press, 1996); John Micklethwait and Adrian Wooldridge, *A Future Perfect* (New York: Times Books, 2000).

3. For the changing state of international law in this area, one important writer is Yaman Akdeniz, whose publications include "Computer Pornography: A Comparative Study of the US and UK Obscenity Laws and Child Pornography Laws in Relation to the Internet," *International Review of Law, Computers and Technology* 10 (1996): 235–261; "Governance of Pornography and Child Pornography on the Global Internet: a Multi-Layered Approach," in Lilian Edwards and Charlotte Waelde, eds., *Law and the Internet* (Oxford: Hart, 1997); "The Regulation of Pornography and Child Pornography on the Internet," *Journal of Information, Law and Technology* 1 (1997), at *http://elj.warwick.ac.uk/jilt/internet/97_1akdz/*; and *Sex on the Net* (London: South Street, 1999).

4. Jeremy Seabrook, *Travels in the Skin Trade* (London: Pluto Press, 1997); Ryan Bishop and Lillian S. Robinson, *Night Market* (New York: Routledge, 1998); Lin Lean Lim, *The Sex Sector* (Geneva: International Labor Office, 1998); Martin Opperman, ed., *Sex Tourism and Prostitution* (Emsford, NY: Cognizant Communication Corp., 1998).

5. MB: Thor, November 10, 1999.

6. MB: Rocky, May 8, 2000; Darkstar, February 22, 2000.

7. MB: January 20, 2000.

8. MB: Helper, January 11, 2000.

9. MB: Darkstar, May 26, 2000.

10. Philip Jenkins, *Moral Panic* (New Haven, CT: Yale University Press, 1998).

11. Philip Jenkins, *Intimate Enemies* (Hawthorne, NY: Aldine de Gruyter, 1992); Ray Wyre and Tim Tate, *The Murder of Childhood* (London: Penguin, 1995); *Organized Criminal Paedophile Activity: A Report by the Parliamentary Joint Committee on the National Crime Authority* (Canberra: Parliament of the Commonwealth of Australia, 1995); Peter C. Bibby, ed., *Organised Abuse* (Brookfield, VT: Ashgate, 1996).

12. For the inmpact of the Dutroux case and its international ramifications, see Philip Jenkins, "How Europe Discovered Its Sex Offender Crisis," in Joel Best, ed., *Spreading Social Problems* (Hawthorne, NY: Aldine de Gruyter, 2001); Robyn Dixon, "Three Top Latvians Are Named in Investigation of Pedophilia," *LAT*, February 19, 2000; Ian Traynor, "Child Abuse Scandal May Topple Latvian Leaders," *HC*, March 10, 2000; MB: Darkstar, February 19, 2000.

13. Dominic Kennedy, "Sex Tourists to Be Tried by Courts in Britain," *The Times* (London), August 27, 1996; *Draft Declaration and Papers Presented to the World Congress Against Commercial Sexual Exploitation of Children, Stockholm, Sweden*, August 27–31, 1996 (Stockholm: Printing Works of the Cabinet Office and Ministries, 1996); Jenkins, "How Europe Discovered Its Sex Offender Crisis"; "Sex Tourists to Be Sent Packing," at *http://www.britain-info.org/bistext/fordom/law/171197.htm.*

14. Edmund L. Andrews, "Compuserve Official Charged in Germany," *NYT*, April 17, 1997; "Ex-Compuserve Chief's Conviction Overturned," *HC*, November 18, 1999; Lesli C. Esposito, "Regulating the Internet," *Case Western Reserve Journal of International Law* 30 (1998): 541–565; MB: Marc, May 29, 2000. For the Dutch experience with Internet regulation, see Edwin C. Mac Gillavry, "Internet Service Providers and Criminal Investigation," paper delivered to the international conference on Combating Child Pornography on the Internet, Vienna, Austria, September 29–October 1, 1999: online at *http://www.stop-childpornog.at/.*

15. Marlise Simons, "French Police Arrest 250 Men Linked to Child Pornography Ring," *NYT*, March 14, 1997; Craig R. Whitney, "French Child Porn Dragnet Is Criticized after Suicides," *NYT*, June 24, 1997; "Dozens Convicted in French Child Porn Trial," Reuters, from *CNN.Net*, May 10, 2000.

16. R. Watson, "EU Backs New Anti-Child Pornography Plan," February 12, 1998, at *http://www.european-voice.com/*.

17. "Pedophiles Use Encoding Devices to Make Secret Use of Internet," *The Times* (London), November 21, 1995; David Connett and Jon Henley, "The Pedlars of Child Abuse," *The Observer* (London), August 25, 1996; Paul Wilkinson and Ruth Gledhill, "Paedophile Priest Circulated Porn on the Internet," *The Times* (London), November 13, 1996; Paul Stokes, "Six Years for Priest Who Broadcast Abuse of Boys to Internet Paedophiles," *Electronic Telegraph*, November 13, 1996; Akdeniz "Regulation of Pornography"; Laurence J. O'Toole, *Pornocopia*, 2d ed. (London: Serpent's Tail, 1999), 261–263.

18. "U.S., Foreign Web Masters Indicted in Child Porn Case," *LAT*, April 14, 2000; Angela K. Brown, "Texas Couple Convicted for Child Porn Web Sites," *Salon* magazine online, December 2, 2000; Toni Heinzl, "Internet Child Pornography Case Led to Global Inquiry," *Fort Worth Star-Telegram*, January 9, 2001.

19. Ian Traynor, "Raid Uncovers Huge Child Porn Ring," *The Guardian* July 17, 1998; idem, "'I Put the Child Porn Together with the Murder and Realized It Was Our Neighbor,'" *The Guardian*, July 18, 1998; Marlise Simons, "Dutch Say a Sex Ring Used Infants on Internet," *NYT*, July 19, 1998; "Dutch under Fire for Child Porn," Reuters report on *CNET News.com*, July 26, 1998.

20. MB: The exchange was posted on May 16, 2000.

21. *R. v. Sharpe*, BCCA 1999 416, June 30, 1999, at *http://www.courts.gov.bc.ca/jdb-txt/ca/99/04/c99-0416.html*.

22. "La Cassazione, a Sezioni unite, ha respinto un ricorso: Se le foto hard sono per uso proprio, il reato non c'e," *La Repubblica*, 31 May 2000.

23. MB: G-Man, May 16, 2000.

24. MB: Grrrrr, December 2, 1999.

25. For the legitimate naturist tradition, see Mikhail Rusinov, *Holy Nature: A Celebration of Naturism in Today's Russia* (Body and Mind Publications, 1998).

26. MB: Strougal, May 29, 2000. For the legal situation in the Czech Republic, see *http://netmag.cz/db/L20000522053846.pARANOIk.html*.

27. MB: RaNDoM, December 13, 1999.

28. MB: Cross, March 5, 2000.

29. MB: January 23, 2000.

30. MB: G-Man, December 23, 1999.

31. Kate Connolly, "Ex-Radio 1 DJ Jailed in Prague for Child Sex Abuse," *The Guardian*, March 16, 2000; J. A. Getzlaff, "Poland Moves to Ban Skin Flicks and Magazines," *Salon*, March 17, 2000.

32. Nicholas D. Kristof, "Threatened by Older Women, Tokyo Men Chase Schoolgirls," *NYT*, April 2, 1997; Jonathan Watts, "Japan Tackles Child Porn," *The Guardian*, April 27, 1999; Stephanie Strom, "Japan's Legislators Tighten the Ban on Under-Age Sex," *NYT*, May 19, 1999; Stephanie Strom, "Rising Internet Use Quietly Transforms Way Japanese Live," *NYT*, May 14, 2000.

33. Strom, "Japan's Legislators Tighten the Ban"; *NYT*, May 19, 1999. Karen Mazurkewich, "The Dark Side of Animation," *Far Eastern Economic Review*, August 10, 2000.

34. MB: December 23, 1999.

35. MB: These responses were posted on March 5, 2000.

36. MB: UKPEDO, December 23, 1999.

37. MB: May 9, 2000.

38. Robert Pear, "Thais Help U.S. Stem Internet Sales of Medicines," *NYT*, March 21, 2000.

39. MB: Jazzjackass and Visitor1, May 3, 2000.

Notes to Chapter 9

1. Mike Cane, *The Computer Phone Book*, rev. and expanded ed., 2 vols. (New York: New American Library, 1986), 287.

2. Elisabeth Rosenthal, "Web Sites Bloom in China, and Are Weeded," *NYT*, December 23, 1999; idem, "China Issues Rules to Limit E-Mail and Web Content," *NYT*, January 27, 2000; "Few Comply as China Enacts Encryption Rules," *NYT*, February 1, 2000.

3. Ian Buruma, "China in Cyberspace," *New York Review of Books*, November 4, 1999, 9–12.

4. Rosenthal, "China Issues Rules to Limit E-Mail"; "Chinese Web Site Operator Arrested on Subversion Charges," AP, June 8, 2000.

5. Lesli C. Esposito, "Regulating the Internet," *Case Western Reserve Journal of International Law* 30 (1998): 541–565.

6. Quoted in Laurence J. O'Toole, *Pornocopia*, 2nd. edition (London: Serpent's Tail 1999), 272.

7. Buruma, "China in Cyberspace"; though see James C. Luh, "The Internet Can't Free China," *NYT*, July 25, 2000.

8. Simson Garfinkel, *Database Nation* (Sebastopol, Calif.: O'Reilly and Associates, 2000); Lawrence Lessig, *Code and Other Laws of Cyberspace* (New York: Basic Books, 1999).

9. Michelle Finley, "Canadian Data: Northern Exposure," May 18, 2000, at *www.wired.com/news/politics/0,1283,36435,oo.html.*

10. Mark Boal, "Freedom Fighters," *Village Voice*, October 19, 1999, 31; Carl S. Kaplan, "Lawsuit Says Web Cookies Allow Illegal Stalking," *NYT*, February 18, 2000; Carl S. Kaplan, "When the Internet Moves Faster Than the Courts," *NYT*, February 25, 2000; Ariana Eunjung Cha, "Your PC is Watching," *Washington Post*, July 14, 2000.

11. Jeffrey Rosen, *The Unwanted Gaze* (New York: Random House, 2000); Charles Jennings, Lori Fena, and Esther Dyson, *The Hundredth Window* (New York: Free Press, 2000); Nadine Strossen, "Cybercrimes v. Cyberliberties," *International Review of Law, Computers and Technology* 14(1) (2000): 11–16; Jeri Clausing, "Commission Will Work to Protect Children after Legislation Fails," *NYT*, March 7, 2000; Daniel Tynan, "Privacy 2000," *PC World*, June 2000, 102–116.

12. Richard L. Berke, "What Are You Afraid Of? A Hidden Issue Emerges," *NYT*, June 4, 2000; Stephen Labaton, "U.S. Is Said to Seek New Law to Bolster Internet Privacy," *NYT*, May 19, 2000.

13. Jeri Clausing, "Worries about Internet Crime Spark Legislative Blitz," *NYT*, February 29, 2000; idem, "Interagency Alliances Aim to Fight Cybercrime," *NYT*, April 25, 2000.

14. Lacy McCrary, "No Wiretap Protection on the Net," *Philadelphia Inquirer*, March 2, 2000.

15. Robert O'Neill, "Free Speech in Academe," *Chronicle of Higher Education*, May 19, 2000, A88.

16. *Encryption, Key Recovery, and Privacy Protection in the Information Age: Hearing before the Committee on the Judiciary, U.S. Senate, 105th Congress, First Session . . . July 9, 1997* (Washington, DC: GPO, 1997).

17. Zhonette M. Vedder-Brown, "Government Regulation of Encryption," *American Criminal Law Review* 35 (1998): 1387–1414; Jeri Claus-

ing, "New Encryption Rules Leave Civil Libertarians Unhappy," *NYT*, January 18, 2000; Carl S. Kaplan, "Wrinkle in Mitnick Case Hints at Encryption Battles to Come," *NYT*, January 28, 2000; Strossen, "Cybercrimes v. Cyberliberties"; James Bovard, "Rise of the Surveillance State," *American Spectator*, May 2000, 68–69; O'Neill, "Free Speech in Academe," A88; Lisa Guernsey, "Secrecy for Everyone, as Encryption Goes to Market," *NYT*, May 18, 2000. Steven Levy, *Crypto: When the Code Rebels Beat the Government* (New York: Viking Press, 2001). Recently, much of the concern over electronic snooping has focused on the FBI's "Carnivore" system, which was intended to intercept e-mails; the issue drew national attention to the issue of Internet privacy. See, for instance, "Reno Says Review Is Under Way on Internet Wiretapping," AP story, in *NYT*, July 14, 2000; Stephen Labaton, "Learning to Live with Big Brother," *NYT*, July 23, 2000; "Congress Probes F.B.I. E-Mail Snooping Device," AP story, in *NYT*, July 25, 2000.

18. Boal, "Freedom Fighters."

19. MB: Licker, March 18, 2000.

20. John Gibeaut, "Image Is Everything," *ABA Journal* 86 (May 2000): 20–21.

21. Tim Tate, *Child Pornography* (London: Methuen, 1990), 13. I feel uneasy quoting Tate with approval, since in the early 1990s he emerged as a leading advocate of the reality for a "Satanic ritual abuse" menace in the United Kingdom, a view on which I feel he was wrong in every particular. See Tim Tate, *Children for the Devil* (London: Methuen, 1991); Philip Jenkins, *Intimate Enemies* (Hawthorne, NY: Aldine de Gruyter, 1992); Jean S. Lafontaine, *Speak of the Devil* (Cambridge: Cambridge University Press, 1997). Nevertheless, Tate's *Child Pornography* is one of the most comprehensive accounts of its kind.

22. Rogier van Bakel, "To Surf and Protect," *Wired* magazine online, July 1996.

23. Frederick S. Lane, *Obscene Profits* (New York: Routledge, 2000), 209–212.

24. Drucilla Cornell, *Feminism and Pornography* (New York: Oxford University Press, 2000); James Elias, Veronica Diehl Elias, Vern L. Bullough, Gwen Brewer, Jeffrey Douglas, and Will Jarvis, eds., *Porn 101* (Amherst, NY: Prometheus Books, 1999); Bosah Ebo, ed., *Cyberghetto or Cybertopia? Race, Class, and Gender on the Internet* (Westport, CT: Praeger,

1998); Jane Juffer, *At Home with Pornography* (New York: New York University Press, 1998); Thomas Foster, Carol Siegel, and Ellen E. Berry, eds., *Sex Positives?* (New York: New York University Press, 1997); Laura Kipnis, *Bound and Gagged* (New Y ork: Grove Press, 1996); Jonathan Wallace and Mark Mangan, *Sex, Laws, and Cyberspace* (New York: Henry Holt, 1996); Bill Thompson, *Soft Core* (London: Cassell Academic, 1994); Linda Williams, *Hard Core* (Berkeley: University of California Press, 1989); Donald Alexander Downs, *The New Politics of Pornography* (Chicago: University of Chicago Press, 1989).

25. Compare Lane, *Obscene Profits*, 226–227. A vast collection of "domestic" and amateur adult porn can be accessed through *http://www.southern-charms.com/*.

26. *http://www.sassysally.com/*; *http://sheasplace.nu/*.

27. Personal interview, 1998.

INDEX

ABOUT THE AUTHOR

Philip Jenkins is Distinguished Professor of History and Religious Studies at Pennsylvania State University. He is the author of numerous books, including *Mystics and Messiahs: Cults and New Religions in America* and *Synthetic Panics: The Symbolic Politics of Designer Drugs*, available from NYU Press.